Luke's Gospel provides a comprehensive and schematic reading of its subject text. Dr Knight introduces the Gospel and discusses how it came to birth. He introduces a narrative approach to the Gospel and compares this with other methods of research. He offers a chapter-by-chapter exposition of Luke and considers alternative perspectives such as feminism and deconstruction. He then examines the principal motifs of the Gospel, particularly the theme of the temple which has been overlooked in previous scholarship, arguing that Luke's Jesus pronounces the present temple forsaken by God to introduce himself as the cornerstone of the eschatological temple. Finally, Knight examines earlier readings of Luke's Gospel from Conzelmann to the present day.

Jonathan Knight presents an accessible and jargon-free introduction to the Gospel which makes a valuable addition to the *New Testament Readings* series.

Jonathan Knight is a priest in the Diocese of Ely who was educated at Cambridge University and subsequently taught at Sheffield University. He is the author of *The Ascension of Isaiah* (Sheffield 1995) and *2 Peter and Jude* (Sheffield 1995). He currently works as Research Assistant to Stephen Sykes, the Bishop of Ely, and is Secretary of the Doctrine Commission of the Church of England.

New Testament Readings
Edited by John Court
University of Kent at Canterbury

Luke's Gospel

Jonathan Knight

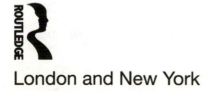

London and New York

First published 1998
by Routledge
11 New Fetter Lane, London EC4P 4EE

Simultaneously published in the USA and Canada
by Routledge
29 West 35th Street, New York, NY 10001

© 1998 Jonathan Knight

Typeset in Garamond by Routledge
Printed and bound in Great Britain by Creative Print and Design
(Wales), Ebbw Vale

British Library Cataloguing in Publication Data
A catalogue record for this book is available from the British Library

Library of Congress Cataloging in Publication Data
Knight, Jonathan (Jonathan Morshead), 1959–
Luke's gospel / Jonathan Knight
p.   cm. – (New Testament readings)
Includes bibliographical references and index.
1. Bible. N.T. Luke–Criticism, interpretation, etc. I. Title.
II. Series.
BS2595.2. K58   1998
226.4' 06–DC21   97–30043
                                                          CIP

ISBN 0–415–17321–3 (hbk)
ISBN 0–415–17322–1 (pbk)

Contents

Series editor's preface

This volume has every right to stand on its own, as a significant contribution to the study of Luke. But equally it is a volume in a series entitled New Testament Readings. Each volume in this series deals with an individual book among the early Christian writings within, or close to the borders of, the New Testament. The series is not another set of traditional commentaries, but designed as a group of individual interpretations or 'readings' of the texts, offering fresh and stimulating methods of approach. While the contributors may be provocative in their choice of a certain perspective, they also seek to do justice to a range of modern methods and provide a context for the study of each particular text.

The collective object of the series is to share with the widest readership the extensive range of recent approaches to Scripture. There is no doubt that literary methods have presented what amounts to a 'new look' to the Bible in recent years. But we should not neglect to ask some historical questions or apply suitable methods of criticism from the social sciences. The origins of this series are in a practical research programme at the University of Kent, with an inclusive concern about ways of using the Bible. It is to be hoped that our series will offer fresh insights to all who, for any reason, study or use these books of the early Christians.

John M. Court
Series editor

Preface

My interest in Luke was kindled when I read for the Diploma in Theology at Cambridge University in 1983. I became aware of the need for literary approaches to the Gospels when I was working at the Department of Biblical Studies at Sheffield University between 1991 and 1994. This book draws on a fusion of methodologies to present what I hope is a balanced reading of Luke.

As I was finishing this book news came from Germany of the sad death of Ernst Bammel, so soon after the death of his wife. Bammel was an inspiring teacher of the New Testament who never stinted with his generosity towards his friends and pupils. This book is dedicated to his memory with gratitude and respect.

The biblical citations in this book are taken from the Revised English Bible (REB) except where stated.

Abbreviations

AB	*Anchor Bible*
CBQ	*Catholic Bible Quarterly*
ET	*English translation*
GAP	*Guides to the Apocrypha and Pseudepigrapha*
HTS	*Harvard Theological Studies*
JSNTSS	*Journal for the Study of the New Testament Supplement Series*
JSOTSS	*Journal for the Study of the Old Testament Supplement Series*
NRSV	*New Revised Standard Version*
NTS	*New Testament Studies*
NTT	*New Testament Theology*
REB	*Revised English Bible*
RSV	*Revised Standard Version*
SBLMS	*Society of Biblical Literature Monograph Series*
SBT	*Studies in Biblical Theology*
SHR	*Studies in History and Religion*
SNTSMS	*Society for New Testament Studies Monograph Series*

Chapter 1

An introduction to the text

This book sets out to provide a reading of Luke's Gospel.[1] Of the writing of books on the Gospels there has been no end, especially not in the last ten years. It is therefore incumbent on a new author to explain where his work differs from the rest and doubtless to acknowledge the many areas of overlap and the sources from which his ideas have been culled. This book is motivated by the belief that it is helpful to read Luke as a narrative – that is to say, as a text which tells a story – and that much can be learned from this approach, which has assumed increasing prominence in New Testament scholarship over the past decade.[2] The Gospels, after all, *do* tell a story. Recent research has shown that they have much in common with the so-called 'Lives' of Hellenistic figures (see below). There is a need for a reading of Luke which examines the nature of its narrative, including matters of structure and content, within the confines of a single volume.[3] This aim shapes the way in which this book has been written. Chapter 1 is an introduction to Luke which explores the Gospel's major features and argues for a common authorship with the Acts of the Apostles (a theory which has implications for the wider interpretation of the Gospel). Chapter 2 offers an introduction to Luke as a narrative and suggests some areas which ought to be considered in a reading of the Gospel. Chapter 3 presents a reading of Luke which works through the Gospel on a chapter-by-chapter basis. Chapter 4 considers some alternative readings of Luke – notably, deconstructive and feminist readings. Chapter 5 examines the themes of the Gospel in the light of this earlier discussion. Finally, Chapter 6 offers a reading of some of Luke's interpreters, beginning with Hans Conzelmann and ending with Stephen Moore, and offers a metacommentary on readings of Luke which tries to guide the unfamiliar reader through the growing maze of secondary material.

It is doubtless true to say that a 'literary' approach to the Bible arose from the recognition that much scholarship was dominated by a theological agenda (which generally meant a *Christian* theological agenda) that ignored developments in other fields of literary research and concentrated on themes in the text rather than on the text itself. Much of what has been done from this perspective in New Testament studies so far has been of the nature of 'catching up' on approaches which have already profitably been adopted in English, Classics and Philosophy. This observation raises an important question of method for the present study. The approach that will be adopted in Chapters 2 and 3 of this book is to read Luke as a text and to ask what holds it together and makes it function as a work of literature. This is a different approach from many previous studies which have asked mainly about Luke's place in the development of Christian ideas. There is a coherent reason for this shift in emphasis. The Gospels certainly illustrate the development of early Christian ideas but they are not in themselves theological treatises. First and foremost, they tell a story about Jesus which (meta)comment(ate)s on his significance as it was perceived in the late first century CE. They incorporate earlier material which each Evangelist arranges in a certain way. Readers interact with this material to form the meaning which they take from each Gospel. It is through this process of reading that the meaning of the text is forged out for the reader.

This book works from the assumption that, since Luke is a narrative, the methods which have been used to interpret secular narratives can and should be applied to Luke as well. This means that we must pay careful attention to issues of plot and characterization which stand at the heart of all narratives. Whatever sources lie behind Luke – and I shall argue that Mark and Matthew were two of them – our interest lies with the interpretation of Luke as it stands and not with an analysis of the elements from which it was composed. This approach does not mean that Luke is without its gaps and problems. Far from it. There are some very obvious gaps in the story, like what Jesus did in his childhood and what he thought about a variety of issues. A continual tension surrounds the character of Jesus in the Gospel. Throughout, the figure of the heavenly Lord dances with the human Jesus because the narrative hero who dies is also the Lord in heaven. Moreover, Luke's Jesus seems to adopt a different perspective from Luke's narrator. The author himself sides in places with Jesus against the narrator.[4] This is an invitation by the author to the reader to ponder the meaning of the text. The gaps and problems are in many ways the most interesting parts of the story for they force the reader to grapple with its meaning and to construct an interpretation which explores and explains the signs that the author has embedded in the narrative.

This approach means that a consideration of the author's theological purpose has been (partially) upstaged in my book by a consideration of what makes Luke's story work. This book draws on a variety of methods in which narrative criticism is aided by composition criticism (especially in Chapters 1 and 5) and by redaction criticism too. The nature of Luke as a Gospel – as a work that uses earlier tradition – makes this multi-faceted approach essential. Narrative criticism is a valuable new approach but, in the opinion of this writer, the older methods have not lost their value. This book will therefore study how Luke works as a narrative and also ask about the themes of Luke's story and about Luke's relation to the other Gospels.

A word is in order about how I as the author would like you as the reader to use what I have written. There are several different ways of reading this book. Some readers may want to read it from cover to cover and digest its contents in the order I have devised. This is a perfectly satisfactory way of reading and I hope that I have placed enough signposts in the text to guide my readers along their way. On the other hand, some readers may find themselves impatient with what has turned out to be quite a lengthy introduction (Chapters 1 and 2). I regard it as equally satisfactory if readers want to begin with Chapters 3 and 4, where some different readings of Luke are explored, and then return (or choose not to return...) to the introduction. Chapter 3 contains the real meat of the book (readers may find my summary of Luke's plot in Chapter 2 a helpful preliminary to this chapter). I hope that readers will come to share the sense of enthusiasm which I have gained for Luke's Jesus with his denunciation of the present temple (13.35) and self-introduction as the corner-stone of the eschatological temple (20.17).

LUKE AS A GOSPEL

The first question we must consider is the question of Luke's genre. What kind of text are we dealing with? The answer is that Luke is 'a Gospel'. A Gospel is a written record of the life of Jesus which tells the story of his adult ministry (or at least what are considered the significant parts of it) and concludes with his death and resurrection (uniquely in Luke with the ascension of Jesus). Matthew and Luke describe the birth of Jesus. *All* the Gospels omit the substantial details of his childhood (apart from one sparse Lucan anecdote). There are four Gospels in the New Testament; Luke is the third in sequence. These Gospels must be distinguished, both in form and in content, from the other so-called 'Gospels' which lie outside the New Testament canon.[5] These non-canonical Gospels were written later than the canonical Gospels and they lack the narrative structure which gives the canonical Gospels their character. In the analysis of the genre, the observation that the New Testament Gospels 'tell a story' – that they have a fundamental narrative structure – is an important one.

Luke was not the first Gospel to be written. That distinction probably rests with (a form of) Mark. It seems virtually certain that Luke knew Mark. It is probable that he also knew Matthew. Luke must be evaluated in the context of the emerging Gospel tradition and in deference to the possibility that some of what he says may be a *deliberate* recasting of the earlier Gospels, for whatever reason this was done (as for instance in the temptation story, chapter 4). Luke did not come to birth in isolation from a literary or from an oral tradition. The latter continued to circulate even in the second century.[6] The author picks up both traditions and gives them new shape and focus through his own distinctive touches.

The Gospel form was an innovation in first-century Christianity but it is broadly related to other ancient literary types. Since Mark was the first Gospel to be written, it is by his standards that the other Gospels must be judged. It is clear that when Mark wrote, some forty years after the resurrection of Jesus, the need was felt to write down the facts about Jesus to yield a more permanent record than was provided by the oral tradition. One can only admire the simplicity with which the earliest Gospel is written. Mark's narrative moves from the story of John the Baptist through Jesus' ministry in Galilee, his identification as the Messiah by the disciples, to the journey to his death in Jerusalem, which is followed in turn by the resurrection. This basic plot supplies the narrative framework which the other Gospels adopt.

The body of Mark's Gospel contains both sayings and deeds of Jesus. The presence of both to the exclusion of neither gives the Gospel its character. Mark's record of the sayings of Jesus is presented in a narrative framework, even if the links at times seem rather perfunctory. His narrative moves towards the trial and death of Jesus which occupy a disproportionately large part of the Gospel. Mark ends, almost mysteriously, with a description of the empty tomb and the women's vision of the angels (16.8).[7] The other Gospels add to this the resurrection appearances of Jesus which allude to the Christian belief in his heavenly existence; Luke also adds the ascension of Jesus to heaven.

The question has been raised of how far the Gospels conform to the style of ancient biography. Comparison has often been made with the 'Lives' of Hellenistic figures written by the classical historians. Richard Burridge examines five such 'Lives' which were written before Mark.[8] Burridge shows that all exhibit a similar range of features within a flexible pattern. He mentions the following points of comparison. Their flexibility operates within perceptible boundaries. The 'Lives' are generally called by their subject's name (cf. Mark 1.1). Their subject dominates the narrative. The way in which the story is told varies from example to example. Some texts adopt a strict chronological sequence. Others mix this with topical analysis. Their scale is limited to the subject's life, deeds and character. The anecdote ('a brief biographical narrative that relates a striking or unusual feature of the hero's character') plays a significant role in them. Many such works conclude with the story of the hero's death. Its cause is sometimes described in much detail. Burridge discerns a variety of reasons for the writing of these Lives, including the need to preserve the hero's memory and to pass on his teaching. He shows that they were read at public occasions such as festivals. They were not originally intended for private consumption but for public edification.

These points of comparison are instructive but we must not ignore some significant differences between the Gospels and the Lives. Graham Stanton observes that only a small number of the features of Mark can be found either in any one ancient biography or in any single type of biography.[9] Moreover, many features of Mark would have puzzled the readers of ancient biography. These include the Evangelist's concentration on the death of Jesus, his seemingly abrupt ending and his evident dislike of anecdotes. In the case of Luke, the Gospel presents something more than the life of Jesus *tout court* for it begins with the birth of John the Baptist and offers a theological commentary on what Jesus does, which paves the way for the writing of Acts, which narrates the sequel to his ministry. The Gospels certainly contain elements of biography, and it may be that this broad Hellenistic influence allowed Luke to conceive of a work in two volumes.[10] Yet the impression remains that Luke describes not so much the life of Jesus as such but what Acts 2.11 calls 'the mighty works of God' (RSV). This is an altogether broader view even though the story of the life of Jesus gives initial shape and coherence to the project.

Perhaps the most important difference between the Gospels and the Lives is the status accorded the heroes in the respective literature. Charles Talbert thinks that Luke has close parallels to those Lives of philosophers which show where the 'living voice' of the tradition can be found once the founder has passed on.[11] This is doubtless true to the extent that Luke provides a more permanent record of Jesus' deeds and sayings than the oral tradition but this comparison potentially obscures a most important point. For the first readers of Luke, Jesus was the heavenly Lord whose presence was experienced whenever they met for worship. He was not a dead prophet but the living Lord whose installation as a heavenly being is symbolized by the ascension in the Gospel and celebrated in the gathered community. The belief that Jesus is 'seated at the right hand of Almighty God' (22.69) colours Luke's narrative to the extent that belief in his divinity is read back into the story of his life. There is thus a dialectical relationship between Luke's story of the historical Jesus and the readers' perception of him as Lord. The experience of reading the Gospel affects the experience of meeting Jesus in worship and vice versa. Talbert's comparison must be qualified by the observation that the living voice of the Jesus tradition was provided as much by the promptings of his Spirit in the Christian community, whatever that meant in practice, as by the reading of an authoritative text. We can now only speculate on the nature of the relationship between the reading of the text and the perception of the heavenly reality which these early readers enjoyed.

Nor should the comparison between the Gospels and the Lives be allowed to yield the conclusion that the Gospels are biographies as we understand the term today. Biographies are two-a-penny at the moment. They fall into different forms ranging from serious historical scholarship to romantic or fictional reconstruction. Those who look to the Gospels to provide a full-blown life of Jesus will be sadly disappointed. Much of the crucial information is missing: what Jesus' parents did, what were the formative influences on his life, and so on. Moreover, some of the information that is included is unconvincing. It is incredible that Jesus should predict his fate in the terms suggested by 9.22 (although I accept that 9.44 is a more convincing prediction). The discrepancies between the Gospels, notably in the trial narrative, pose a serious problem for historians which must not be ignored. This demonstrates the point that the Gospels must be read on their terms and not on ours (even though we bring our agenda to the act of reading). When this point is acknowledged it is possible to make snatches at the elusive Jesus of history, even to reconstruct an outline of his career. But there is much that we cannot say from a reading of the Gospels, and much that we might not want to say. This problem of information is created by the texts themselves.

One of the problems with some research in this area is that it tends to treat the Gospels as uniform documents and to ignore the differences between them.[12] Luke is by no means necessarily the same kind of text as Mark or Matthew. Luke has his own interests and methodology, notably his avowed contact with Hellenistic literature. These parallels with Graeco-Roman writing, and the nature of the text which they produce, distinguish Luke among the Gospels. This point must be duly acknowledged in the discussion of genre.

Luke's affinity with Hellenistic literature is historiographical as well as biographical. Luke self-consciously sets his work in a tradition of research which supplies the meaning of the facts recorded (1.1–4). Comparisons are often drawn with the opening part of Josephus' *Against Apion* (a near contemporary of Luke's) which is dedicated to Epaphroditus and which initially sets out the author's purpose in writing.[13] There is a similar Preface at the beginning of *Apion* Book II which recalls the Preface that opens Acts (Luke's second volume). Several features of Greek historiography are mirrored in the Gospel.[14] Luke attempts to fix his history with reference to various authorities in 1.5 and (especially) 3.1. He follows Hellenistic conventions in translating foreign words (e.g. 8.54; 23.33) and in assimilating Jewish concepts to more familiar Greek ones (e.g. the reference to 'tiles' in 5.19). Hellenistic too is Luke's interest in moral topics, such as his attitude to wealth in 16.14. His writing of Acts as a companion to the Gospel supports the theory that Luke conceives his work as history of a kind. This again distinguishes him from Mark and Matthew and brings Luke closer to Hellenistic modes of writing through which the Gospel genre is apparently modified.

A variant of this hypothesis observes that the Lucan Preface is closer to Hellenistic scientific writing than to historiography as such.[15] Loveday Alexander defines the 'scientific' tradition widely to include medicine, philosophy, mathematics, rhetoric and even magic and mantic sciences. She argues that it well explains the brevity of the Preface with its tortuous vocabulary. This is not to say that Luke lacks affinities with historiography but that the Gospel extends that sphere of influence to include a wider gamut of literature. The philosophical literature in particular is held by Charles Talbert to explain Luke's form; notably, Talbert cites the third-century CE writer Diogenes Laertius and his *Lives of Eminent Philosophers*.[16]

This diverse information can be summarized in the following way. We are left with a picture of Luke as writing after the model of Mark and with a knowledge of Matthew but at points adapting his sources and perhaps even trying to correct what he regarded as unhelpful tendencies in the earlier literature. Part of his method was to use Greek literary conventions. Our thoughts about genre must be broad enough to accommodate the similarities with wider Hellenistic literature (and sufficiently critical to observe Luke's differences from it). Perhaps it matters rather less to classify Luke as a precise literary type – for such precision inevitably begs questions – as to identify those features of Luke which give the Gospel its character. It is perfectly possible to read Luke without reaching an exact judgment about its genre, even when this is acknowledged to be an important question.

LUKE AND ACTS AS TEXTS WRITTEN BY THE SAME AUTHOR

One of the ways in which Luke differs from the other Gospels is in its affinities to another New Testament text, the Acts of the Apostles. The two texts are strikingly similar in style, language and ideas. The overwhelming consensus of scholarship is that Luke and Acts were written by the same author and form a two-volumed work. This view deserves brief examination since it bears on the interpretation of the Gospel and on Luke's overall purpose.

The two texts certainly display a family resemblance. This is obvious from their openings. Both are dedicated to a Theophilus (Luke 1.1; Acts 1.1). The introduction to Acts clearly presupposes an earlier work ('In the first part of my work, Theophilus, I gave an account of all that Jesus did and taught from the beginning', Acts 1.1). Given the reference to Theophilus in Luke, it stretches credulity to suggest that this can be another Gospel or a lost text when Luke fits the bill so well. Moreover, the narrative description of the ascension in the two works (despite the differences between them), which is absent from the other New Testament documents, suggests a common authorship (see Luke 24.50–1; Acts 1.9–11). This hypothesis is reinforced by the observation that both works describe a geographical progress. Luke ends in Jerusalem and Acts in Rome. This mode of construction confirms that the texts are related and that Paul's appearance in Rome matches that of Jesus in Jerusalem in what seems to be a deliberate parallel.

It would, however, be wrong to say that Luke and Acts are two halves of a composite work, still less that they were once a single text that is now disjointed. They are in fact quite independent of each other. Each has features which are not shared by the other. Acts is the sequel to the Gospel (and we have no idea how much later than Luke it was written). The view taken in this book is that Luke and Acts were written by the same author, whom we will call Luke, and that this observation affects the interpretation of both texts. In practice, however, we shall be concerned here with Luke and shall examine Acts only when this is relevant to the argument in hand.

THE AUTHOR AND THE DATE OF COMPOSITION

Next, we must consider Luke's identity and the probable date that his Gospel was written.

Luke as an author gives few clues about his identity. Papias (c.125 CE) does not mention him but the Muratorian Canon (late second century CE) says that: 'after the ascension of Christ, Luke, whom Paul had taken with him as an expert in the way, wrote under his own name and according to his own understanding. He had not, of course, seen the Lord in the flesh, and therefore he begins to tell the story from the birth of John on, insofar as it was accessible to him'. Eusebius (*Hist. Eccl.* 3.4.6) adds that Luke was from Antioch but the reliability of this report is uncertain. The only Luke mentioned in the New Testament is 'Luke, the beloved physician' of Colossians 4.14, Philemon 24 and 2 Timothy 4.11 whom the sources indicate was a Gentile. There is a broad case for supposing that this Luke was the author of the Gospel and Acts, especially since his connection with Paul would have lent him prestige in the Christian communities; but the case falls short of formal proof. Luke-Acts has been studied assiduously to discern whether it displays authentic medical terminology,[17] but again the evidence for this is inconclusive. All we can say is that Luke was probably a Gentile; that he possibly had a connection with Paul (and may have accompanied the apostle on some of his journeys – although the 'we'-passages in Acts are confined to maritime travel); and that he had a literary expertise which makes his Gospel for the most part a pleasure to read.

Recent scholarship has drawn attention to the importance of the 'implied author' as a feature of a text. The 'implied author' is the impression of the author which the reader reconstructs from the story. This of course depends on the view of his or her identity which the actual author chooses to disclose there. I shall say more about the role of the 'implied author' in Chapter 2 but I note here that this is a fruitful path to Luke given the little that we know about him from external evidence. We should not, however, confuse the implied author with the actual author or assume that the implied author necessarily remains consistent from text to text (i.e. from Luke to Acts), or even from one part of a text to another.

We do not know when the Gospel was written but we can date it within broad parameters. Some scholars, observing that Acts ends with the house-arrest of Paul, think that Luke and Acts were written in the 60s of the first century. This date is almost unbelievably early. Luke is dependent on Mark and probably also on Matthew. Mark may not have been written until after 70 CE (its earliest accepted date is 64 CE). Luke was certainly not written before the Fall of Jerusalem (see 21.20). The generally-agreed date is in the 80s or 90s, perhaps towards the end of this span if the theory that Luke knew Matthew is adopted. This date coheres with the view, recorded by the Muratorian Canon, that Luke was a companion of Paul but not an eyewitness of Jesus.

We have no idea where Luke was written and where the first readers lived. Many suggestions have been made; Rome is prominent among them. About the only thing that we can say with confidence on this issue is that Luke was written outside Palestine. Again, however, we can gain a broader picture by asking about Luke's 'implied readers'. These are those for whom the narrative with its particular set of emphases was apparently designed. This reconstruction of the evidence will be attempted in Chapter 2.

THE 'PROTO-LUKE' HYPOTHESIS

An issue that has often been discussed is whether the form in which we know Luke is the form in which the Gospel was originally written. Some scholars think that the Infancy Narrative (chapters 1–2) was added later and that a 'proto-Luke' (an earlier version of Luke) originally began with the preaching of John the Baptist in 3.1. This suggestion is perhaps not as unlikely as it seems. Luke itself contains evidence that different versions of the Gospel circulated at an early period. Chapter 22 exists in two different forms in the manuscript tradition. Some 'Western' manuscripts omit the full text of the eucharistic words of Jesus (22.19–20), perhaps because a scribe was reluctant to disclose what was regarded as sacred tradition to a reader outside the Christian community.[18] There is a similar omission in 22.43–4 concerning the behaviour of Jesus on the Mount of Olives. We have no proof that a more primitive form of the Gospel stands behind our present text but the way in which 3.1 is introduced, which seems out of place given the information presented in chapters 1–2, makes this a reasonable possibility. We do know that the other Gospels passed through different recensions: Mark acquired a longer ending (16.8b–20) and John another chapter (chapter 21). It would perhaps be perilous to assume that we have *any* of the Gospels in the form in which they were originally written. Our interest in this book is primarily with the final form of Luke; but clearly the question of earlier editions is an intriguing one which affects the interpretation of the text.

THE SOURCES OF THE GOSPEL

The question of Luke's sources may be discussed quite briefly. It involves consideration of what has come to be called 'The Synoptic Problem'.

The problem of the relationship between the Synoptic Gospels is a vexed issue in New Testament scholarship. The problem, simply stated, concerns the question of which Gospel was written first and what sources – including the other Gospels – were available to the first three Evangelists. It should be said straight away that this problem is virtually insoluble. No resolution of it has yet been proposed which is able to escape some form of criticism. Study of the problem has, however, produced some well-defined positions which may be explained here.

The majority of scholars who have worked on the Synoptic Problem accept the possibility that Mark was the first Gospel to be written. The exception is the group of scholars who support the 'Griesbach hypothesis' (see below). The majority hypothesis needs careful statement for we cannot necessarily assume that our canonical Mark is its original form. Mark was certainly expanded by the addition of material at the end of chapter 16 and it may have existed in a now-lost but abbreviated version which stands behind the present text (the so-called *Ur-Markus*, or proto-Mark, theory). To argue for Marcan priority is thus not to argue that Mark reached its *present* form before the other Gospels were written.

The grounds for accepting Marcan priority have been stated in an article by Geoffrey Styler.[19] Styler observes a number of passages where individual points of style and detail suggest that Matthew and Luke were written with a knowledge of Mark. So far as Matthew is concerned, Styler notes his description of the death of John the Baptist (Matthew 14.3–12 = Mark 6.17–29). There are features in Matthew's story which he thinks betray knowledge of Mark's. The words 'and the king was sorry' are integral to Mark but alien to Matthew, who has already said that Herod *wanted* to kill John. Matthew also forgets that the story is told as a 'flashback' and builds a smooth transition to the next pericope at its conclusion (14.12–13). Another example of Marcan priority is Pilate's offer to release a prisoner in Matthew 27.15–18 (= Mark 15.6–15). Mark's sequence is clear and intelligible but Matthew blurs it badly. He removes Mark's logic by *first* making Pilate offer a choice between Jesus and Barabbas (27.17) but *then* stating that 'he knew it was from envy that they had delivered him up' (27.18). The confusion in Matthew suggests that he knew Mark but inexpertly retained his flow of thought. The six examples which Styler produces have a certain cumulative force. They explain some features of Matthew which are otherwise difficult to account for.

It might be objected, as I shall show in a moment, that there are places in the Synoptic Gospels where the similarity between all three Gospels is best explained on the hypothesis that *Matthew* and not Mark is the 'middle term'. I do not think that this invalidates the case for Marcan priority once we recognize that Mark itself possibly passed through more than one version. It is probably true to say that in places Matthew does represent the most original form of text. It is however in general easier to support Marcan priority over Matthew than the other way round (and very difficult to support Lucan priority over either). Marcan priority over Matthew is thus a hard-and-fast rule but not an absolute rule. It claims more supporters than detractors today. (There *are* no absolute rules in the study of the Synoptic Problem.)

Styler also argues for Marcan priority over Luke. This hypothesis is easier to sustain because Luke follows Mark's order more closely than does Matthew. Styler identifies several passages where it is easy to believe that Luke's version is 'secondary' and hard to believe otherwise.[20] The best example is the sermon in the Nazareth synagogue, Luke 4.16–30. Here Luke retains themes that are prominent in Mark 6.1–6 but he works many of them in artificially and presents what appears to be a 'secondary' version of the story. In the story of Jairus' Daughter (Luke 8.40–56, cf. Mark 5.21–4, 35–43) Luke blunders in allowing the mother to enter the house – for she has been there all the time – and appears to stumble in suggesting that the inner group who witness the miracle scoff at Jesus. This statement, however, is comprehensible when Mark's version is read, for there Jesus allows only three disciples to accompany him and the people scoff when Jesus says that the child is merely asleep. Luke compresses Mark's account. In so doing he is guilty of a carelessness which betrays his source. Luke is clearly secondary at this point to a Gospel which has a fuller narrative.

Belief in Marcan priority has often been combined with belief in another source which is cryptically called Q, after the German *Quelle* ('source'). Q has never been found, evidently because it was never committed to writing, but several scholars offer confident (in some cases, rather *too* confident) reconstructions of it.[21] This fusion of sources yields what has come to be called the 'two-source' hypothesis, according to which Matthew and Luke used Mark and Q independently of each other (and their own private material too). Its advantage, it might unfairly be said, is that a putative source can never be examined and so it can be held to contain anything a Gospel critic would like it to. That Luke used Mark and Q and worked independently of Matthew has been the dominant theory in the past century. Only quite recently has a scholarly consensus begun to emerge that this is not correct.

There are greater objections to the 'two-source' theory than its protagonists are prepared to concede. These have been cogently stated by Sanders and Davies.[22] The theory's fatal flaw is the strong evidence that Matthew and Luke were not written independently of each other but that one of them used the other. The 'triple tradition'

– incidents which occur in all three Synoptists – throws up about a thousand agreements between Matthew and Luke against Mark. These are far too many to be coincidental. They suggest that Matthew and Luke did *not* use Mark independently of each other. This calls into question the existence of Q (and shows that belief in the priority of Mark is hypothetical and neither finally proven nor even finally provable). We must also consider those places where Mark and Q overlap (e.g. in the temptation story). This overlap, noted by B. H. Streeter in 1911, raises the possibility that Mark himself knew Q.[23] That would mean the defeat of the 'two-source' hypothesis because Mark could not then be held to be uncontaminated by Q.

If Q is regarded as an invalid hypothesis, this must mean that either Matthew or Luke used the other. Sanders and Davies observe that, in places in the triple tradition, Matthew and not Mark (but never Luke) is the most plausible middle term.[24] This indicates that, of all three Synoptic Gospels, Luke is the most likely to be dependent on the others. The hypothesis that Luke used Matthew, which they form from this information, requires careful statement. To prove it, we must look for something more precise than just Luke's knowledge of Matthaean passages or even of Matthaean themes. These would indicate only that Luke knew Matthew's sources which brings us back to the beginning of the Synoptic Problem. We must find hard evidence that Luke knew Matthew's *style and editorial activity* to place his knowledge of Matthew beyond doubt. According to Sanders and Davies, such evidence is indeed forthcoming from the text of Luke.[25]

I reproduce here their argument which seems to me quite plausible. In the story of the many from east and west, Luke 13.28 preserves the phrase from Matthew 8.12 that there will be 'weeping and gnashing of teeth' among those who deserve eschatological punishment. It is easier to suppose that Luke copied Matthew in this than that both independently copied Q because Matthew often uses the phrase but Luke never does again (and Mark never does at all). In the Commission of the Twelve (Luke 9.1–6 = Mark 6.6b–13 = Matthew 9.35; 10.1, 7–11, 14) there are several agreements between Matthew and Luke. One of them is very striking. In 9.5 Luke says that the disciples, if rejected, must shake off the dust from their feet when they leave 'that town'. This phrase agrees verbatim with Matthew 10.14 but the context is strikingly different: Luke 9.4 says 'whatever *house* you enter' and nothing about towns.

Matthew 10.11 has the words 'whatever town or village you enter' which make the succeeding phrase relevant. Luke 9.4 is based apparently on Mark 6.10 ('when you enter a house . . . ') and not on Matthew. The best explanation is that Luke has used both Matthew and Mark. The alternative – that Luke's reading is coincidental – is not at all convincing.

Thirdly, in the story of John the Baptist (Mark 1.2–3 and parallels) Mark's statement about John ('Behold I send' . . .) is from Malachi 3.1 or Exodus 23.20 but not a precise citation of either. Matthew and Luke lack the 'Behold I send' (but agree in placing it elsewhere; see Matthew 11.10 = Luke 7.27), and have their own version of the scriptural citation which in both cases ends with the words *emprosthen sou*, 'before you'. *Emprosthen* is a favourite word of Matthew's, and here Luke agrees with Matthew against Mark, Exodus and Malachi. This makes the suggestion that Luke used Matthew an irresistible one, for otherwise Luke would coincidentally have produced a citation which Matthew also records. That would stretch credulity to breaking point.

Sanders and Davies also include a discussion of the Griesbach hypothesis (the view that Mark is a redaction of Matthew and Luke).[26] They see it as 'mechanically feasible' but ask why Mark should have written a Gospel that contains so many omissions of consequence which are balanced merely by trivial insertions. The lack of a convincing reason for the writing of Mark is the Achilles heel of the Griesbach hypothesis. This argument represents a substantial objection to the theory that Mark is the third Gospel in chronological sequence. And the observation that Mark is more often the middle term than Matthew tends to support the theory of Marcan priority, with the proviso noted here that there may have been more than one edition of Mark.

I conclude therefore that Luke's sources were (or included) Mark and Matthew and I am far from convinced that it is necessary to posit the hypothetical Q, a version of which has never been discovered (and which I think constitutes a substantial problem for the theory). Luke was thus the third Gospel in the chronological sequence but I repeat that we do not know for sure that our version of Luke is the original one. Such uncertainty continues to make all study of Gospel relations a troublesome area.

If Luke used the other Synoptists, it is a reasonable assumption that part of his intention was to rework what they say. At this point we must briefly mention the theory of Eric Franklin that Luke was an interpreter of Paul and a critic of Matthew.[27] Franklin thinks that Luke reinterprets Paul's theological position in the light of his perception that Christianity is the fulfilment and logical outcome of Judaism.[28] Luke used Mark as a primary source. Mark determined the overall shape and outlook of the Gospel. Franklin thinks that Luke redeployed Matthew with a freedom related to his post-Pauline view that the Law no longer has a part to play in defining the boundaries of the people of God.[29] Luke tones down Matthew's attitude to the Law and is less hostile than he to the Jews. Luke is less confident about the present than Matthew and depicts the kingdom, although actually in the heavens, as hovering over but not yet realized in the contemporary situation.

I shall examine Franklin's views more closely in Chapter 6 and mention them here only to indicate that Luke may be a polemical text of sorts. Franklin is certainly wise to acknowledge the possibility, against Michael Goulder, that Luke may have used *other* sources besides Mark and Matthew.[30] This is intrinsically plausible although we cannot necessarily say what those sources were. The oral tradition must not be neglected in this assessment. It is sobering to recollect how little we actually *know* about the complex process which yielded the canonical Gospels.

A SYNOPSIS OF LUKE

Before reading Luke it will be helpful to take a broad panorama on what the Gospel contains.

Luke begins with a description of the births of John the Baptist and Jesus (chapters 1–2) which is not found in Mark (or for that matter in John). This material resembles Matthew's Infancy Narrative in style but not for the most part in content. The Lucan Infancy Narrative makes Jesus the promised Messiah born of the tribe of David. The significance of his mission is demonstrated by the Canticles (especially 2.29–32). The presumed death of Simeon after the *Nunc Dimittis* ('I have seen with my own eyes the deliverance you have made ready', 2.30–1) demonstrates that eschatological salvation has arrived with Jesus. This is crucial to the Gospel's plot where the story of salvation forms the major undercurrent to the story of Jesus and gives that story its meaning.

Chapter 3 tells the stories of John the Baptist and the baptism of Jesus. It counters the suggestion that John is Messiah and reserves this accolade for Jesus (3.15–17). Immediately after the baptism, a dominant tendency in Luke becomes evident. Geography is a powerful tool in the Gospel (as it is in Acts). There is a sense in which the spread of the Christian gospel can be compared to a ripple as Luke describes it. It begins in Galilee, spreads to Jerusalem, then beyond Palestine and finally, at the end of Acts, to Rome so that the two cities of prominence in the author's mind are visited in the two texts.

This process of expansion begins early in Luke. Chapter 4 records Jesus' sermon in the synagogue at his home town of Nazareth (after the temptation story, 4.1–13). Jesus here announces that the prophecy of Isaiah 61 ('the Spirit of the Lord is upon me') has been fulfilled in the presence of the congregation, with the implication that he is the one through whom God's eschatological enfranchisement is being discharged (4.14–30). From Nazareth Jesus goes to Capernaum (7.1) and thence to the towns and villages of Galilee (8.1). In the course of this journey he imparts teaching (notably in chapter 6) and works miracles, particularly the casting-out of demons which is an important feature of the plot because it demonstrates the onset of the kingdom of God.

There is a watershed in the Gospel in chapter 9 where Simon Peter identifies Jesus as the Messiah and the narrator says that Jesus forbids the promulgation of this knowledge (9.21). This incident is followed by the Transfiguration (9.28–36), in which Jesus appears to three disciples as a heavenly being, and the report of his decision to go to Jerusalem (9.51). The connection between the two events is far from incidental in the Gospel's plot. The journey has, in Luke's eyes, the status of a messianic visitation which will be emphasized in the story of the triumphal entry (see below). The Gospel gains its pathos from the fact that Jesus journeys to Jerusalem as Messiah only to be rejected by the Jewish authorities and crucified by the Romans. There is, however, the hint that he will visit Jerusalem again and that this time his visitation will be for judgment (see especially 13.35b).

The 'central section' of the Gospel (chapters 10–19) reads somewhat lamely after the drama of chapter 9. This section contains a large amount of teaching which is held together by loose narrative links that seem rather artificial and are not always consistent. They do, however, demonstrate that Luke retains the form of a story even when the author is not concerned directly with narrative. The teaching in this section is both ethical and eschatological in content. It is addressed to Luke's readers. For this reason it is significant that it should begin with an affirmation of the Christian mission. In chapter 10 Jesus sends out seventy (seventy-two?) messengers and tells them to prepare for his visit to the towns and villages bordering the Jordan (10.1–12). Instructions are given for the provision and reception of hospitality. The seventy-two exult in their mission on their return, says the narrator (10.17). They tell Jesus that even the demons had submitted in his name. This is followed by a vision of Jesus which states the meaning of his mission: 'I saw Satan fall, like lightning, from heaven' (10.18). The Christian mission, confirmed by Jesus, continues his own preaching activity. The passage directly encourages readers to participate in the mission.

In this central section of the Gospel we find many familiar sayings and parables of Jesus. Here are the good Samaritan (10.25–37), the Lord's Prayer (11.2–4) and the prodigal son (15.11–32). Despite the awkward transitions we would be much the poorer without this material. Luke was content to let the narrative serve loosely as a framework for the teaching. If this jars on modern readers, that is how it is. It would be wrong to skim through these chapters just because the links are awkward and imprecise.

Nevertheless the device of geographical progress is preserved in 18.35 and 19.1 by describing how Jesus approaches and then enters Jericho. Jesus' journey to Jerusalem is a journey towards his death as Luke explains it. The inexorable progress is emphasized by Luke's geographical interest. 19.28 describes how Jesus 'set out on the ascent to Jerusalem' and 19.29 how he came to the Mount of Olives. This is followed by the story of the triumphal entry (19.29–40) which has the nature of a messianic visitation of Jerusalem. The Messiah arrives in the Jewish capital only to be rejected by the leaders of the Jewish religion.

The cleansing of the temple is briefly described in 19.45–6. Luke describes how Jesus drives out the traders from the temple. This significant episode, reported only briefly, is followed by the statement that the powerful people want to bring about his death but are powerless to do so because the people hang on his words (19.47–8). It is only at this point in the Gospel that the authorities decide to kill Jesus (this should be contrasted with Mark 3.6).

The rest of the Gospel describes the growing hostility to Jesus. At the beginning of chapter 20 the chief priests and others ask a trick question to undermine his authority (20.1–8). This is followed by the parable of the vineyard (20.9–16) in which the landlord's only son is killed by the tenants (as Jesus will soon be killed). Again, the chief priests want to seize Jesus but are 'afraid' to do so (a nuanced statement) because of the people (20.19). They 'sent agents in the guise of honest men, to seize on some word of his that they could use as a pretext for handing him over to the authority and jurisdiction of the governor' (20.20). These agents, testing him again, ask whether it is lawful to pay taxes to Caesar (20.21–6). They are given a suitably discreet answer (20.25). The Sadducees next question him about the resurrection (20.27–38), after which 'nobody dared put any further question to him' (20.40). The substance of this section is that no-one could convict Jesus of misbehaviour no matter how hard they tried.

Chapter 21 is Luke's version of the Synoptic eschatological discourse. 21.20 is a prediction of the Roman destruction of Jerusalem which took place in 70 CE. The verse undoubtedly shows knowledge of that event. This dates Luke after this time and presents 70 CE as a stage in the eschatological process which Jesus himself had predicted. It reminds the readers that many of the eschatological signs have been accomplished already. It is in this light that they are reminded of the hope for the coming of the Son of Man 'in a cloud with power and great glory' (21.27). This verse sounds a note of eschatological imminence. The chapter ends with a warning that the end might happen at any time: 'Be on your guard; do not let your minds be dulled . . . so that the great day catches you suddenly' (21.34). This warning represents the heart of Luke's eschatological teaching.

Chapter 22 begins the dénouement of the Gospel. The Passover is approaching (22.1). The chief priests and scribes want to dispose of Jesus (22.2). Satan enters into Judas Iscariot (having bided his time since 4.13). Judas goes to the priests and offers to betray Jesus for money (22.3–6). The main part of chapter 22 describes the Last Supper. Jesus vows not to eat bread and drink wine until he does so new in the kingdom of God (22.16, 18). After supper Jesus goes with the disciples to the Mount of Olives where a crowd appears with Judas to arrest him. Jesus is taken to the house of the High Priest for a summary trial whose purpose is to gain evidence to denounce him to the Romans (22.66–71). Pilate is not convinced by this evidence. He wants to release Jesus but cavils under pressure from 'the chief priests, councillors, and people' (23.13), having sent Jesus to Herod for review (23.6–12). Jesus is given over 'to their will' (23.25) and led away for execution (23.26). At the moment of his death the centurion pronounces that 'beyond all doubt, this man was innocent' (23.47). Jesus is laid in Joseph of Arimathea's tomb, carefully watched by the women (23.49–56).

Luke concludes with the resurrection of Jesus. There are two kinds of story in chapter 24. This chapter describes both the discovery of the empty tomb and the resurrection appearances of Jesus. Their combined force is to create the impression that the resting of Jesus' body in the tomb is not the end of him. Whatever the cause of the empty tomb – and more than one reason has been proposed to explain it – it makes the point that the absence of the body is related to the heavenly Lordship of Jesus which is attested both by the resurrection appearances and by the ascension narrative (24.50–1).

Luke closes by describing the departure of Jesus. This raises the question of his heavenly presence through which the whole Gospel gains its meaning and which is developed more coherently in the early chapters of Acts, especially in the speeches (e.g. Acts 2.22–36).

Chapter 2

Luke as a narrative

We have seen that Luke tells the story of Jesus, albeit selectively, from the period before his birth until after his death with the resurrection and ascension. Any interpretation of Luke must take account of this fundamental narrative structure. In this chapter I want to examine the narrative basis of the Gospel and to ask how this can best be approached from the perspective of literary criticism.

To do this demands an initial explanation of 'narrative criticism' and of what constitutes a narrative. Much has been written about both matters in the field of literary studies. We must consider a variety of issues including plot, readers, characterization and manner of narration.

WHAT IS NARRATIVE CRITICISM?

'Narrative criticism', as an approach to the Gospels, recognizes the primacy of the present form of text and assumes that, although the Gospels are part of the scriptural canon, they can be interpreted by the same kinds of methods as secular narratives. Narrative criticism is one of the newer approaches to the Gospels which have been explored in the twentieth century. It will be helpful initially to review its predecessors.

The early part of the twentieth century was dominated by the approach called 'form criticism'.[1] The form critics believed that the Gospels (like the Hebrew narratives) represent the fusion, and presentation in written form, of traditions which had previously enjoyed oral circulation. They held that these oral traditions were shaped by the circumstances which they addressed in the life of the primitive church. In order to interpret a particular passage, the form critics argued, it is necessary to identify how a particular saying was used in the church, and then to ask how the church adapted a saying of Jesus to support that usage (if indeed the saying really originated with Jesus). Rudolph Bultmann divided the Synoptic material into 'sayings' and 'narratives'.[2] Martin Dibelius went so far as to distinguish six kinds of material in the Gospels: sermons, paradigms, tales, legends, passion story and myth.[3]

It will be seen from this brief summary that form criticism is essentially an historical method. It involves seeing the text as a repository of earlier traditions and combing the material for the different layers of tradition that lie behind it. Form criticism exudes the confidence that this procedure can successfully be undertaken and that the results which are obtained in this way are valuable ones.

Form criticism has two main weaknesses. First of all, it tends to divert interest from the present form of text through its interest in the traditions that lie behind it. This has the effect, secondly, of presenting the Evangelists mainly as compilers of material and not themselves as creative writers. On this view, the differences between the Gospels are explained through recourse to the theory that each Evangelist handled the traditional material in a different way. Attention rests with the generic classification of forms and not with the interests of the Evangelists themselves.

A second major approach to the Gospels is called 'redaction criticism'.[4] This approach was introduced in the 1950s in two books: Conzelmann's *Luke* and Willi Marxsen's *Mark the Evangelist*.[5] Redaction criticism analyzes the way in which the material is arranged in a particular Gospel. The form critics compared the Evangelists to threaders of beads on a string. The redaction critics showed that they threaded their beads in a particular way. Their arrangement of material is by no means a haphazard one. Redaction criticism agrees with form criticism that much of the Gospels' material is traditional but argues that the examination of how that material is handled reveals the perspectives of the different Evangelists. The redaction critics examined literary factors like vocabulary, style and compositional techniques to see how the Gospels vary from each other.

It should not be assumed that redaction criticism produces an overall 'theology' of the Evangelists. Its aims are more limited than this. A redactional study of Luke does not study all of Luke's theological convictions but merely his *handling* of the traditions he received and the consequences which this has for determining

Luke's purpose in the Gospel. Redaction criticism tries to isolate the unique theological purpose of each Gospel but not to produce a comprehensive theology of the Gospels.

Many redaction critics assume the 'two-source' solution to the Synoptic Problem. They posit that Matthew and Luke used Mark and Q independently of each other. More recently, with the growing challenge to this solution, redaction criticism has focussed on Luke's use of his sources, particularly on the possibility that he used Matthew as well as Mark. This is the special feature of Michael Goulder's book, *Luke: A New Paradigm* (1989).

A variant on redaction criticism is 'composition criticism'. Composition criticism extends the scope of redaction criticism by focussing on those themes and words which are considered important for the Evangelist's theology.[6] It places theology at the forefront of a reading of the Gospels and offers a more comprehensive view of the theology than redaction criticism. An example of Lucan composition criticism is Robert O'Toole's *The Unity of Luke's Theology* (1984).

With narrative criticism, the emphasis is different. Narrative criticism represents a turning-away from theology in a reading of the Gospels and an interest in the structural mechanics of the text. The difference in outlook from the older methods should not be minimized. Moore goes so far as to argue that narrative criticism represents an *importation* into biblical studies and that it is not simply the child of redaction and composition criticism.[7] Narrative criticism does not deny the importance of theology but it does observe that theology, far from being brought into the text as it were from an outside store-cupboard, is part of the Gospel's form and does not (and cannot) precede the form of the narrative. In order to understand the Gospels we must consider their structure and the way in which the story is told. This demands attention to plot and characterization, aporias and irony. The story that the Gospels tell is not just a vehicle for its theology but a significant entity in its own right.

Several books on the Gospels employ a narrative-critical approach. An example is Alan Culpepper's *Anatomy of the Fourth Gospel* (1983).[8] Culpepper cites Murray Krieger's distinction between the use of a text as window and mirror. The 'window' approach is one in which scholars use the Fourth Gospel (like other New Testament literature) to reconstruct a picture of the Johannine community. They peer *through* the text to see what lies behind it.

The mirror approach, by contrast, locates the meaning of the text in the relationship between the text and the reader. Culpepper comments:

> Meaning is produced in the experience of reading the text as a whole and making the mental moves the text calls for its reader to make, quite apart from the questions concerning its sources and origin. As one reads the gospel, the voice of the narrator introduces the narrative world of the text, its characters, values, norms, conflicts, and the events which constitute the plot of the story. The narrator conveys the author's perspective to the reader and sends signals which establish expectations, distance and intimacy, and powerfully affect the reader's sense of identification and involvement. The narrator's claims and the norms of the story woo, beckon and challenge the reader to believe that the story, its narrative world, and its central character reveal something profoundly true about the 'real' world in which the reader lives.[9]

Culpepper includes chapters on the role of the narrator in John, on narrative time, plot, characters, implicit commentary and implied reader. This represents a sea-change from the older Johannine scholarship which was preoccupied with the history of the Johannine community, not least with the question of how the Fourth Gospel relates to the Johannine Epistles. Narrative criticism has the effect, initially, of shifting attention from the question of whether there is historical tradition in the Fourth Gospel (as in other texts) to the recognition that the Johannine Jesus is first and foremost a character in the story. This is the matrix through which the historical questions must be asked. Such questions cannot be posed at all until we take account of John's literary character.

'Narrative criticism' is also explored in a book published by Mark A. Powell in 1990.[10] Powell points out that the term has a peculiar reference to biblical studies and lacks a precise counterpart in secular criticism: 'If classified by secular critics, it might be viewed as a subspecies of the new rhetorical criticism or as a variety of the reader-response movement.'[11] Powell here identifies the variegated nature of the method and refuses to accept that it can be reduced to a simple or convenient formula. He draws attention to the role of the reader and his or her response to the text. Powell discusses the work of Fish and Iser on the approach of the first-time reader, and Fish's later work on the function of 'interpretive communities'. He introduces the concept of the 'implied reader' and defines 'a story' as encompassing events, characters and settings: 'Somebody does something to someone, somewhere, at some time. The "something" that is done is an event, the "somebody" and "someone" are characters, and the "somewhere" and "sometime" are settings.'[12]

It should be clearer from this review what I am trying to do in this book. My aim is to offer a reading of Luke which takes account of its literary character and to examine the features that make the story work. This will include consideration of Powell's three areas: events, characters and setting. I have called his 'events' the plot, and his 'settings' narrative time, but otherwise my approach is similar to his. Although I shall not ignore historical and redactional questions, my aim is first and foremost to read Luke as a story and to examine how it makes its effect on you and me, the readers. This takes precedence (at least initially) over the attempt to construct a morphology of Lucan ideas.

In setting out my programme, I want to express one fear that came to me from a reading of Culpepper's book. This is the worry that 'narrative criticism' can be used as an excuse for presenting the Gospels as homogeneous documents by explaining their tensions and problems with reference to the potentially obscure nature of the reader's response. (I am not accusing Culpepper of doing this but presenting my response to a reading of his work.) There is the constant danger that 'narrative criticism' can become the vehicle for disguising or even removing problems from the text when in fact the act of reading throws up new problems at every step. This is in the nature of the reading process itself. A brief example from Luke will show what I mean. For years I simply assumed, having been told it was true, that Matthew and Luke both advocate the doctrine of the virgin birth. It was only when I was writing this book that I saw that Luke's account is more ambiguous than is often acknowledged, and that the virgin birth has to be *inferred* by the reader from the text and is not definitively stated there. Some readers may choose not to find it there at all. Emphasizing the absence of a definitive statement is a valid reading of what Luke says about the virgin birth. This makes reading Luke a dangerous process for those who see the virgin birth as a *sine qua non* of Christian theology and whose presuppositions are challenged by the discovery that the narrative is not quite so forthright on this point.

Even more dangerous – or challenging – is the paradigm shift that is currently taking place in New Testament studies whereby the belief in a metaphysical 'other' – for instance the existence of God or the necessary validity of Christianity – is removed as a presupposition for reading the literature. Moore has an interesting comparison between what is happening now and what took place earlier in the twentieth century when Rudolph Bultmann announced his 'demythologizing' programme: 'Today, it is biblical criticism itself that cries out for demythologizing. And whereas the modernist demythologizer, Bultmann, found it necessary to wrestle critically with the New Testament's rendering of the metaphysical in terms of the contingent, "the other side in terms of this side", the postmodern demythologizer will find it necessary to address the New Testament critic's propensity to render "this side in terms of the other side".'[13]

Moore is right to say that narrative criticism may not turn out to be the comforting thing it could be assumed to be. My aim here is not to argue the case that we can, or should, attempt exegesis without Caputo's 'celestial, transcendental justifications',[14] but to make the more restricted point that reading Luke can be a dangerous and even a subversive business as well as a reassuring one. This is because readers continually discover a range of meanings there and because the readings offered by some people may subvert those which others hold dear.

No single reading can exhaust the range of meaning in Luke (or any other text). Luke itself proves this point in the parable of the sower (Luke chapter 8). The form critics say that this parable was developed into an allegory in the primitive church. Originally, perhaps, there were only two kinds of ground: that which bore fruit and that which did not. The allegorical interpretation Luke gives the parable means that it has acquired a potentially unlimited range of meaning. The different meanings which it is given in books, articles and sermons confirm that this is so. We read this story of Jesus and construct its meaning as we hear and talk about it. The sower reminds us that we should not think that any single interpretation of the parable – not even Luke's interpretation of it – has a final and decisive significance. What emerges is the need for further and continual interpretation. This is enjoined upon the reader by Luke's own allegorical interpretation.

Or take the view that the Last Supper is really the last supper.[15] The title 'Last Supper' comes from Jesus' statement that he will not eat bread or drink wine until he does so new in the kingdom of God

(22.16, 18). The finality of this statement is however controverted not much later in the Gospel by the further statement that Jesus breaks bread with the disciples whom he joins on the road to Emmaus (24.30). This is not to descry the narrative integrity of Luke 22 but to observe that the fraction in Luke gains its weighty meaning through repetition. It is repeated whenever the Gospel is read. The fraction is repeated again at every Christian eucharist in a further demonstration of the point that Jesus' hopes about the future have yet to be realized.

This brings us to the area of deconstruction and to the ground inhabited by Derrida. My aim in Chapter 3 is not to offer a Derridean reading of Luke which exposes its contradictions and subverts some dominant meanings (although I shall move in that direction in Chapter 4). I do however want to note the problems which the text raises and to explain how I have (provisionally) dealt with them. In doing this, I want to argue that Luke is less homogeneous than some scholars suggest and in particular to explore the contradictions in the narrative whereby layers of meaning are suggested to the reader. It would be wrong – indeed dishonest – to pretend that this is not the case and to make the act of reading a simplistic exercise which looks only for harmony and continuity.

WHAT IS A NARRATIVE?

Our next task is to consider the nature of narrative. I begin with a citation from a theorist in the field:

> Whenever a piece of news is conveyed, whenever something is reported, there is a mediator – the voice of a narrator is audible. I term this phenomenon 'mediacy' (*Mittelarkeit*). Mediacy is the general characteristic which distinguishes narrative from other forms of literary art.[16]

Stanzel here introduces 'a narrative' as a story *mediated* to the reader by the narrator. The fact of mediacy makes it a narrative. Narratives occur in every area of human life and in a plenitude of forms. We are concerned here with Luke as a narrative *text* (rather than say, a tone poem or stained-glass window). A text is 'a finite, structured whole composed of language signs'.[17] The designation of Luke as a *narrative* text depends on the fact that, in it, a sequence of events – a story – is related by a narrator. The narrator in Luke is undramatized – that is to say, he does not play a part in the story. One of the features of Luke's narrator is that he does not agree at every point with the implied author or the central character. Nevertheless, he is a crucial feature of the text. Luke's story is composed of a variety of smaller units (many of them derived from the earlier Gospels). The narrator is responsible for the (in)coherence which emerges when these units are read together. His story comes to life in the act of reading. It impacts on the readers in such a way as to provoke a response in and from them.

As with other narratives, the readers' response depends on *what* the story is and *how* it is told. No two stories are the same, nor are two story-tellers or ways of telling a story (and thus no two Gospels). Narrative as a process involves an infinite variety, hence Stanzel's description of it as an 'art-form'. The artist's skill lies in shaping the different possibilities and in constructing the various elements to yield the finished product.

WHAT MAKES THE GOSPELS NARRATIVES?

The question arises of what makes the Gospels narratives. This should be formally answered (and the answer not merely assumed). The point is that the Gospels relate a story which is mediated to the reader by the narrator. The narrator introduces the plot and explains the conditions under which it operates. He tells the reader the meaning of the plot and the motives of the characters (notably Jesus) as well as what happens in the drama.

The story which the four Gospels tell – their 'plot' – is different in every case. In Luke, the narrator introduces the reader to Jewish history through his description of John's birth with its background in Hebrew literature. The main part of the story concerns the events of the life of Jesus and the tragedy of his death. Luke continues his story in his second volume which is, broadly speaking, the story of the primitive church. A further theme in Luke's plot is the attention which is given to external events, including the information specified by 3.1 and the affinities I have noticed with Greek historiography.

Since Luke is a mediated story, we must examine the nature of that story and the conditions of mediacy under which it operates. This is what I shall do in the rest of this chapter. I begin with a further consideration of the question of authorship (which is more complicated than we have so far assumed).

THE REAL AUTHOR

All narratives are written by a 'real author'. The real author is the person who puts the pen to paper and leaves the text in its finished form. We may or may not know who the real author is but his or her's is the abiding genius which leaves its mark on the text. In the case of Luke we have seen that the 'real author' is a more or less anonymous Christian of the late first century who was perhaps a Gentile, a companion of Paul and who may have been a doctor.

One of the contentions of this book is that all the Gospels probably passed through different recensions. We do not not know how many recensions but a simple answer to the question of how the Gospels evolved is unlikely to be convincing. This view has implications for evaluating the question of the 'real author'. Is the real author the person who wrote the original Luke or the person who left the Gospel in the form that we now know Luke? The answer, of course, is that we do not know. The 'real author' is as much the reader's construct as the 'implied author' whom I will introduce in a moment. We reconstruct the real author from what we learn about him or her from internal and especially from external evidence. In the case of Luke we do not have very much evidence to work on. I shall assume that one person was responsible for the main part of the text but that others may have expanded what he wrote. The most intriguing question is whether this person wrote the Infancy Narrative (chapters 1–2). To this there is no definite answer, but perhaps some indication that he did write this material.

THE IMPLIED AUTHOR

Luke as we know him is essentially an 'implied author'. The 'implied author' is the author as he or she is reconstructed by the reader from the narrative. Wayne Booth illustrates the 'implied author' by discussing the work of Henry Fielding:

> The author of *Jonathan Wild* is by implication very much concerned with public affairs and with the effects of unchecked ambition on the 'great men' who attain to power in the world. If we had only this novel by Fielding, we would infer from it that in his real life he was much more single-mindedly engrossed in his role as magistrate and reformer of public manners than is suggested by the implied author of *Joseph Andrews* and *Tom Jones*

— to say nothing of *Shamela* (what would we infer about Fielding if he had never written anything but *Shamela*!).[18]

It goes without saying that the stance adopted by 'implied author' can vary from text to text, although the real author is the same, and even from one part of a text to another. The implied author should not be confused with the real author, especially not in the absence of concrete information about the real author (let the reader of the Gospels beware!). He is however related to the real author in that he is the real author's own creation and the product of his literary skill and judgment.

The recognition that there is an *implied* author in every text compensates for the fact that, as so often with ancient literature, we know little or nothing about the actual author. We shall now introduce ourselves to Luke's implied author.

William Kurz proposes the following points about Luke's implied author.[19] In the Preface Luke introduces himself as a careful historical investigator who sifts evidence and presents it in a coherent narrative. In this context he uses terms which occur in non-biblical history. Luke is moreover the only Gospel to be addressed to a named patron. The agreement in this with Josephus' *Against Apion* shows this self-conscious literary outlook as the primary face of Luke's implied author.

Kurz also presents him as an 'insider' or Christian. The use of the first-person plural, again especially in the Preface, makes this Luke the representative of the Christian community who presents an(other) ordered version of the story of Jesus. This in turn explains his choice of material, which is determined by his membership of the church and his knowledge of the oral and written records about Jesus. He chooses to write in a style that recalls earlier Jewish narrative like the books of Samuel, the Kings and the Maccabees. The implied author takes upon himself the catechetical purpose of confirming the truth about which Theophilus has been orally instructed (1.4).

Luke's style presents him as an author who knows both Hellenistic and biblical Greek. Kurz thinks that the abrupt transition from the elegant and extended complex Preface to the biblical paratactic style 'seems too deliberately conspicuous to be overlooked'.[20] It is not just a stylistic variation but the conscious declaration of purpose or intention in the Gospel. Luke begins with the claim to investigate matters in the style of Greek historiography but his language quickly makes the point that the plot is essentially a biblical one and the story rooted in the context of Jewish eschatology. This is a good example of the need for readers to examine *how* something is said as well as *what* is said in the Gospels. Luke is writing, as it were, with double vision. He has an eye to the Greek world but he reminds readers who approach from that perspective that his subject-matter cannot be understood apart from Jewish hopes about the future.

A point worth considering is whether the implied author of Luke is identical with the implied author of Acts given that Acts incorporates 'we'-passages whereas Luke does not. Kurz notes that Luke's eyewitness claims are more moderate than Josephus' and that the 'we'-passages demand only limited participation in Paul's maritime travel. Yet there *is* a difference in perspective given that in one text the implied author admits to not being an eyewitness of the events he records (Luke 1.1–4), but in another claims to have participated in Paul's journeys. We should not too readily accept that the *persona* of the implied author is identical in the two texts mentioned.

We should add to Kurz's assessment Dawsey's point that the implied author knows how to distinguish between the words of Jesus and the commentary of the narrator and presents himself as a complex figure who allows ambiguities to remain in the text.[21] His claim to have investigated things carefully is substantiated by this observation. Luke has certainly edited the words of Jesus but his attempt to preserve earlier tradition (i.e. tradition about Jesus) is an honest one. Luke was aided by his knowledge of Mark and Matthew which he has reworked but by no means entirely recast.

THE NARRATOR

Distinct from the implied author (and the characters) is the narrator. The narrator is a rhetorical agent who guides the reader through the narrative, introduces him to its world and characters and supplies the perspective from which the action can (or should) be viewed. The narrator may or may not be a character in the story (he is not in Luke). He may disagree with the implied author, in which case he is known as an 'unreliable narrator'.

Luke's narrator speaks with a distinctive voice and has his own characteristic phrases and expressions. Dawsey shows that the narrator avoids some of the most important christological titles in the Gospel, such as 'Son of Man', 'King', 'Son of David' and 'Prophet', and habitually calls Jesus 'Lord' (e.g. 3.4, 10.1, 22.61).[22]

This title is shared with other speakers (e.g. Elizabeth, 1.43; the disciples, 10.17). In this, the narrator associates himself with those characters in the Gospel who are aware of Jesus' power and of their own dependence on it. In other words, 'the narrator defines himself as part of the believing community'.[23] He is a Christian of the late first century who tells the story of Jesus to readers of his own day. He calls Jesus 'Lord' to emphasize the connection between the narrative and the liturgical Jesus which reflects the Gospel's first use in the context of worship.

The narrator's mode of speech is shown by the shift in style that takes place between the Preface and the Infancy Narrative. This shift is the author's own deliberate manoeuvre. Eduard Norden thinks that it was done to remind the reader that the story *could* have been told in Attic Greek but that this was not in fact the preferred mode of exposition.[24] The language of the Infancy Narrative links the story to the world of biblical narrative and presents the narrator in that light. This change in the style of speech is accompanied by the change from first-person to third-person reporting. That draws attention to the narrator and puts him on the centre of the stage even when the characters are delivering their most memorable lines.

Dawsey notes that the narrator's speech is weighted very heavily with particles – 'and' and 'but' are foremost among them.[25] The narrator's short, simple sentences have their matrix in an oral setting. (This orality is a not insignificant feature of the distinction between ancients and post-moderns as 'actual readers' of the text.) Dawsey also shows that the narrator uses certain expressions which are not employed by the characters: 'and it happened', 'answering, he said' and 'praising God' are examples of this.[26] These formulae are found in the Septuagint but were apparently not otherwise characteristic of speech in the first century CE. Dawsey follows Matthew Black and Fred Horton in arguing that the domain of this speech is the specialized language of early Christian worship. This means that the Gospel is not only addressed to a worshipping community but that it also reflects the language of that community. That explains the narrator's distinctive but nevertheless affected voice (which is accentuated by the way in which, these elements apart, it generally coheres with good Hellenistic style).

Luke's narrator is on the face of it an omniscient creature who knows not just the sequence of the narrative but also the meaning of what happens there. There is an example of this in 9.51: 'As the time approached when he was to be taken up to heaven, (Jesus) set his face resolutely towards Jerusalem'. This statement mixes reporting with interpretation and tells the reader what significance the journey to Jerusalem has in the Gospel's plot. It is through the narrator's commentary, so it seems, that the readers avoid the characters' misunderstandings. The narrator tells people who Jesus is at the beginning of the Gospel (e.g. 2.26). This compensates for the fact that the Lucan Jesus is remarkably unwilling to disclose his own identity.

This impression of the narrator's omniscience, however, is controverted by the formal conclusion which Dawsey fails to draw and for which he is taken to task by Stephen Moore.[27] This is that Luke's narrator is an 'unreliable narrator' who adopts a different perspective from the implied author in the Gospel. We can discover the implied author's view by examining the way that the Gospel is structured. Dawsey shows that the implied author generally endorses what Jesus says and organizes the Gospel to support Jesus' view of events.[28] Dawsey produces two examples of this structural policy. The first is the sharp break between chapters 1–2 and 3–24 of Luke. In the Infancy Narrative John the Baptist and the other speakers are oriented towards Israel. Chapters 1–2 make John much more than just the forerunner of Jesus. He is a significant figure in his own right. This is borne out in the direct speech of Jesus which disagrees with the narrator about John's identity. Jesus thinks of the Baptist as the eschatological Elijah who heralds the kingdom of God. This is evident in 7.27 where Jesus calls John the herald who is more than a prophet. The implication is that John heralds the kingdom which arrives with the ministry of Jesus (cf. 17.21; 19.11). The narrator, however, makes John precede *Jesus* and not the kingdom. This is evident in the way he makes Jesus' statement follow John's question: 'are you the one who is to come, or are we to wait for another?' (7.19). The narrator's interpretation allows a longer time for the kingdom to emerge (and thus includes the readers in the kingdom). But the Infancy Narrative supports Jesus' view and not the narrator's, for there the kingdom arrives with the birth of Jesus and this is what John heralds.

The second example is drawn from the motif of rejection in Luke. Jesus constantly emphasizes his own rejection by 'the people of this generation' (e.g. 11.29–32; 13.34). Through this rejection, which leads to his death, Jesus sees himself as becoming Christ (24.26). This is a major structural element in the Gospel which describes how Jesus goes to his death but is then revealed as Christ. The narrator tones down Jesus' emphasis on his rejection (a) by attributing it only to the authorities, (b) by emphasizing Satan's role in it and (c) by setting it within the context of a history that is predetermined by God. We find this reinterpretation in several narratorial passages. Throughout the Gospel, (a) the narrator indicates that 'the people' receive Jesus but that various Jewish authorities dislike him. The best example is 7.29–30: 'When they heard him, all the people, including the tax-collectors, acknowledged the goodness of God, for they had accepted John's baptism; but *the Pharisees and lawyers*, who had refused his baptism, rejected God's purpose for themselves.' Here, the rejection is assigned to a specific group in the Jewish community and not to the community as a whole. Satan's role (b) is explained in two key passages in the Gospel. Ominously, at the end of the temptation story, the narrator says that 'the devil departed, biding his time' (4.13). Satan reappears at the beginning of chapter 22 where he enters into Judas to instigate the betrayal of Jesus (22.3). The implication is that, without Satan, there would have been no betrayal or passion. The narrator's belief that everything is predetermined by God (c) is exemplified by his addition to Jesus' words in 24.26–7. Jesus asks the Emmaus disciples: 'was not the Messiah bound to suffer in this way before entering upon his glory?' (24.26). The narrator adds: 'then, starting from Moses and all the prophets, he explained to them in the whole of scripture the things that referred to himself' (24.27). This makes the emphasis fall, not on the last phrase ('before entering upon his glory') but on the word 'bound' which refers the death of Jesus to divine or scriptural necessity and neglects the point that this is the first time that Jesus has called himself 'Messiah' in connection with his mission.

The narrator's softening of the portrait of rejection is significantly not supported by the structure of the story. Jesus himself does not want to die. We can see this from his impassioned plea to God on the Mount of Olives (22.39–46).[29] The narrator admits that Jesus does not want to die through his realistic description of the agony (22.43–4). The story does not even say that *God* wants Jesus to die: neither Jesus nor the narrator present the divine will in such terms. The development of the story does not disguise the fact that Jesus is rejected and not merely misunderstood. The trial narrative confirms this impression when it indicates that Jesus is *rejected* and by *everybody*. In 23.13 the narrator himself states that the 'chief priests, councillors *and people*' denounce Jesus before Pilate. This must mean, not just a minority of the population, but the whole population. This statement agrees with Jesus' words about the Son of Man in 17.25: 'He must endure much suffering and be rejected by *this generation*' where the highlighted term is again an inclusive one. Even the disciples abandon Jesus, including Peter who had earlier trumpeted his support (22.33). This rejection by the disciples is particularly heinous for they form part of the believing community and profess their faith in Jesus throughout the Gospel (notably in 9.20). Their denial serves to illustrate the point that Jesus is rejected and rejected by *everybody* in Luke. It is a universal rejection – and it is a rejection, not just a misunderstanding.

The fact that Luke's implied author agrees with Jesus means that there is a continual dissonance between Jesus and the narrator in the Gospel. Dawsey analyzes their direct speech to contrast their different understanding of things. While the narrator speaks the language of worship, Jesus speaks the language of prophecy.[30] Jesus calls himself a 'prophet' during his ministry (4.24) and 'Christ' only after his resurrection (24.26). For Dawsey, this means that Jesus in Luke 'is not the Christ until he dies on the cross and is raised. . . . Until such time he is a prophet'.[31] The narrator never calls Jesus 'a prophet' at all. He thinks that Jesus is Christ from the beginning (2.26) and introduces the messianic secret to explain why Jesus does not proclaim his Messiahship before the resurrection (9.21). For the narrator Jesus is not a rejected but a *misunderstood* Messiah. He emphasizes Satan's part in the crucifixion (e.g. 22.3) when Jesus states that Satan's power has already been broken in his own ministry (10.18).[32]

Both the structure of the Gospel and the unreliable narrator are the author's own creations. We must presume that he has arranged things so for a purpose. This purpose is apparently the fact that the narrator comments on the significance of Jesus from his faith-perspective that Jesus is the Lord. He thereby interprets the story of Jesus for a later generation of readers. Part of this reinterpretation is to make subtle changes to Jesus' message which suit the altered situation. He tones down the emphasis on rejection and reinterprets the preaching of the kingdom to allow for second-generation discipleship (see below). It is significant, however, that Luke retains the tradition of the sayings of Jesus in a form which controverts the narrator's perspective. There is a fundamental tension in the Gospel which our reading must not obscure.

Luke's narrator is thus not the neutral figure that he seems on first appearance. The author has fashioned his narrator against the grain of his beliefs about Jesus. His distance from Jesus puzzles the readers and teases them into asking questions about the meaning of the story and the identity of the central character. This in turn makes them reflect on their stance as Christians in the late first century CE.

THE READERS

Recent study has drawn attention to the reader as a significant agent in the interpretation of a text.[33] No longer is it possible to see the reader as a passive vessel who waits to be filled with information. A text only comes to life in the act of reading. The reader plays an active part in the creation of its meaning.

Part of the reader's task is to decode the signs which the author has placed in the narrative. A sign is a symbol of meaning. A collection of signs yields a pattern of thought. A text conditions its reader to react in a particular way, as for instance through the comments and presuppositions of the narrator, but the final assembly of meaning rests with the reader and not with the author. This means that a reader can quite appropriately find meanings in a text which were not consciously placed there by the author – even meanings with which the author might not have agreed. One school of scholarship questions whether it is appropriate to speak about 'authorial intention' at all given the nature of the reading process.

Just as there is a 'real author' of a text, so there is an 'actual reader'. The actual reader is the person who reads the text, be they a Christian in the first century or a reader of Luke today. We should not restrict the term to either category, although clearly a reader today will find Luke a different text from a reader in the first century. We cannot say much about Luke's first-century readers since we do not know where the Gospel was written and first read. But we can make a series of judgments about the 'implied reader' by asking how we as readers react to the signs which the author has placed in the text.

There is, of course, an element of provisionality in any such reconstruction. It is typified by the statement of Jesus in 9.23: 'Anyone who wants to be a follower of mine must renounce self; day after day he must take up his cross, and follow me.' Does this mean that Luke was written for people who were *already* bearing the cross, or for people who needed a reminder that they *should* be doing this?

Most commentators (including me) assume the latter but this is of course a deduction and not an 'assured result' of research. We do not *know* the precise circumstances of Luke's first readers. This is why the reconstructed portrait remains a provisional one.

Kurz cites Fitzmyer's assessment as among the most helpful treatments of Luke's implied readers.[34] Fitzmyer notes that Luke shows fewer Jewish traits than either Matthew and Mark and that the Gospel has a Hellenistic Preface. Luke uses the term 'Judaea' to designate the whole of Palestine. This accentuates the Christian outreach to the Gentiles because it presents Judaism as a single, identifiable category. Luke also tries to relate Gentile Christianity to Judaism as if the text is written for readers who live outside Palestine and are either Gentiles or else Christians of Jewish birth who are concerned to preserve the continuity between Judaism and Gentile Christianity.

Luke's heavy use of biblical Greek, and the implied readers' presumed knowledge of the Septuagint, identifies them as people with expertise in this area and thus as Christians rather than as interested Romans who had not been instructed in Jewish matters. That the readers were Christian and not Jewish is suggested by the comparative lack of interest in specifically Jewish issues in the Gospel. The Preface makes it virtually certain that the implied readers are Christians.

In support of this point it can be said that Jesus' eschatological discourse in Luke 21 is Christian in content and contains little material of relevance to Jews. It probably even distances Jews through the use of polemic. Most Jews would not have shared the hope for the return of Jesus as the Son of Man which is the major feature of the Gospel's eschatology. Luke was written for Christian readers. The contents of the Gospel define the religious group for which it was written.

We can extend this portrait by returning to the fundamental confusion that I noticed in the text of Luke. This confusion focuses on the identity of Jesus as the central character. Jesus remains a continual paradox in Luke. This is evident especially in his dealings with opponents. The narrator makes the Pharisees oppose him (e.g. 7.30; 11.53–4), yet in their direct speech they appear more confused than hostile. Their question about fasting (5.33–5) and their warning to Jesus (13.31) reveal an uncertainty about Jesus which is mirrored by other characters. Those responsible for Jesus' death are clearly fasci-

nated by him. Their condemnation of Jesus works from the false
and deeply ironic assumption that they know who he is. They ask
him questions to substantiate their presumed knowledge but, as
Jesus says to them, 'if I tell you . . . you will not believe me'
(22.67).

The paradox of Jesus is evident, too, in the way that the author
teases the readers into comparing him with some familiar Hebrew
figures such as Moses, Elijah and David. Luke's story indicates that
Jesus is like but also unlike such people. In the case of David, for
example, Jesus is like David in that he will occupy the royal throne
(1.32) but unlike David because he refuses to be constrained by that
role and asks a question about the Messiah's enthronement in
heaven (20.41–4; cf. Acts 2.34). This makes Jesus a continually
enigmatic figure in the Gospel despite the narrator's provision of
commentary.

This confusion impacts on the readers and encourages them to
respond to it. They are invited to consider Jesus through the information provided by the Gospel. Dawsey shows that the Emmaus
scene, as the dénouement of the Gospel, reveals its major purpose.[35]
The two disciples tell Jesus their disappointed hope that he was to
be a mighty prophet and the liberator of Israel (24.19–21). Jesus
then comments on his mission: 'Was not the Messiah bound to
suffer in this way before entering upon his glory?' (24.26). This first
use of the 'Messiah' title on the lips of Jesus makes the sentence
significant. It explains that the exaltation of Jesus depends on his
passion. Jesus says that it is only through this that he can truly be
perceived as Christ. The disciples had *contrasted* his suffering with
their hopes for liberation. Jesus says that his status *depends* on that
suffering. The sub-text of this statement is that the liberation of
Israel has not been thwarted, as they suppose, but that it derives
from a different understanding of events in which the cross plays a
crucial role. This is principally where the narrator differs from Jesus
(and the author) in the Gospel. Like the Emmaus disciples, he does
not fully understand the need for Jesus' suffering or the implications which this has for contemporary Christianity.

There is thus a tremendous irony – by no means obvious at the
beginning of the Gospel – in the (unreliable) narrator's claim to pass
on reliable information to Theophilus.[36] The narrator himself, as
the representative of the Christian community, is the recipient of
Jesus' ironic criticism in 13.23–30 where he is told: 'Then you will
protest, "We used to eat and drink with you [cf. 22.17–20], and

you taught in our streets." But he will repeat, "I tell you, I do not know where you come from. Out of my sight, all of you, you and your wicked ways." . . . Some who are now last will be first, and some who are first will be last.' That the title 'Lord' is used in this passage means that it is addressed primarily to the Christian community (and not, say, to the narrative opponents of Jesus like the Jews). It implies that there are some in that community who have not grasped the need for humility and who need reminding that only the humble path of suffering and service which Jesus exemplifies is truly the one of Christian discipleship. There is a further reminder in the Last Supper where Jesus speaks about his 'appointed way' (22.22) – which the readers have already been told is the way of suffering and rejection (9.22) – and a dispute begins among the disciples as to which of them is the greatest. Jesus replies: 'The greatest among you must bear himself like the youngest, the one who rules like one who serves. . . . I am among you like a servant' (22.26–7). The fact that Jesus is the speaker makes the words reliable. Here he speaks directly to the Christian community and warns them against the desire for prestige and precedence which was evidently a major temptation there.

There are a variety of situations to which such a perspective could have been addressed. Dawsey lists some possibilities: 'Through the narrator, a proud church might have relived its own tendency to exalt Jesus, and therefore its denial of the suffering Son of God. Through the narrator, a socially insensitive community might have experienced its own blindness in perceiving the present kingdom'.[37] We should add the possibility that the emergence of a more institutional form of Christianity in the late first century, which is documented by the *Didache* and Ignatius and criticized by the *Ascension of Isaiah*, could also have been responsible for this call for a radical and Christ-centred humility in which the leaders are reminded that they are appointed to serve and not to rule. Luke does not allow us to be precise about the nature of the situation. Such imprecision is a feature of the way in which it operates. The dissonance between Jesus and the narrator can in fact apply to a variety of situations as readers insert their self-awareness into the story. The narrator's misunderstandings draw them into the narrative, make them interact with it, and help them to take a meaning from it. The perceptive reader will see that Jesus is criticizing the narrator and his friends and no doubt make an appropriate deduction from that observation.

THE PLOT

An essential part of a narrative is its plot. A plot is the outline or framework of events that happen in the story. It is, we might say, the 'what' of the narrative. All the Gospels have plots. This distinguishes them from the New Testament letters which are not narratives. A plot often employs the device of 'cause and effect' (explaining why the events happen as they do). In the Gospels, this 'cause and effect' concerns the reason for the death of Jesus which is presented variously in terms of the will of God, the climax of eschatology, the hostility of the Jews, the involvement of the Romans and the general need for suffering. Not all plots have a 'happy ending' − tragedies, for instance, do not − but there is at least a sense that conflict is resolved in many if not most plots. One might almost say that conflict is an essential feature of plot given that human emotions and relationships are involved in it. Plot is bound up with characterization as the different characters interact with each other against the backcloth of external events.

Luke's plot is on the face of it a simple one but this simplicity is deceptive as we have seen in the case of the narrator. The Gospel tells the story of Jesus from before his birth to his death. It concludes with his resurrection appearances and ascension. Interwoven with this material is the sense of eschatological anticipation and purpose which is symbolized by Jesus' journey from Galilee to Jerusalem. This means that the plot functions on more than one level. On a simple level, we have the story of Jesus as he journeys to Jerusalem to be rejected and killed by his contemporaries. On another level, Jesus is drawn towards Jerusalem by the belief that the kingdom of God (and all this meant in terms of the biblical promises to Israel) will soon be fully realized. Thirdly, Luke is engaged in the business of reinterpreting eschatology through the mouthpiece of his narrator to allow for the continuing existence of Christianity after the ascension and before the final manifestation of the Kingdom. Fourthly, the plot has a future aspect in its assertion that Jesus will return as Son of Man from heaven. This makes the readers heirs of the same eschatological hopes that motivate the characters in the Gospel.

The basic story of Jesus is common to all four Gospels (the ascension apart), but the Gospels are different texts and their plots are not identical. Luke's plot has some distinctive features. His Preface speaks of 'the events that have been fulfilled among us' (1.1) and of those things in which Theophilus has been instructed (1.4). The first phrase implies that Luke's story is not a disinterested biography but incorporates both theological and eschatological reflection. The verb 'instructed' indicates that this material constitutes a form of tradition which was handed on to new Christians and derived from the 'eyewitnesses and servants of the gospel' (1.2). It gives Luke's plot the purpose of supplying information about the present orientation of Christianity and of emphasizing the reliability of what was believed about Jesus (including the hope for his return from heaven). Only in Luke is this purpose formally articulated at the beginning of the text. Luke's Preface might be compared with the statement of John 20.31: 'these (things) are written so that you may come to believe that Jesus is the Messiah' (NRSV). For 'Messiah' in John read 'Lord' and 'Christ' in Luke (cf. Acts 2.36).

Luke ends with a description of the ascension of Jesus (24.50–1). This too is unique among the Gospels. For Luke, the ascension is the confirmation that Jesus is Christ and Lord following the Gospel's dénouement on the road to Emmaus (24.26). It has a symbolic relevance for those who have not seen the risen Jesus. For the original Christians, with their tradition of apocalyptic revelation (notably the resurrection appearances), the appearance of the risen Jesus had been a significant thing. Later readers lacked this advantage. They had only the reports about Jesus, the oral tradition of his sayings, the written Gospels and the (probably quite enigmatic) experience of encountering Jesus in worship. The ascension reminds them that the heavenly Lord is the same Jesus who had suffered. This is a major theme in the Gospel. The ascension tells readers that the exaltation cannot be believed without the suffering, and *vice versa*.

The basis of Luke's plot is the rejection of Jesus the Messiah by the Jewish people and the promise that, despite this, he will still bring in the kingdom of God (see 9.26; 21.27–31). The plot in this sense has a wide orientation. Its background is not just the birth of Jesus (the point where the Gospel begins) but the whole history of Israel conceived as the prelude to the messianic age. The rejection of Jesus in Luke is nothing short of a tragedy as the frequent irony indicates. This tragedy is exemplified especially in the parable of the vineyard (20.9–16) which presents the ministry of Jesus as God's eschatological challenge to the nation (and I think to the temple) which the authorities misunderstand and reject. The basis of the tragedy is that the one who would bring restoration and wholeness (see especially 13.34–5) is denounced by the authorities as a messianic pretender whose claims are subversive (23.2). There is however a strong note of reversal in the resurrection and ascension narratives (notably in 24.26) where it is said that the suffering is a *necessary* part of the eschatological task. The plot thus has an ironic logic whose basis is the Jewish rejection of the Messiah and the complex set of paradoxes which emerge from this.

Since Luke's plot is the substance of the narrative, and ought not to be considered merely in terms of theology, it is worth spending a little time on what Luke says and on the essential elements of the plot. Readers who find this exposition irritating can jump to Chapter 3; but I hope that at some point they will return to consider my understanding of Luke in microcosm.

I begin with the death of Jesus to which the plot works forward. The reasons for Jesus' death in Luke needs careful statement. There is more than one level of understanding in the text. Jesus sometimes predicts his own suffering, in places with great accuracy. 9.22 is an early example: 'The Son of Man has to endure great sufferings, and to be rejected by the elders, chief priests, and scribes, to be put to death, and to be raised again on the third day'. The reason for the 'has to' is not given but it is perhaps suggested by the 'Son of Man' title. This is because Jesus will only become Christ by enduring the cross which is the pattern of discipleship Luke impresses on his readers.

The narrator, as we have seen, takes a different view of Jesus' death. He refers it to the demands of scriptural necessity (24.27) – and in places Jesus himself seems to take this view as well (see 18.31). The narrator keeps his silence about the suffering of Jesus and does not apparently understand the first reason for his death.

The structure of the story suggests a third reason for the death of Jesus. This concerns his attitude towards the temple. Prior to Jesus' arrival in Jerusalem, his opponents are confused (13.17) but not overtly hostile. It is only after the cleansing of the temple (19.45–6) that we read: 'the chief priests and scribes, with the support of the leading citizens, wanted to bring about his death' (19.47). The cleansing (and the teaching in the temple associated with it) gives Jesus a new status in the eyes of his opponents. From then on, they seek to kill him (see especially 20.19).

This observation means that we must investigate the temple strand in the Gospel with some care. And, in doing this, we must ask whose perspective we can trust on the matter. We have seen that the narrator is an unreliable figure who diverges from the views of the author (and of Jesus). But is Jesus any more reliable? The structure of the story indicates that the journey to Jerusalem is bound up with Jesus' concern for the temple. But Jesus never says: 'The Son of Man is going to Jerusalem to purify the temple' or 'to do something that will cause a rumpus in the temple and thereby bring about his death'. He always says (and I paraphrase): 'The Son of Man is going to Jerusalem to suffer and to die.' There is, of course, nothing exceptional in the fact that Jesus does not offer a commentary on the story. That, after all, is the narrator's job. Yet there *is* a sense of unease in the fact that the story places the temple in the centre of the stage but that Jesus never makes a clear statement about the role of the temple in connection with his ministry. We must conclude from this, either that the structure of the story disagrees with the way that Jesus sees things (a view which we have rejected already), or else that there is more to the words of Jesus than at first sight meets the eye. A little investigation shows that the second alternative is the better one.

The Infancy Narrative tells the reader that the temple is going to be an important theme in the Gospel. In a sense, the Infancy Narrative offers a microcosm of the plot. It describes two journeys of Jesus to the temple before his ministry begins. His first recorded expedition is in 2.22–4. This is as a babe for purification. What happens on his arrival sets the conditions for the plot. Jesus is greeted by Simeon who states that God has finally revealed 'the deliverance' which he had made ready in view of the nations (2.30–1); and by Anna, who 'talked about the child to all who were looking for the liberation of Jerusalem' (2.38). Simeon is also said to have 'watched and waited for the restoration of Israel' (2.25). He calls 'the deliverance' he had witnessed 'a light that will bring revelation to the Gentiles and glory to [God's] people Israel' (2.32).

This is a clear textual indication that Jesus' appearance in the temple has eschatological implications. Simeon's hymn recalls Isaiah 60.3 ('nations will journey towards your light') which was an important theme in Jewish eschatological speculation (see below). The references to 'restoration' and 'liberation' imply that some form of change is impending. Given that 2.11 makes Jesus the Messiah, the reader rightly concludes that the arrival of Jesus in the temple means the messianic age is nigh.

A short narrative link (2.39–40) separates this visit from Jesus' second journey to Jerusalem. In 2.41–52 Joseph and the family head for Jerusalem to celebrate the Passover. On the way home Jesus gets lost and is found eventually in the temple. This anecdote is included (exceptionally in the Gospels) because it shows that Jesus is inextricably connected with the temple (and also because by implication it criticizes those who do not associate him with the temple). Jesus' parents trawl Jerusalem for three days before searching in the holy building. It was clearly the last place they had thought of looking. They find Jesus astonishing the teachers with his learning (2.46–7) much as he will later offend them with his words (19.47). The incident climaxes with his rebuke: 'Did you not know that I was bound to be in my Father's house?' (2.49). These words have an ominous ring. They express the sense of purpose which impels Jesus to the temple. When he goes there again, it will lead to his death (19.45–7).

I want to pause at this point to explore the reason for Luke's interest in the temple and to suggest that Luke reflects the Jewish belief that the temple is the focus of eschatological hope. We find evidence for this belief in a variety of Jewish literature.[38] Several passages anticipate the renewal of the temple by God in the eschatological age. Isaiah 60.1–14 links the coming of the Gentiles to Israel's light (cf. Luke 2.32) with the glorification of 'my holy sanctuary'. Isaiah 56.1–8 anticipates the regathering of the 'outcasts of Israel' (cf. Luke 13.34) and the purity of sacrifice at that time, 'for my house will be called a house of prayer for all nations' (Isaiah 56:7). According to Micah 4, the 'mountain of the Lord's house' will be made the highest mountain where many nations will come to learn the law. This eschatological interest is continued in post-biblical literature. The theme of the rebuilding or replacement of the temple is introduced there. Tobit 14.5 says that 'the house of God will be rebuilt [in Jerusalem] with a glorious building for all generations for ever'. In *1 Enoch* the author states that 'the Lord of the sheep brought a new house greater and loftier than the first, and set it in place of the first' (90.29; cf. 91.13). *Jubilees* 1.15–17 predicts that national repentance will be accompanied by the construction of God's sanctuary in Israel. This expectation is found also in the *Psalms of Solomon* (17.32). It extended to the Qumran community, to judge from 4Qp Psalms 37 3.11: 'They shall possess the High Mountain of Israel [for ever], and shall enjoy [everlasting] delights in His Sanctuary' (cf. 11QTemple 29.8–10).

This complex of passages, which represents the hopes of many centuries, expects that in the eschatological age a renewed or even a replacement temple will emerge through the intervention of God.

We should not obscure the different forms in which this hope is found, but nor should we minimize its significance in this literature cited. An equal number of passages mention the hope for the reconstitution of the Israelite tribes at this time.[39] Isaiah 49.5 is an example: 'The Lord has formed me in the womb to be his servant, to bring Jacob back to him that Israel should be gathered to him.' In the post-biblical writings, there is relevant material in *Ben Sira* 48.10 (Elijah will 'restore the tribes of Jacob'); the *Psalms of Solomon* (chapters 11 and 17); and 1QM (where the heads of the tribes offer twelve loaves of bread). Again, we must not be dogmatic about the form of this future hope, which varies across the literature. Nevertheless, the hope that God will restore the tribes of Israel, which is tantamount to the hope that he will restore the fortunes of Israel, is a prominent theme of Jewish literature and reflects its concern for the land. Jewish messianism, as Klausner observes, has 'earthly ground . . . under its feet'.[40]

Such material shows why the temple occupies a prominent position in Luke's plot. My reading of the Gospel sees Jesus as supposing that God will replace the temple with a heavenly or eschatological counterpart of which he is the chief corner-stone. The theme of the new temple is introduced allusively at first and one can only see it on a complete reading of the Gospel. But the evidence for it is, I think, striking. The replacement of the present temple at the climax of the ages is a major theme of Luke's plot. It must be considered in company with the belief that the tribes of Israel will be restored under the Messiahship of Jesus and the presidency of the twelve disciples.

This reading of the Gospel depends on several passages. I continue with two incidents in the first half of the Gospel. The first is the temptation of Jesus. Luke reverses Matthew's order to make the temptation for Jesus to throw himself from the parapet of the temple the last in the series and by implication the most significant (4.9–11). The devil insinuates that, if Jesus does this, the angels will catch him and he will make a spectacular demonstration to draw attention to himself as the Son of God. By such a ruse, it is implied, the kingdom of God will be visibly revealed. The location of this temptation in the temple is highly significant given what will be said later about Jesus in 20.17. It tempts Jesus to reveal himself as Messiah (the devil, like the demons, knows the truth about him) by forcing God's hand and thus for the eschatological age to be introduced at his own behest – before the passion and without the suffering which is a crucial theme in Luke.

The next reference to the temple is in 6.1–5. This story justifies the behaviour of the disciples in rubbing ears of corn on the sabbath by citing David's example in eating shewbread from the temple. The story is set ostensibly in the context of a sabbatarian dispute (cf. the subsequent story in 6.6–11) but it is obvious that its focus is wider than the sabbath. The David analogy is not in fact about the sabbath at all but about the temple. The logic of the story is that the disciples break one Jewish rule; Jesus justifies their behaviour by saying that David's men broke another. The focus of the comparison is that Jesus' status as Messiah gives him a similar (indeed a greater) authority over Jewish institutions, including the sabbath and the temple. Jesus here apparently cites David's behaviour as a messianic visitation of the temple by which its normal rules of operation are suspended. This prepares the way for chapter 19 where he, too, will do something exceptional in the temple. The passage provides a preliminary justification for that act by referring to the deeds of the prototypical Messiah.

We turn now to 13.34–5. I hold this passage absolutely central to the Gospel and think that it gives the meaning of the plot: 'O Jerusalem, Jerusalem, city that murders the prophets and stones the messengers sent to her! How often have I longed to gather your children, as a hen gathers her brood under her wings; but you would not let me. . . . Look! There is your temple, forsaken by God. I tell you, you will not see me until the time comes when you say, "Blessings on him who comes in the name of the Lord!"'

It is important at this point to note that the Revised English Bible provides an interpretative translation of 13.35 (as do several English translations of this passage). My view is that its emphasis on the divine element in the 'forsaking' is the correct one but it will be helpful briefly to compare another translation so that we can be sure about the precise nuances of the verse. My own (very literal) translation is: 'Behold, your house is left to you.' The verb 'left to you' is intransitive but in fact there can only be one referent for the 'forsaking'. This is that the temple has been forsaken by *God*. The passive is a 'divine' one. For this reason Jesus calls it 'your house', whereas in Judaism the temple was universally known as the house of God. The force of 13.35 is that the (present) temple is pronounced by Jesus devoid of the divine presence.

This reading of the verse needs further justification. Let me consider an alternative reading. One of the characteristics of Jesus in Luke is that, from the standpoint of the readers, he foretells the destruction of Jerusalem which was effected by the Romans in 70 CE. In 21.20 he says: 'when you see Jerusalem surrounded by armies, then you may be sure that her devastation is near'. There is another prediction of Jerusalem's downfall in 19.43–4 ('your enemies will set up siege-works against you'). Several scholars see a similar reference in 13.35. Three objections, however, must be considered before that interpretation is accepted. First of all, the wording of the passage suggests a different understanding of 13.35. Jesus does not say that the temple *will* be *destroyed* by the *Romans* (a future event from his point of view) but that it has *already* been *forsaken* and evidently by *God* (a past action with a different agent). Secondly, 21.20 rather obviously predicts the Roman destruction of Jerusalem but this passage says nothing specific about the destruction of the temple (cf. the silence of 19.43–4 on this matter). This is a most significant silence given that Jewish sacrificial worship ceased in 70 CE and that the destruction of the temple was regarded by Judaism as the worst part of the catastrophe. We should surely have expected some such indication in 13.35 if this is the real meaning of the verse. Thirdly, chapter 21 distinguishes the downfall of the temple (21.6) from the destruction of Jerusalem (21.20) which, in the logic of the passage, is said to *precede* the event specified by 21.6 (see below). This makes it difficult to identify the destruction of the temple (the result of its forsaking by God) with the Roman destruction of Jerusalem.

The meaning of 13.35 can be explained with reference to the Jewish literature just considered. This is that Jesus denounces the present temple in the hope of its eschatological renewal or replacement by God. Jesus does not say why the temple needs restoration, nor how this would be done, but there is the unspoken assumption in the Gospel that it does need to be replaced or purified for the eschatological age. This interpretation is supported by the cleansing of the temple in 19.45–6 which has been seen both as a symbol of its future purity and also as a symbol of impending destruction (see below). The view that the present temple is defiled is in fact a feature of sectarian Judaism. The Qumran community advocated this view and thought that true worship was no longer offered there (see CD 5.6–7; 1QpHab 12.7–9). A similar understanding of defilement is found in *1 Enoch* 89.73.

The question of whether this view was held by the historical Jesus (although an interesting one) does not detain us here because we are concerned with an assessment of Jesus the Lucan character. Clearly, the statement is hyperbolic, as befits the language of prophecy. But it is nevertheless very firmly made. The second half of the verse gives the reason for it. Jesus says that the next time that Jerusalem sees him will be when its inhabitants exclaim, 'Blessings on him who comes in the name of the Lord!' This phrase, which derives from the Psalter, was used by pilgrims as they went up to Jerusalem for religious festivals. It here anticipates Jesus' (so-called) triumphal entry into Jerusalem when the words are used again (19.38). In both passages the benediction has christological significance. It designates Jesus as 'the one who comes in the name of the Lord'. This presents him as Messiah (especially in 19.38 which adds the words 'comes as king' to the Psalm citation). The acclamation makes Jesus' journey to the city a messianic visitation. The God-forsaking of the temple is thus connected with the Messiah's arrival in Jerusalem, whatever might be meant by this assertion.

A further statement of interest is made before 13.35. 13.34 picks up the Jewish belief that the tribes of Israel will be restored in the eschatological age: 'O Jerusalem, Jerusalem, city that murders the prophets and stones the messengers sent to her! How often have I longed to gather your children, as a hen gathers her brood under her wings; but you would not let me.' Jesus complains that Jerusalem rejects all God's messengers and spurns his attempt to gather 'her brood'. The brood are surely the twelve tribes which had been scattered abroad. The thought is that Jesus would gather them together under his rule as Messiah. This implies that the restoration of the twelve tribes is also on the agenda of Luke's Jesus (cf. 22–30).

For this reason the sense of anticipation grows as Jesus nears the Jewish capital. In 19.11–27, just before Jesus sets out on the ascent to Jerusalem (19.28), he tells the parable of the absent king. This qualifies the sense of drama in chapter 13 by warning that the kingdom of God will *not* appear when Jesus reaches Jerusalem. The narrator says that: 'he was now close to Jerusalem and they thought the kingdom of God might dawn at any moment' (19.11). The parable which follows concerns delay and expectation. It tells the story of how a nobleman goes on a long journey (19.12) but finally 'return[s] as king' (19.15) to effect an act of judgment. The sub-text of the parable, introduced by 19.11, is that the emergence of the kingdom is connected with the Messiah's arrival in Jerusalem but that there will be a period of waiting before this is fulfilled. This suggests that there is perhaps a deliberate ambiguity in 13.35b where Jesus refers to his future greeting by the inhabitants of Jerusalem. That verse anticipates, not just his triumphal entry which is accomplished in chapter 19 of the Gospel, but also the second coming of the Son of Man for judgment (9.26), which lies beyond the pages of the Gospel.

In 19.28–40 Jesus comes to Jerusalem. He enters the city in 19.45 and goes immediately to the temple. Jesus drives out the traders with the words: ' "My house shall be a house of prayer"; but you have made it a bandits' cave' (19.46). The saying in 19.46 is made up of two scriptural allusions: to Isaiah 56.7 ('my house will be called a house of prayer for all nations') and Jeremiah 7.11 ('Do you regard this house which bears my name as a bandits' cave?'). In both cases we should assume that the allusion is to the context in which these words are found and not narrowly to the words themselves. The context of the Isaiah citation gives the cleansing an eschatological reference: Isaiah anticipates that the Gentiles will be included in the final act of salvation when acceptable sacrifices would be offered in the temple. This agrees with what Luke says about the inclusion of the Gentiles in the *Nunc Dimittis* (2.32) and elsewhere. The Jeremiah citation (Jeremiah 7.8–11) criticizes those who think they are safe in the temple when they commit heinous offences. Jeremiah's thrust is that the slogan, 'This place is the temple of the Lord' (Jeremiah 7.4), is a lie for that reason. For Luke, who cites Jeremiah, the words indicate that the present temple is the subject of an over-optimistic confidence from people who refuse to accept the ethical consequences of worship. Jeremiah adds to Isaiah the veiled hint that the temple may be over-run which I think looks back to 13.35 and is also reflected in what Jesus does in the temple on this occasion.

Much has been written about the cleansing of the temple, both as the deed was done by the historical Jesus and as part of the story which the Gospels tell.[41] My reading of Luke tends towards the conclusion that it is an ambiguous event whose meaning must be constructed by the reader from the text. In the light of 13.35 the implication is that the cleansing demonstrates the God-forsakenness of the present temple. But, as yet, the reader lacks sufficient information to place a definitive meaning on this information. Several possible interpretations arise. Is Jesus cleansing the temple by driving out the money-grabbing traders? Is he symbolizing the repristinization of the present temple by briefly interrupting the sacrificial worship? Or does he anticipate the replacement of the temple by God in the eschatological age? Any or all of these interpretations can be deduced from the text so far. Luke has yet to provide sufficient information to let the reader decide between these possibilities.

Further (and I think decisive) information about the plot is provided by 19.47–8 and especially by chapters 20–1. 19.47 makes two significant statements. The first is that 'day by day [Jesus] taught in the temple'. The second is that 'the chief priests and scribes, with the support of the leading citizens, wanted to bring about his death'. This verse indicates that Jesus is condemned because of his teaching in the temple as much as for his behaviour in the temple. Luke tells us what Jesus taught in chapter 20. The chapter records a series of disputes about his status and authority. The most important element is the parable of the vineyard and its interpretation in 20.9–18. This parable has the form of an allegory. There has been no shortage of allegorical interpretations of it. The most common interpretation takes the owner as God, the vineyard as Israel, the messengers as the prophets, the Son as Jesus and the new tenants as the Gentiles. There is, however, a different interpretation which makes better sense of the context by referring the vineyard to the temple. This interpretation was proposed by Lohmeyer.[42] It circumvents the problems of the other interpretation by explaining why the tenants think they will gain the vineyard by abusing the messengers (for the tenants are the Jewish authorities who are removing a threat to their security). On this reading the messengers are indeed the prophets. They include Jeremiah who spoke against the temple (Jeremiah chapter 7) as the parable implies. The final messenger is the 'beloved Son' (20.13). The tenants decide to kill the Son when they had (merely) mistreated the other messengers because he has threatened the temple in his teaching and behaviour. The tenants want to remove someone who has disturbed their confidence in the holy place. This interpretation of the parable is strongly implied by its conclusion: 'The scribes and chief priests wanted to seize him there and then, for they saw that this parable was aimed at them' (20.19) which links back directly to 19.47 and the statement that the leaders wanted Jesus dead. There is, of course, a considerable irony in this, for 19.46 has already indicated that the Son's intention is the eschatological restoration of the temple and not its destruction in a negative sense. But this is lost on the other characters who, as chapter 8 says, see and hear what Jesus does and says but strikingly fail to understand it.

The parable of the vineyard is appended by commentary from Jesus in the form of a scriptural citation: 'The stone which the builders rejected has become the main corner-stone. . . . Everyone who falls on that stone will be dashed to pieces; anyone on whom it falls will be crushed' (20.17–18). If the parable concerns the temple, it is natural that the language should turn to stones. The source for the first half of this citation is Psalm 118.22 to which Luke has appended some words based on Isaiah 8.14–15 about the Lord of hosts: 'He will become a snare, an obstacle, and a rock against which the two houses of Israel will strike and stumble. . . . Many will stumble and fall and suffer injury.' The words as they stand refer to Jesus, but Luke again does not indicate the precise sense in which they should be understood. Here, too, the reader must exercise imagination in interpretation. The citation seems almost deliberately intended to make them ponder what it means. Unless Jesus is speaking entirely in a metaphor, the reference must be to a building. It is not said *for which building* Jesus is the corner-stone but the context of the parable throws up the strong possibility that it is the temple. The temple in question cannot be the present temple, which was standing when the historical Jesus spoke but was destroyed before the writing of the Gospel. The implication is that Jesus is thinking of the heavenly or eschatological temple and that he is presenting himself as the main part of that temple which has yet to be fully revealed. This makes for a contrast between the present temple, rejected by God (13.35) and the heavenly temple whose key feature is Jesus, the stone rejected by the Jews (cf. 2.35).

Chapter 21 develops this picture by explaining clearly the fate of the present temple. 'Some people were talking about the temple and the beauty of its fine stones and ornaments' (21.5). Jesus warns them that 'the time will come when not one stone will be left upon another; they will all be thrown down' (21.6). My reading of the plot devotes careful attention to the progress of thought in Chapter 21. The chapter is introduced by this statement about the temple which is made the cue for the disciples to ask: 'When will that be? What will be the sign that these things are about to happen?' (21.7). It follows from this that the bulk of the material in Chapter 21 is devoted to the explication of the *signs* of the end. These signs precede the destruction of the temple which is mentioned by 21.6.

Looking through the chapter we can see that the eschatological climax is described in 21.27: 'Then they will see the Son of Man coming in a cloud with power and great glory'. The 'then' at the beginning of 21.27 indicates that the eschatological 'signs' have at last been completed as the Son of Man appears. The whole of 21.8–26 describes the sequence of signs which precedes this climax. These include the Roman destruction of Jerusalem in 21.20–4. The fact that 21.20–4 occurs within the context of the 'signs' means that it is formally distinguished from the destruction of the temple in 21.6. 21.6 is by contrast connected with 21.27 as an indication of what will happen at the eschatological climax. The chapter associates the coming of the Son of Man (21.27) with the collapse of the (present) temple (21.6) for the reason I have discerned in 20.17. This is that the appearance of the eschatological temple makes the present temple redundant. In this chapter Luke sees the Roman destruction of Jerusalem as the divinely-instituted punishment of the Jews which is completed before the new and perfect temple makes its appearance in the holy city.

This view of the matter draws us back to the cleansing of the temple in 19.45–6. Whatever Jesus does on that occasion, it is difficult to believe that the event is unconnected with the eschatological information supplied by 13.35, 20.17 and 21.6. The cleansing anticipates the appearance of the eschatological temple and is significant for the fact that it is undertaken by the corner-stone of the eschatological temple. Jesus not only anticipates the true purpose of the temple but he embodies the future of the temple which his death and return from heaven will disclose.

The theme of eschatological restoration recurs in 22.30. Jesus tells his disciples: 'in my kingdom you shall eat and drink at my table and sit on thrones as judges of the twelve tribes of Israel.' The notion of judgment reflects the belief that the Son of Man is the eschatological judge (9.26). The Twelve assist him in his work. Their number reflects the number of the tribes of Israel. The implication is that the Twelve are tribal presidents of the restored Israel who will assist the Messiah when the kingdom comes.

At the moment of the death of Jesus, the curtain of the temple is torn in two (23.45). This is a further symbol of destruction which links the promise of the heavenly temple with the death of Jesus. The final verse of Luke contains another reference to the temple. After the ascension the disciples 'returned to Jerusalem full of joy, and spent all their time in the temple praising God' (24.52–3). As in Acts, they go to the temple because the temple is expected to be the focus of the eschatological climax.

Stephen's speech (Acts chapter 7) confirms that Luke has an eye to the eschatological temple when it criticizes the present building on the grounds that (like its predecessors) it is made by human beings and therefore far from adequate for its purposes: 'The Most High does not live in houses *made by men*; as the prophet says, "Heaven is my throne and earth my footstool. What kind of house will you build for me, says the Lord; where shall my resting-place be? Are not all these things of *my own making?*"' (Acts 7.48–50). Stephen's speech is an expansion of Luke 13.35 and develops the view that God has forsaken the present temple. There is perhaps the hint in Acts 7.50 ('are not all these things of my own making?') that God will make his own temple which I think reflects the thought of Luke 20.17.

Luke's plot is thus based around the theme of eschatology in which the replacement of the temple by God is a crucial motif. The motif may be submerged at first but it emerges more clearly as the Gospel unfolds. What Luke does not tell us is what it means for Jesus to be the corner-stone of the eschatological temple and what that temple will be like. But he does say enough to indicate that the temple occupies a large place in his eschatological hopes and that it is related to the person of Jesus. He expects the climax of the ages to bring to completion the events that are inaugurated in the ministry of Jesus.

CHARACTERIZATION

Characterization is a further feature of narrative. It goes without saying that an ancient Christian Gospel does not have the detail or style of characterization, say, of the classic English novel. Luke is not a writer like Dickens or Austen whose concern is with the full-blown development of his characters. Luke hardly develops his characters at all. He introduces one major character, Jesus. What is said about Jesus is far from complete, particularly in areas like his emotional life and what he did before his ministry. Luke introduces a fair variety of other characters. They include disciples, women and Jews of different kinds. Most are stock or representative figures who highlight the onset of the kingdom of God as it is manifested in the ministry of Jesus.

The function of these other characters, including the Twelve, is to engage with Jesus and let him produce a response, either in word or deed; and to chart their (often quite enigmatic) responses to Jesus. In this sense the plot controls the characterization and not the other way round. One should always remember that God is the unseen and most important character in the Gospel. His purposes are invincible and his promises to Israel, it is implied, secure. That God is bringing in the kingdom through the person of his Son is the message which Luke conveys.

JESUS AS A CHARACTER

Luke's characterization of Jesus is based on the Gospels of Matthew and Mark. Luke chooses not to alter the substance of their portraits but he does change some of the narrative and he edits the words of Jesus. We are thus not dealing with a character called Jesus created *de novo* but with a narrative where tradition plays a decisive role.

I start by observing that there is no 'docetism' in the Gospel. Docetism is the presentation of Jesus, as it were, with superhuman powers. It was a second-century tendency which allowed the divinity of Jesus to triumph over his humanity, initially for reverential reasons. Docetism has sometimes been detected in the Fourth Gospel but even there the humanity of Jesus is not 'qualified' as it is in other sources.[43] *None* of the Gospels makes Jesus evade his passion, as Basileides did, nor suggests that there was anything unreal about his need for food after the manner of Valentinus.

In contrast to John, Luke has no 'incarnational' christology. By this I mean that he does not describe the descent of a heavenly being who appears as Jesus or becomes associated with Jesus. Luke's christology is one in which Jesus becomes Messiah through his death on the cross (24.26). This is similar in many ways to the christology of the hymn that Paul includes in Philippians 2.6–11.

Luke's portrait of Jesus is a very 'human' one in which the belief that he is Lord does not reduce his credibility as a human being. Luke makes the reader infer belief in the virgin birth. He is less explicit on this point than Matthew (1.18–25). It is interesting that Luke, who claims to have researched all things carefully (1.1–2), should write in this way. Luke also presents a credible portrait of Jesus' anguish on the Mount of Olives (22.39–46).

Luke's favourite description for Jesus after 'Lord' is 'prophet'. Jesus himself uses this title (4.24; 13.33). There is perhaps a deliberate element of ambiguity concerning what kind of a prophet Jesus is. Is he like Moses or Elijah, both or neither? There is a sense in which 'both and neither' is the correct answer. Luke teases with parallelism and lets his readers make their own deductions. Jesus as prophet does however provide an authoritative interpretation of the scriptures. This is clear from chapter 4 where he visits the synagogue in Nazareth and reads the scroll from Isaiah 61 ('The Spirit of the Lord is upon me . . . '). He tells the congregation that 'today this scripture has been fulfilled in your hearing' (4.21). In this context Isaiah 61 is understood as a prophecy about Jesus: *he* is the one to whom the prophet's words apply, so that one prophet fulfils the words of another. Luke thinks that Jesus has realized Isaiah's vision and that Joseph's son (as he is called contemptuously in 4.22) is the prophet through whom Isaiah's eschatological vision is being effected (4.24).

As this kind of prophet Jesus is possessed by the Spirit of God (4.18). This characterization is sustained throughout the Gospel, not least in the implicit (but allusive) dialogue with other figures such as Moses, Joshua and Elijah. It is particularly evident in the miracles. In Luke the miracles support the portrait of Jesus as the eschatological prophet because they are signs of the kingdom of God. The miracles make two points about Jesus. First of all, the demons – in contrast to the ordinary people – know that he is 'the Holy One of God' (4.34) and 'the Son of God' (4.41). There is the sense – clearly an ironic one – in which such knowledge confirms that his power is greater than theirs. Secondly, the miracles leave the bystanders in awe of Jesus: 'with authority and power he commands the unclean spirits, and out they come!' (4.36, NRSV). This aura of power and yet uncertainty surrounds Jesus throughout Luke and explains the different responses of people towards him.

Jesus is portrayed as the leader of a band of followers. Chapter 5 describes how he calls certain people. 6.13–16 says that these are twelve in number. The number twelve was not invented by Luke but features throughout the Gospel tradition (the names of the Twelve vary according to which list is consulted). Luke 22.30 (= Matthew 19.28) implies that in the eschatological age the Twelve will sit on thrones and judge the tribes of Israel. We have seen that Jesus designates the tribal presidents of the restored Israel in advance of his impending death.

Jesus does not call himself 'Messiah' until after the resurrection

(24.26). Prior to this, he uses 'Son of Man'. The history and precise meaning of this title has been the subject of a protracted dispute in scholarly literature. 'Son of Man' clearly *is* a title in Luke. It coheres and contrasts with 'Messiah' in the Gospel. 'Messiah' is what Jesus says he is after the resurrection; 'Son of Man' is what he calls himself beforehand. 'Son of Man' does not *deny* that Jesus is Messiah before the resurrection. The reader knows that he is on the basis of 2.11. But it is a feature of Luke that Jesus avoids 'Christ' until 24.26. This is why 'Son of Man' features so often in the Gospel. The term denotes Jesus before his passion. It is a special feature of his direct speech. 'Son of Man' in this sense denotes Jesus in advance of his heavenly enthronement (22.69; cf. Acts 7.56) and no more excludes belief in his divinity than does 'Christ'.

In chapter 9 Jesus begins to talk seriously about his death. After Peter's identification of him as Messiah (9.20) Jesus says that: 'the Son of Man must undergo great suffering, and be rejected by the elders, chief priests, and scribes, and be killed, and on the third day be raised' (9.22, NRSV). This thought is repeated later in the chapter: 'the Son of Man is going to be betrayed into human hands' (9.44, NRSV). This second prediction is of interest because it is quite unspecific about the manner of Jesus' death. It is possible that here Luke preserves the most primitive form of the passion predictions that we can recover. This would suggest that he really has made an attempt to unearth authentic material, as he claims in the Preface.

There is sense of deliberateness about the way in which Jesus submits to his destiny. Luke expresses this resolve in geographical terms. After Jesus' preaching in Galilee the narrator says that: 'when the days drew near for him to be taken up, [Jesus] set his face to go to Jerusalem' (9.51). 'Taken up' refers to the ascension which Luke understands as heavenly exaltation (see Acts 2.36). The journey to Jerusalem, as Luke presents it, is not the final journey of a man desperate to force God's hand, which is what Albert Schweitzer believed about the historical Jesus, but the self-conscious acceptance of a destiny in which Jesus knows and accepts his impending death. This enables the portrait of his passion as a willing submission to God's will (cf. especially 22.42). It makes, it must be said, for a curious psychology in which Jesus appears as an utterly determined character.

The central section of the Gospel (chapters 10–19) has been criticized for its narrative imprecision but it discloses important teaching which is a crucial feature of Luke's characterization of Jesus. This teaching is addressed to Luke's readers. It calls them to ethical action and to eschatological vigilance. A feature of this teaching is the repeated command for Luke's readers to follow Jesus' own path of suffering and service. Some but not all of the teaching has an eschatological orientation. Examples are the passage about the 'days of the Son of Man' in 17.22–37, and almost the whole of chapter 21.

At the Last Supper Jesus pledges himself not to taste bread and wine until he tastes them new in the kingdom of God (22.16, 18). This links his death with the coming of the kingdom and makes him say that he will preside over the kingdom's inaugural banquet. Jesus also knows that his betrayer is present (22.21). This presents *him* in control of the situation despite what the events suggest.

In 22.39–46 – on the Mount of Olives – we find Jesus at his most convincing as a character. He displays his fear of death in a realistic portrait, but yields to the will of God and goes to his passion. It would have been unthinkable for Luke to present Jesus as having tried to evade it. Luke does however say that Jesus' decision is a hard one, even if the outcome is assured.

The arrest presents Jesus as again in control of the situation. One of the disciples cuts off the ear of the High Priest's servant (22.50). Jesus touches the wound and it is healed instantly (22.51). Jesus' perseverance under suffering is contrasted with Peter's fickleness in 22.54–62, particularly in the crisp statement that 'the Lord turned and looked at Peter' (22.61). The Jewish trial is a sham which fails to find any convincing proof of guilt (22.66–71). Jesus refuses to say that he is the Messiah (22.67) but speaks instead about the heavenly enthronement of the Son of Man (22.69). There is a substantial irony in the fact that at his trial, when the High Priest could have used his prerogative to identify Jesus as the Messiah, Jesus' true status is discussed by the Jewish authorities who fail to recognize it. They identify Jesus as 'the Son of God' (22.70) but ignore the implications of their identification.

In chapter 23 Jesus is brought before Pilate. Pilate is told that Jesus has subverted the nation, opposed the payment of taxes to Caesar and claimed to be Messiah, 'a king' (23.2). The reader knows that none of this is true for Jesus has carefully resisted the title 'Messiah' (see especially 9.20–2; 22.67) and he supports the payment of taxes (20.19–26). Pilate asks whether Jesus is the king of the Jews; Jesus replies that the words are his (23.3). The irony again is that someone beyond Jesus' circle should pronounce Jesus Messiah but fail to appreciate the implication of this identification. It is crucial for Luke's characterization of Jesus that in 23.4 Pilate announces: 'I find no case for this man to answer.' None of the charges made by the Jews – especially the charges of disaffection and insurrection – are found to be proven. There is an apologetic aspect to this aspect of the characterization. The figure of Jesus serves to this extent as the ideal Christian whose testimony cannot be refuted (cf. 21.15) except by mob violence. Even Herod, the quisling king, is reported as finding no crime in Jesus, despite his mockery of him (23.15). Jesus is further pronounced innocent by one of his fellow victims (23.41); and then, after his death, by the Roman centurion (23.47).

The Gospel ends with the story of the resurrection. This is crucial to the characterization. The narrator tells the reader what to believe about the resurrection. In 24.3 people 'did not find the body of the Lord Jesus'. The angel visitors, with their supernatural knowledge, give the reason for this in 24.5: 'Why search among the dead for one who is alive?' Jesus for Luke is not a dead hero but the living Lord whose heavenly presence dominates the Gospel. The ascension shows in pictorial form that Jesus is waiting in heaven for the time of his return. He will soon return to earth to carry out the judgment in the manner described by 9.26.

THE OTHER CHARACTERS

Luke mentions a variety of other characters besides Jesus. We have mentioned God already. He is the one unseen character in the story and, as Luke presents him, the veritable director of the action. God chose Israel in ancient times and revealed his will in the Hebrew Bible. He sends John the Baptist and identifies Jesus as his Son at the Baptism. He introduces the plan of eschatological salvation that is fulfilled through Jesus. Ultimately, he sanctions the crucifixion and brings good out of the tragedy. He raises Jesus from the dead and gives him his position as Lord in heaven. God must not be ignored even though he does not appear in person.

God's demonic counterpart in Luke is Satan. Satan is the chief demon (also called Beelzebul) who organizes the opposition to Jesus. His activity is discerned, not just in the temptation and passion, but also in the numbers of sick people from whom Jesus casts out demons. It is implied that Satan has a real power over people but

Jesus says that this has been broken at the onset of the kingdom of God (10.18). Nevertheless, Satan is sufficiently alive and well at the end of the story to inspire the betrayal of Jesus (22.3). We can see from Acts 5.3 and 26.18 that his activity is not finished even at the end of the Gospel. His final removal awaits the eschatological judgment.

John the Baptist is the most prominent human character after Jesus in the Gospel. The Infancy Narrative presents him as a significant figure and makes him herald the kingdom of God. Jesus identifies John as the eschatological Elijah in 7.27. The narrator, however, makes John the herald of Jesus to include his own readers in the offer of salvation.

Jesus is accompanied by the Twelve and by unspecified other disciples. These are not quite 'minor characters' but their activity does little to affect the development of the plot. The disciples interact with Jesus. Their misunderstandings contrast with his knowledge and resolve. It is implied that the Twelve will only come into their own after the story (and indeed the story in Acts) has finished. They are to be the tribal presidents of the renewed Israel (22.30). In Acts they undergo substantial development. They change from being fearful half-believers to bold preachers of the truth about Jesus. This contrast, which Luke assigns to the influence of the Holy Spirit, is an important difference between the two texts.

As the intimate followers of Jesus the disciples leave much to be desired in their understanding of his mission. Simon Peter may identify Jesus as Messiah (9.20) but he denies him at the trial (22.54–62). No disciples are mentioned at the foot of the cross. They are as much prone to misunderstanding as the other characters. The disciples are told explicitly about the passion in Luke but they fail to understand what they hear (9.44–5). One of the Twelve is even inspired by Satan to inaugurate the events which lead to the death of Jesus (22.3). This misunderstanding, which ties in with the misunderstanding that Luke assigns to the narrator, is one way in which the author challenges the readers to examine their understanding of discipleship, to see how it conforms to the desired pattern of suffering and service.

The Jewish religious authorities play an important role in the story. They are distinguished by the narrator from 'the people' but, at the height of the drama, it is said that even the people agree with them that Jesus must be killed (23.13). There is a sense in which the distinction between 'the leaders' and the 'people' is the only significant division of 'the Jews' which Luke makes. Luke discriminates between different kinds of Jewish authorities in name alone. It is not certain that he really knew the precise distinctions between them. We read in the Gospel of the Pharisees, the Sadducees, the scribes, the lawyers, the teachers of the Law, the chief priests, the High Priest, the captains of the temple, the elders, and the rulers. These people are presented as the opponents of Jesus in a quite monochrome way. The Pharisees are sometimes presented in a redeeming light (e.g. 13.31; cf. the portrait of the Jewish elders in 7.3); Luke's criticism of them is by no means so harsh as Matthew's.

Distinct from the Jewish authorities are 'the people'. 'The people' are essentially neutral towards Jesus in Luke. They do not share the public commitment of the disciples, but neither do they side with the religious authorities until chapter 23. At many points 'the people' receive Jesus warmly, as they had received John. Luke 7.29–30 makes a distinction between the people and the Pharisees in this respect. The people think that Jesus is a prophet (9.18–19) but they do not see him as Messiah and Lord, which for Luke are the ultimate christological accolades. In Acts, 'the people' respond to the preaching about Jesus in large numbers (e.g. Acts 19.26).

There are quite a few 'minor characters' in Luke who react to Jesus for good or for ill. Those who are well disposed towards him include Elizabeth, his mother Mary and the people who bring the paralytic on the stretcher (5.17–26). The Gospel mentions a number of nearly anonymous people whom Jesus heals. They of course are in favour of him, whenever their response is described (e.g. 17.16). Those who are opposed to Jesus include Herod and Pilate. In the passion narrative, certain minor characters do what the disciples should have done: Simon of Cyrene carries the cross, and Joseph of Arimathea organizes Jesus' burial. These characters highlight the disciples' lack of understanding and to this extent act as a foil for them. This again draws attention to the idealizing presentation of discipleship in the Gospel.

These minor characters show how characterization operates in Luke. Luke's interest in the characters is not with them as fascinating people, still less as characters whom he can develop, but with the way in which they interact with Jesus as the central character. Even the disciples are rather wooden characters to this extent. All the characters make a foil for Jesus. This leaves it open for Jesus to speak authoritative truth which conveys the message that the readers hear.

NARRATIVE TIME IN LUKE

Luke's Gospel operates on more than one time-scale. The main part of the text describes Jesus' ministry in Galilee (of unspecified duration) and his journey to Jerusalem. The central section of the Gospel, where diverse teaching is held together by loose narrative links, creates the impression of a relatively substantial preaching ministry but with no exact indication of how long it lasted. It is from John's Gospel that the traditional three-year scheme of Jesus' ministry is derived. By contrast, the trial and death of Jesus in Luke occupy quite a short time, being confined to a long weekend. This means that they occupy a disproportionately large part of the Gospel so as to emphasize the importance of these events. Such variation in the Gospel's time-rhythm brings a heightened sense of drama to the final chapters, appropriate to the narration of a tragedy.

The main part of the Gospel describes the adult ministry of Jesus but a wider time-scale is introduced by the Infancy Narrative. This describes the birth of Jesus. Its biblical allusions recollect the whole history of God's dealings with Israel which, it is implied, reaches its climax with the coming of Jesus. Behind the story thus stands the whole time-span of the Hebrew Bible from Adam onwards.

Luke also has an eye to secular chronology (3.1). The Gospel does not make much of this but nevertheless mentions it. It reminds the reader that the significance of the story is not confined to Palestine but affects the whole earth. This point is vividly demonstrated when Paul comes to Rome at the end of Acts.

A fourth time-scale is provided by the distance between the story and the readers. Acts describes some but not all of this period. We have seen to some extent that the readers' situation is incorporated in the Gospel, at least in terms of questions that the author wants them to ponder. This fourth time-scale is reflected in the dissonance between Jesus and the narrator. The narrator is a contemporary Christian who comments on the words of Jesus. The passage of time explains why he feels the need to reinterpret what Jesus says for a later generation. The fact that the author sides with Jesus in the Gospel means that everything that Jesus says is held to be true despite the passage of time. This is an important insight, not least for the study of Lucan eschatology.

THE SETTING OF LUKE

Luke operates within the geographical confines of Palestine. The Gospel describes Jesus' initial ministry in the region of Galilee, followed by his journey to Jerusalem. Luke's general imprecision about geography suggests that he is not familiar at first hand with the region (see e.g. 5.17). His use of the 'journey to Jerusalem' motif has a narrative function to which geography in the narrow sense is subordinated. 'Jerusalem' is the centre of the Jewish nation and the place where the prophets died and must die (13.33). Acts continues the theme of journeying by describing how the chief apostle comes to Rome. Paul's arrival there parallels the arrival of Jesus in Jerusalem.

THE STRUCTURE OF THE GOSPEL

Luke as a Gospel takes its structure from the developing ministry of Jesus, first in Galilee and then in Jerusalem. The structure of the Gospel is determined by its place in the two-volumed series. This implies the belief that the Gospel is incomplete by itself and that the Messiah's preaching and death in Jerusalem must be matched by Paul's preaching (and presumed death) in Rome. Of all the structural devices which the Gospel employs, geography is the most obvious. The career of Jesus involves suffering and death. This point is made in many places in the Gospel (e.g. 9.22), from the Infancy Narrative onwards (1.34–5). The journey to Jerusalem is thus a journey by Jesus to his death. This is explained in 13.33 where the place-name 'Jerusalem' is held synonymous with the fate of those who preach the words of God. The device of geographical progress denotes the expansion of Jesus' mission, but also his sequence of steps towards the cross.

Jerusalem is foregrounded because it is the centre of Jewish eschatological hope. Isaiah 2.3 illustrates the underlying belief: 'Many peoples shall come, and say: "Come, let us go up to the mountain of the LORD, to the house of the God of Jacob; that he may teach us his ways and that we may walk in his paths." For out of Zion shall go forth the law, and the word of the LORD from Jerusalem' (RSV translation). This prophecy makes Jerusalem the centre of what God is expected to do in the future of the Jewish nation. Luke stands firmly in this tradition of hope, like the other Evangelists. His Gospel describes how the Messiah comes to Jerusalem – to fulfil what God had intended – and how he is tragically rejected and crucified there. The Gospel nevertheless contains the hint that Jesus will finally be acclaimed as Messiah in the Jewish capital (13.35) when he returns there from heaven.

Christopher Evans thinks that the central section of the Gospel is modelled on the theme of Israel's wilderness journey in the book of Deuteronomy.[44] He cites a variety of evidence for this view which has a certain cumulative effect. The parallels include the sending out of the apostles (= spies) and the appointment of seventy missionaries (= elders). We should, however, observe that Luke is too subtle an author merely to imitate an existing theme. He plays around with it, not least in the temptation story, by explaining that Jesus is both like but also unlike Moses (as other figures). Jesus differs particularly from Moses in that he is expected to lead his people into the promised land – the kingdom of God – when he returns from heaven. In 16.18 Jesus intensifies a Mosaic regulation to make the point that he is a speaker of even greater authority. We should therefore bear Evans' comparison in mind but remember that Luke is unlikely to be using the Deuteronomy analogy in a straightforward or literalistic way.

The Gospel is also structured round the theme of the fulfilment of prophecy. The deliberate change from Attic to biblical Greek after the Preface tells the reader that the Bible is an important text for the plot. This expectation is not disappointed in what the Gospel says. The birth of John recalls the birth of Samuel (as well as of Samson). John is presented as the Elijah who has come (7.27). This raises the question of who Jesus is and where he stands in relation to the prophetic tradition. We have seen that Luke teases with this motif. He appears to answer it in Acts by his reference to the prophet like Moses (Deuteronomy 18.15) in Acts 3.22 and elsewhere.

A major part of the plot is the demonstration that the biblical hopes are being realized. This is indicated programmatically in chapter 4 where the prophecy of Isaiah 61 is held realized before the eyes of the synagogue congregation. This passage presents Jesus as the person who gives the scriptures their authoritative interpretation. That should be compared with the function of the Teacher of

Righteousness in the Qumran *Habakkuk Commentary*. It is essentially an eschatological view.

The passion predictions are important structural elements in Luke. 9.22 says that: 'the Son of Man *has to* endure great sufferings . . . etc'. The basis of the 'has to' lies in the fact that God is the unseen director of the plot. His will must be obeyed although he himself remains unseen. Behind this statement stands a whole Jewish tradition in which the righteous suffer at the hands of the ungodly. This is altogether broader than Deutero-Isaiah's 'servant' where that tradition is reflected (cf. 20.10–12). Jesus thereby aligns himself with a view in which the righteous suffer which he, as the prophet of the end-time, can hardly circumvent. The passion predictions are of course a form of prophecy in themselves. They structure the narrative by explaining what will happen later and to this extent provide more reliable information than the narrator, who suppresses the suffering of Jesus. Jesus both fulfils and makes prophecies in an authoritative way as the one whom God has empowered for the eschatological task.

None of this information disguises the fact that the journey of Jesus from Galilee to Jerusalem is *the* major structural element in the Gospel. The journey to Jerusalem is a journey by Jesus to his death but, as the passion predictions indicate, also to resurrection and heavenly glory (cf. Acts 2.36). It is (only) through the death of Jesus that the new covenant is inaugurated (22.20). The implication is that what Jesus and the prophets have said about Jerusalem will soon be realized with the full appearance of the kingdom of God.

IRONY IN THE GOSPEL

Irony plays an important role in Luke. 'Irony' denotes the different levels of understanding which emerge when the narrator or Jesus expresses a view which embodies information that is denied to other characters. 'Double irony' occurs when one of the characters unwittingly says something that is true but without realizing that the statement is true. Irony is a feature of many narrative texts. In Luke it occurs because the other characters lack either the authoritative knowledge of Jesus or the information imparted to the readers by the narrator.

The conditions for the Gospel's irony are established in the Infancy Narrative. This presents Jesus as no ordinary person but as the Messiah whom Judaism had long expected. The Infancy

Narrative tells the readers what they need to understand the story. Their expectations are raised particularly by the Canticles which explain how God has 'come to the help of Israel his servant' (1.54); how 'the dawn from heaven will break upon us' (1.78); and how God has prepared 'deliverance . . . in full view of the nations' (2.31). This means that, when the mission of Jesus is introduced in chapter 4, little of what is said there comes as a surprise.

We have seen that the characters in Luke enjoy different levels of understanding about Jesus. No-one understands him completely but we can nevertheless distinguish three levels of comprehension. The disciples are committed followers (for all their misunderstanding). The people are basically neutral. The Jewish leaders are generally opposed to Jesus (at least by the end of the Gospel). Only the readers know the full truth about him. They are guided by the words of Jesus and, it must be said, by the blundering of the narrator into realizing that Jesus is Christ and that his status as Messiah is achieved only through the suffering and death of the cross.

The first indication of irony is the healing of the possessed man in 1.40–1. The devil identifies Jesus as 'the Son of God' when he is cast out of the man. This is ironic because the demon utters knowledge which is true but which the other characters understand only incompletely. That the demons should identify Jesus in this way, but have their correct identification ignored by the other characters, is a prominent theme of the early chapters.

There is irony also in the interaction between the author and the narrator. In chapter 9 Peter identifies Jesus as Messiah. Jesus says nothing to contradict this identification (9.20). The narrator, however, says that Jesus 'gave them strict orders not to tell this to anyone' (9.21). The irony lies in the fact that, in suppressing the Messiahship of Jesus which he does on the conscious level, the narrator fails to recognize that he is suppressing the need for the suffering of Jesus which he does on an unconscious level (and which the author holds against him in the Gospel). Jesus and the author have a greater insight than the narrator for this reason. The reader shares this deeper perspective because he has access to the complete text of the Gospel and to the thoughts of Jesus as well as of the narrator.

Irony is most readily apparent in the trial narrative. The irony rests on the premise that Jesus is in control of the situation and that – to paraphrase a famous analogy – the judged is revealed as the judge in a remarkable reversal of roles. The trial narrative is prefaced by the Last Supper in which Jesus demonstrates his control over the situation by telling the disciples that they will be met by the owner of the upper room (22.7–13). Next, Jesus says that his betrayer is at the table (22.21) in a context where there has been no hint of betrayal so far but where it is said that Satan enters into Judas to denounce Jesus to the authorities (22.3). The irony is that Judas is apparently ignorant of Jesus' knowledge of the situation, and evidently also of Satan's role in the events which unfold.

The trial itself redounds with irony. The irony is that Jesus is the victim but that everything he says proves he is in control of the situation. In 22.66–71 Jesus is brought before the Sanhedrin and investigation ensues. It is the High Priest's job to identify the Messiah. Instead, the assembly asks Jesus whether he is the Messiah. Jesus says that if he tells them the truth they will not believe it (22.67). He then proceeds to tell them the truth about the situation: 'from now on, the Son of Man will be seated at the right hand of Almighty God' (22.69). As he predicts, they do not believe it; but then, in a celebrated case of double irony, they themselves pronounce the truth about Jesus but fail to realize what they say: 'You are the Son of God, then?' (22.70). When Jesus refuses to deny this – for how could he deny the truth? – they think they have found conclusive evidence and abjure the need for further witnesses (22.71).

There is further irony in the trials before Pilate and Herod. Both men examine Jesus but find no crime in him. Jesus refuses to answer all charges. This is followed by the Barabbas episode (23.13–25) which is introduced in a curious way. The crowd call for the release of Barabbas for a reason that the narrator does not explain. Luke omits the Marcan statement that 'at the festival season the governor used to release one prisoner requested by the people' (Mark 15.6). This turns the demands of the crowd from legitimate prisoner-bartering to wilful insurrection. The crowd appear as an angry mob who call for the release of an insurrectionary (as Barabbas is called in 23.19) and the death of an innocent man. This is ironic because it is an exact reversal of the situation outlined by 23.2 where *Jesus* is accused of insurrection. The Jews prove their inability to understand Jesus when they unwittingly side with a person who is guilty of an offence of which Jesus has been accused but of which he is manifestly innocent. Nevertheless, Jesus is delivered to be crucified (23.24) and Barabbas released (23.25) according to their demands.

The crucifixion completes the picture. Jesus, the victim, is sufficiently in control of things to predict the future destruction of Jerusalem (23.28–31). Impaled on the cross, he is mocked by the crowds: 'Let him save himself, if this is God's Messiah' (23.35). The irony is that Jesus could save himself, for the narrator has already hinted as much in his description of Jesus' agony on the Mount of Olives (22.39–46). So, too, has the devil in 4.9–11. The Messiah freely dies at the hands of his people. At the same time he is identified most ironically as the Messiah, both by the *titulus* (23.38) and by the crucified criminal (23.39). Here, supremely in the Gospel, the connection is made between Messiahship and suffering in a way that the crowd predictably fails to understand.

Irony reminds the reader that there is more to the Gospel than meets the eye. Through the frequent misunderstandings they are confronted with a portrait of what it means to call Jesus 'Christ' and shown that he is a suffering Messiah who demands the same of his followers (9.23). It reminds them to persevere with the path of suffering when they in turn are misunderstood.

OTHER LITERARY DEVICES IN THE GOSPEL

Finally, we must consider some other literary devices which give the Gospel its structure. Repetition is an important literary tool in Luke. At the beginning of his ministry Jesus announces his mission in the words taken from Isaiah 61 (4.18–19). There is a sense in which all the people whom he heals are stereotypes (or at least 'flat characters') who illustrate Isaiah's basic point that the broken ones are being healed. The reader is not overly encouraged to see the different miracles in isolation from each other or from Jesus' designated purpose in 4.18–19. The healed appear in general to be variations on Isaiah's list of victims. Such repetition makes the point that the kingdom of God is appearing in the ministry of Jesus. The miracles, presented in this way, are signs that this is so.

Another repeated theme is the journey to Jerusalem which is foregrounded through repetition. The Infancy Narrative describes more than one such journey. This repetition alerts the reader to what will be a major theme in the Gospel. Both the narrator (9.51) and Jesus (13.33) comment on the status of Jerusalem in such a way as to confirm that Luke sees the city as central to God's eschatological purpose. The frequent references to the journey draw the reader to the Gospel's plot and prompt consideration of the link which it makes between the journey to Jerusalem and Jesus' rejection in the Jewish capital.

At the same time we must notice that the theme of Jerusalem as the centre of eschatological hope is juxtaposed with Jerusalem the city destroyed by divine anger. Alone of the Evangelists, Luke makes Jesus predict the Roman destruction of Jerusalem (21.20). He insists that the punishment of the Jews for their rejection of the Messiah had taken place already. This mirrors a tension that exists within Hebrew prophecy. Time and again, the prophets express contradictory feelings of divine anger and love towards Jerusalem. (The city was of course overrun in 587 BCE at the beginning of the Babylonian Exile.) Luke plays on this ambivalence and includes it in his Gospel. The fact that the necessary punishment has already been discharged (see 21.20) means that Luke does not contemplate a future punishment of the Jews. This is part of his assertion that a time of *liberation* is impending.

Parallelism is a different kind of repetition in Luke. There are several kinds of parallelism in the Gospel. Luke includes links with earlier Jewish literature (for instance, with Deuteronomy). He also includes parallelism within the Gospel, and parallels between Luke and Acts.

The Infancy Narrative provides an example of this. The births of John and Jesus are described in parallel but in such a way as to indicate that Jesus is the more important figure to whom John defers. The Infancy Narrative at the same time hints that the, both rather strange, births of these children reflect earlier miraculous births. This sets them in the wider context of God's dealings with the Jewish nation. One might even say that the birth of Jesus is paralleled by the birth of the church in Acts.

At places in Luke one story looks back to another so that parallelism is a feature of the narrative style. An example of this is the story of the Roman centurion (7.1–10) which is followed by that of the widow of Nain (7.11–17). This recalls the earlier references to Elijah and Elisha (4.26–7), again to demonstrate that Isaiah's eschatological vision is being realized.

The parallelism between Luke and Acts is striking and significant. Luke often matches events in his two volumes, notably perhaps the trials of Stephen (and Paul) and Jesus. Acts 7.56 ('I see the heavens opened and the Son of Man standing at the right hand of God') is a deliberate evocation of 22.69. The parallelism gains its meaning from the structural consideration that both Luke and Acts describe journeys which have eschatological significance. The conclusion of Acts in Rome mirrors the conclusion of Luke in Jerusalem. Readers of the two-volumed series are left to ponder what still remains to happen before the promise of Luke 21.27 is fulfilled.

Chapter 3

A reading of Luke

We shall now read Luke as a text and see how the story unfolds. We shall read the Gospel on a sequential basis. I shall pause to explain the more difficult textual allusions as and when we come across them.

CHAPTER 1

Luke makes a change from the earlier Gospel(s) at the beginning of his text. He includes a Preface (1.1–4), in the style of Hellenistic scientific writing, which sets out his purpose in writing the Gospel. Luke does not claim to be substantially different in his story of Jesus from the earlier Gospels – and his use of Mark and Matthew confirms this – but he introduces his own as an 'orderly account' (1.3) that concerns the things about which Theophilus has been instructed. Theophilus may or may not have been a concrete historical individual; it is impossible to discern his identity at this distance. There is no firm evidence in the Gospel that he was a high-ranking Roman official, but this suggestion has sometimes been made by the commentators.

Luke's statement that he has 'investigated everything carefully from the first' (1.3a, NRSV) should not be taken to imply that the Gospel is a piece of historical research in the modern sense. The purpose of this 'orderly narrative' is given in 1.3–4 by the assertion that it concerns 'the matters of which you have been informed'. This means that its suits the demands of primitive Christian catechesis. In this sense it follows 'the traditions handed down to us by the original eyewitnesses and servants of the gospel' (1.2). The contribution made by the traditional element to Luke should not be under-estimated. The opening reference to 'the events that have taken place among us' (1.1) includes the period of the church in this assessment. This means that Luke is better described as a story of salvation in Christ than as a story about the life of Jesus as such.

The question arises of who is speaking in the Preface. It is tempting to conclude that here we hear the voice of the real author who briefly appears at this point to state his aims and intentions before the narrator takes over in 1.5. It is possible that we do meet the real author in this way, but his chosen vehicle for communication is writing and this means that we cannot ignore the presence of the narrator as co-speaker in the Preface. The Preface also introduces the 'implied author' who presents himself as a Christian catechist sifting evidence and presenting it in a coherent narrative. The use of the first-person form is striking, made even more so by the deliberate change in tone in 1.5 where the narrator introduces his own speech-pattern which is reminiscent of biblical language. It is worth noting the reference to 'many' previous writers in 1.1. On my reading of the text, Luke was written with a knowledge of Mark and Matthew. The phrase, however, possibly implies that there were more written records than these. One wonders whether Luke knew more sources than we do or whether his language is hyperbolic. The fact that the implied author introduces himself as a source of earlier material means in any event that the story is presented as further commentary on material which is already familiar to the readers.

Luke begins his story with the conception of John the Baptist (1.5–25). The shift to biblical Greek draws the reader to the world of the Hebrew Bible where Luke's plot (and time-scale) in one sense begins. The style and language support the first stages in the plot which describes the miraculous conception of one baby to prepare for the miraculous conception of another.

The Infancy Narrative is crucial for the delineation of plot. The structure of the Preface makes John the Baptist a significant figure. Jesus will later identify him with Elijah (7.27). The assumption of the Infancy Narrative is that John heralds the kingdom which arrives with Jesus. The narrator, however, tends to downgrade John in Luke and to make him the herald of *Jesus* because he wants to allow a longer period for the kingdom of God to emerge and to include his own readers in the offer of salvation.

In this opening story we are introduced to the parallelism which is a significant feature of Luke's Gospel. The birth of John precedes that of Jesus. The parallelism is not without its ambiguities, however. There is no clearly articulated delineation between John and Jesus to match the Elijah analogy in chapter 7. This is because, although Jesus is greater than John – he is the Messiah (2.11) – John is by no means an inferior figure. *John* is said to be the one who will 'lead his people to a knowledge of salvation' in 1.77 and in whose ministry the 'dawn from heaven' (1.78) is expected. The bystanders ask approximately the same question about John in 1.66 as Herod does about Jesus in 9.9 ('what will this child become?'). John is mentioned first in the Gospel and he is described with a greater detail than any other character besides Jesus. He is in every sense a significant figure for Luke's history of Christian salvation.

Zechariah is offering the daily incense when he witnesses an angelophany (1.8–20; cf. Judges 13). The angel's heavenly origin indicates that authoritative knowledge is disclosed at this point (1.13–17). His speech sets the scene for the story and describes the conditions under which the plot will operate. The angelophany is to this degree an important structural element in the Infancy Narrative (and the Gospel). The angel predicts the birth of John and explains his role. He calls John the one who will 'prepare a people that shall be fit for the Lord' (1.17). The echoes here of biblical narrative set the plot firmly within the tradition of the divine promises to Israel. The birth of a child to old and barren parents recalls the births of Samuel (1 Samuel chapters 1–2) and Samson (Judges 13). Both were important figures in biblical history. John will be more so. He will 'bring back many Israelites to the Lord their God' (1.16). This is an appropriate introduction to the plot which concerns the eschatological restoration or reconstitution of Israel.

The importance of the angelic announcement is emphasized by the dumbness of Zechariah (1.18–20). This recalls the dumbness of Ezekiel (Ezekiel 3.26) and the seer's response to the angelophany in Daniel 10.15. It is a helpless human response to divine revelation which renders human speech redundant. The bystanders realize that Zechariah has seen a vision (1.21–2) but at this stage its details are not disclosed. Elizabeth conceals her pregnancy (1.24) to emphasize the miraculous nature of the conception (which was achieved through natural means).

The spotlight now turns on Mary (1.26–38). Another angelophany discloses more authoritative knowledge: 'In the sixth month the angel Gabriel was sent by God to Nazareth, a town in Galilee, with a message for a girl betrothed to a man named Joseph, a descendant of David; the girl's name was Mary' (1.26–7). The 'sixth month' relates to the timing of Elizabeth's pregnancy (cf. 1.24). Mary is said to be betrothed to a Davidide, the Israelite tribe of Judah from which the Messiah was expected to come (cf. 20.41–4). Jesus' messianic credentials are firmly established in this speech: 'You will conceive and give birth to a son, and you are to give him the name Jesus. He will be great, and will be called Son of the Most High. The Lord God will give him the throne of his ancestor David, and he will be king over Israel for ever; his reign shall never end' (1.31–3). This is a clear statement about Jesus at the beginning of the Gospel. It shows how strange the 'messianic secret' is when it is introduced in 9.21. Readers know on the basis of 1.31–3 (which constitutes divine revelation, mediated by the angel) that Jesus *is* the promised Messiah who will reign over Israel for ever. There is nothing secret about this for the readers. For readers who live in the period between the ascension of Jesus and his return from heaven, the angelic statement represents the promise that the Messiah's earthly reign *will* take place ('he will be king over Israel for ever') even though Jesus is now in heaven (and his return seems delayed). The emergence of the kingdom is an assured feature of Lucan eschatology even though its timing remains uncertain. This angelic statement introduces some of the complexities of the plot whereby the liberation of Israel is achieved through the death, ascension and return from heaven of Jesus.

The angel deals with Mary's objection that she is a virgin (1.34–8). Luke writes with a knowledge of Matthew's Gospel which includes the prophetic demonstration that Jesus would be born of a virgin (Matthew 1.23). This makes Luke's quite circumspect description of the virgin birth somewhat surprising. Matthew's scriptural justification for the belief and his statement that Joseph refrained from intercourse with Mary (Matthew 1.25) are both omitted here. Luke says only that 'the Holy Spirit will come upon you, and the power of the Most High will overshadow you' (1.35). This phrase is capable of more than one interpretation. It probably means that the Holy Spirit will impregnate Mary, who remains a virgin; but it does not exclude the possibility that Joseph impregnated Mary. That Jesus is virginally conceived has to be *inferred* by the reader from the narrative. It is not explicitly stated there. Perhaps this is because Luke thinks that virginal conception might be frowned on by some of his readers.

The parallelism between John and Jesus is emphasized when Mary visits Elizabeth (1.39–45). John stirs in Elizabeth's womb when Mary arrives (1.41), as if he knows who Jesus is. Elizabeth blesses Mary and calls her 'the mother of my Lord' (1.43). Here, we find another title for Jesus that will be important in the Gospel. Jesus for Luke is 'Lord and Christ' (Acts 2.36). Both titles are used in chapter 1, but Jesus' direct speech avoids 'Messiah' until after the passion (24.26). Luke nevertheless tells the readers the full truth about Jesus before the story begins.

In this context the *Magnificat* is set (1.46–55). The *Magnificat*, ostensibly a hymn about Mary, is in fact a hymn about Jesus, at least in its second half. The opening verses echo Elizabeth's greeting. All generations will count Mary blessed (1.48) for God has done great things for her (1.49). 1.50–5 describes what God will achieve through Jesus. There is a strong note of reversal in 1.51–3 which states that the mighty will be cast down from their thrones and the hungry be filled with good things. This anticipates the Nazareth sermon in chapter 4 where Isaiah's eschatological prophecy of good news for the poor is said to be fulfilled with the coming of Jesus (4.18–19). There is an interesting parallel to this theme of reversal in the Jewish work called *The Similitudes of Enoch* (*1 Enoch* 37–71; first century CE) which describes the overthrowing of the powerful in connection with the heavenly enthronement of the Son of Man (e.g. *1 En.* chapter 62). The *Magnificat* thus reflects a Jewish apocalyptic background, just as the body of the Gospel (notably 22.69) presents the Son of Man as an enthroned heavenly mediator in agreement with the *Similitudes of Enoch*. The notion of reversal is an eschatological one as Luke presents it. It anticipates the yet-to-be fulfilled aspect of the kingdom of God which Luke connects with the return of Jesus from heaven. The *Magnificat* ends by reiterating the theme of 1.32–3 that God's mercy to Israel (the 'children of Abraham') will last for ever (1.54–5). This again locates the centre of the Gospel's eschatological hopes in the tradition of the biblical promises to Israel.

Mary returns home before John's birth (1.56). She is removed from the scene to permit the description of John's naming and destiny in 1.57–80. At the child's circumcision he is given the name, John (1.63). Zechariah is permitted to speak after he has insisted on this name, just as in Ezekiel the prophet's tongue is loosened to proclaim God's message to Israel (Ezekiel 33.22). The bystanders' question, 'what will this child become?' (1.66), is answered by Luke in the *Benedictus* (1.68–79). Zechariah says that God has 'turned to his people and set them free' (1.68). He has 'raised for us a strong deliverer from the house of his servant David'

(1.69). The *Benedictus* has an implied christological content but we should not ignore its high evaluation of John. John is the one with whom the age of salvation is said to begin. The *Benedictus* makes the point that, although the full realization of the eschatological hope still lies in the future, 'knowledge of salvation' (1.77) is present already.

CHAPTER 2

Chapter 2 describes the birth of Jesus. The introduction (2.1–2) makes this an important event with its reference to the census when Quirinius was governor of Syria. This is a census for which, it must be said, historical scholarship has failed to find precise corroboration. By this ruse Joseph travels from Nazareth to Bethlehem so that Jesus is born in David's own city (2.4–6). One could not imagine that the Messiah should be born anywhere else (whatever the historicity of the tradition). Mary wraps Jesus in swaddling clothes and lays him in the manger because there is no room for them at the inn (2.7). The description of the birth is not embroidered through any description of animals or by reference to hardship. One should not romanticize the scene any more than the story allows. 'Swaddling clothes' are held appropriate to a Jewish monarch in *Wisdom* 7.4 ('no king begins life in any other way'). It is obvious from what follows that the manger becomes a throne in Luke.

The first people to be told about the birth are the shepherds (2.8–20). The shepherds have symbolic value in the story. David was a shepherd before his enthronement. 'The shepherds of Israel' are the Jewish kings in the Hebrew Bible (see Ezekiel 34.2). The shepherds who hear of the Messiah's birth recall the narrative of 1 Samuel 16 where David's anointing took place among shepherds.[1] An angel tells the shepherds what the readers know already: 'Today there has been born to you in the city of David a deliverer – the Messiah, the Lord' (2.11). This authoritative declaration recalls Gabriel's words from 1.32–3 ('he will be king over Israel for ever') and reinforces their meaning through repetition. The fact that the manger and the swaddling clothes are mentioned again in 2.12 confirms they have symbolic value in the narrative. The 'manger' perhaps recalls the words of Isaiah 1.3 ('an ox knows its owner and a donkey its master's stall; but Israel lacks all knowledge, my people has no discernment'). The swaddling clothes are probably a royal sign (see above). The whole passage redounds with messianic symbolism. The noun 'Saviour' in 2.11 (NRSV) and the reference to 'peace on earth' (2.14; cf. 1.79) reflect what was believed in the Hellenistic world about Augustus and his age of peace and present the birth of Jesus in similar terms. Both Jewish and Greek imagery is employed in this passage to describe the birth of the eschatological redeemer.

The shepherds go to the manger and tell their story (2.15–20). The manger is the focus for the narrator's revelation of Jesus to the world. Into the private world of Mary and Joseph step unspecified others who lend it dignity through their astonishment (2.18). This seems an incongruous element in the story but it anticipates what will be said about the reaction to the adult Jesus in the Gospel (e.g. 4.22).

The naming of Jesus in 2.21 recalls that of John in 1.57–66. The description of John's circumcision is longer because it supplies the foil for that of Jesus. Jesus, like John, is given a name disclosed by an angel.

Journeying to Jerusalem is an important structural theme in Luke. The Infancy Narrative describes two such journeys in advance of the final journey to Jerusalem. Both of these are journeys to the temple. 2.22–3 (the purification) allows the narrator to explain the plot. Onto the stage steps Simeon, 'one who watched and waited for the restoration (literally 'consolation') of Israel, and the Holy Spirit was upon him' (2.25). 'Restoration' in this context is an eschatological term. It signifies the climax of Israel's history which had been anticipated by the prophets and which Luke believes is inaugurated in the ministry of Jesus. Luke says that Simeon has been told by the Spirit that he will not taste death until he sees the Lord's Messiah (2.26). He is guided into the temple when Jesus arrives there (2.27). He takes the infant into his arms and utters the words of the *Nunc Dimittis*. His canticle, and presumed death afterwards, is a vivid conviction that the time of restoration has arrived: 'I have seen with my own eyes the deliverance you have made ready in full view of all the nations' (2.30–1). This statement embodies the substantial basis of Luke's plot as we have seen. 2.32 strikingly includes the Gentiles in the promised 'deliverance' and emphasizes this point with an unusual order of words (Gentiles first, Jews second). Simeon predicts the rejection of Jesus in this context (2.34–5). He thereby anticipates the nature of the Messiahship which the Gospel emphasizes.

Simeon's testimony is reinforced by that of the prophetess Anna

(2.36–8), for in Jewish law there must be more than one witness. Anna 'talked about the child to all who were looking for the liberation of Jerusalem' (2.38). This, too, sets Jesus in the context of Jewish eschatological expectation. One should beware of seeing here a 'nationalized' reference to the liberation of Jerusalem from the Romans. Luke stands his distance from such a revolutionary interest (see 20.19–26) and presents the Roman destruction of Jerusalem as one of the eschatological signs that was foretold by Jesus (21.20). This liberation of Jerusalem is an eschatological liberation. It will be accomplished by God alone. Anna too anticipates the time when the biblical promises about Israel will be fulfilled.

Luke is the only (canonical) Gospel to tell us anything about the childhood of Jesus. Anecdotes were a feature of Hellenistic biography. Luke records but one anecdote (2.41–52). The material is carefully selected. It describes another journey to Jerusalem, again to the temple. Jesus goes missing and is eventually found by his parents in the temple, disputing with the Jewish teachers. It seems almost as if he cannot be kept away from there. He tells his bemused parents, 'Did you not know that I was bound to be in my Father's house?' (2.49). This warns the reader that journeying to the temple is going to be a major theme in the Gospel. We have seen that it is decisive for the plot.

CHAPTER 3

Chapter 3 returns to John the Baptist and to his preaching. Again, Luke sets this on the international scale with his reference to the reign of Tiberius, the procuratorship of Pontius Pilate and the jurisdiction of other figures of authority (3.1). At the end of this (deliberate and self-conscious) scene-setting the narrator pronounces: 'The word of God came to John son of Zechariah in the wilderness' (3.2). The biblical tone of this statement is equally deliberate and self-conscious (cf. 1 Samuel 15.10). John's commission results in his proclamation of a 'baptism in token of repentance for the forgiveness of sins' (3.3). Luke makes John's a penitential movement which he thinks has a preparatory nature. The Gospel cites part of Isaiah 40 in 3.4–6 to present John as the one who 'prepare[s] the way for the Lord'. Luke here follows Mark's use of Isaiah but the last phrase of the citation ('all mankind shall see God's deliverance') is not found in Mark and is introduced here to include the Gentiles in the sphere of salvation.

John's preaching falls into two parts. In the first place there is ethical instruction which has an eschatological basis (3.7–14). John warns people to expect judgment and not to trust in their status as 'children of Abraham' as the guarantee of salvation (3.8–9). This material is held in common with Matthew (Matthew 3.7–12). Luke removes Matthew's suggestion that it is addressed to the Pharisees and Sadducees and sets it more generally against the crowd (3.7). They are told to prove their repentance by bearing fruit (3.8–9). Luke also introduces further material, not found in Matthew, to warn people about the need for simple and honest living (3.10–13).

The second half of John's preaching mirrors the crowd's uncertainty about whether he is the Messiah (3.15). Readers already know that John is not the Messiah but he supplies a formal denial of this point (3.16–17). John contrasts his water baptism with Jesus' future baptism of people 'with the Holy Spirit and with fire' (3.16). He states also that Jesus would be the agent of judgment (3.17). We are veering here towards the view that John is the herald of Jesus which is adopted by the narrator. The statement about Jesus' baptism with fire and with the Holy Spirit has a mainly theological purpose in the Gospel. It can be elucidated with reference to a passage in Acts. Acts 8.14–17 is an account of how the Holy Spirit entered into the Samaritan Christians at some point after their baptism through the laying-on of hands by the apostles. That passage reflects the fact that, whereas in its earliest period, Christian baptism was administered 'in the name of Jesus' (e.g. Acts 2.38), later in the first century a Trinitarian formula of invocation was felt desirable (see especially Matthew 28.19–20). My view is that Acts 8.14–17 explains Luke 3.16 when it develops the baptismal formula in a Trinitarian direction. 'Baptism with the Holy Spirit' means Christian (i.e. initiatory and water-based) baptism and not some exceptional experience that is distinct from it. The reference to baptism with fire anticipates the final judgment which 9.26 defers until the return of Jesus. The second baptism mentioned here is thus an eschatological one.

Luke's sense of chronology is neat and precise. He removes John from the scene *before* Jesus' baptism (3.18–20) so that there is no formal overlap between the two figures (as there is, for instance, in John 3.22–3). This creates uncertainty as to who baptized Jesus. If we take the chronology seriously the baptism takes place *after* John's imprisonment so that John himself could not have conducted it. Luke does not say that Jesus was baptized by John. Those who wish to believe that he did must again infer this from the text. Jesus is said to have undergone the rite 'during a general baptism of the people' (3.21). This statement certainly gives it an anonymous air. The description of the event in 3.21–2 has four distinct parts: the baptism itself; Jesus at prayer; the descent of the Spirit from the open heaven; and the heavenly address to Jesus. Only the last two mark Jesus out as someone exceptional. In Mark the heavenly address has the nature of a private vision in which Jesus alone is told the significance of his ministry (see Mark 1.9–11). Luke partially reworks this impression by leaving out the words 'he saw' (i.e. the descending Spirit) but nothing is said to indicate that the heavenly words make a deep impression on other people. The heavenly voice nevertheless supplies an authoritative identification of Jesus similar to the angelic pronouncements in the Infancy Narrative.

Jesus is introduced as God's beloved, or only, Son with whom the divine favour rests. The first half of this address comes from Psalm 2.7 which in the Hebrew original is addressed to the Jewish king. First-century Judaism and Christianity used 'Beloved' as a title for the Messiah. The second half of the address is based on Isaiah 42.1 which was originally spoken of the servant of Yahweh, who seems to be a cipher for Israel in that passage. Luke's heavenly voice here identifies Jesus as the Messiah, echoing what is said in 2.11. The descent of the Spirit on Jesus indicates that he is the person uniquely possessed by the Spirit. This is an important theme in the Gospel (see below on chapter 4). The comparison of the Spirit with a dove perhaps recalls the opening verses of Genesis (Genesis 1.2) where the Spirit of God is said to hover over the waters. This means that, at what was regarded as the climax of Jewish history, a link is made with its beginning as the Spirit settles on the person who will carry out the final judgment.

The baptism is followed by the genealogy of Jesus (3.23–38). Matthew too has a genealogy (1.1–17) but there are significant differences between the two versions. Luke's version probably represents, at least in part, a reworking of Matthew's genealogy. Matthew begins from Abraham and works forward; Luke begins from Jesus and works back to Adam. Luke's list is longer than Matthew's. It is not certain that it is accurate but it does at least show that Jesus is a Davidide (3.31) and mentions the patriarchs (3.34). If Luke is reworking Matthew he may have wanted to avoid the statement that Jesus was descended from Abraham, which presents him exclusively in Jewish terms. The descent from Adam (3.38) shows that Jesus is connected with the nations as well. It is possible that Luke is influenced by Paul's description of Jesus as 'the second Adam' (e.g. 1 Corinthians 15.45) for both Jesus and Adam are called 'Son of God' in the Gospel (3.22, 38). Luke's order of presentation ends the list with the phrase 'Son of God', as if to draw attention to this title.

CHAPTER 4

In chapter 4 Jesus is led by the Spirit into the wilderness for the temptation. There are echoes here of Israel's wilderness wandering (especially in the 'forty days' of 4.1; cf. Numbers 14.34); but, in contrast to the Hebrew story, Jesus' desert sojourn is a time of victory over Satan and not of disobedience. The place of this story in the Gospel – before Jesus' ministry formally begins – makes it paradigmatic of Satan's defeat which is described in the later chapters. The fact that Jesus uses Scripture to refute Satan suggests that he has the authority to give the Bible its authoritative meaning, which we saw is an eschatological property (cf. 1 Corinthians 10.11; 1QpHab 7.1–6). The beginning of the temptation story tells the reader what kind of contrast is in play: Jesus is 'led by the Spirit and tempted by the devil' (4.2). This explains Jesus' unwavering loyalty to God in a single sentence and shows why the downfall of Satan's kingdom is assured.

The three temptations derive from pre-Lucan tradition. Luke reverses Matthew's order to draw attention to the third temptation which takes place in the temple. The temptations have both individual and cumulative significance. The request to turn stones into bread (4.3–4) is the temptation to misuse divine power. It possibly recalls the miracle of the streaming rock (Exodus 17.1–7) which occurred after God had promised to rain down bread from heaven (Exodus 16.4). This is answered by the citation of Deuteronomy 8.3 LXX ('man is not to live on bread alone') which Matthew preserves in a longer form ('but on every word that comes from the mouth of God'; Matthew 4.4). Luke's truncated statement makes the reader wonder what is more important than bread. The rest of the Gospel contains some clues to answer that question. God supplies daily bread (11.3); the breaking of bread becomes Jesus' distinctive action in the Gospel (22.19; 24.30, 35); for Luke, it is the symbol of the kingdom of God (14.15). The kingdom of God – obedience to God – is the thing that is more important than bread.

The next temptation (4.5–8) concerns the nature of God's kingdom. Jesus is offered all the kingdoms of the world if he will worship the devil as their lawful owner. Luke recognizes the devil's supremacy in the human world – the demons, after all, possess people in the Gospel – but he insists that Satan is retreating before the kingdom of God (see especially 10.18). The second temptation is a pictorial demonstration of the conviction that, with the arrival of Jesus, Satan's ability to do what he claims – to distribute the kingdoms under his patronage – has been removed, for someone stronger is overpowering him (11.22). The scriptural citation in 4.8 summarizes this belief by saying that God alone must be worshipped. Dawsey finds here the hint that Jesus is being compared with Joshua.[2]

The third temptation (which Luke highlights) is the temptation to take Jerusalem by surprise. The devil takes Jesus to Jerusalem and offers him a means of instant recognition as the Messiah. If he jumps from the parapet of the temple, the devil insinuates, God will send the angels to catch him (4.9–11). This is the temptation for Jesus to capture Jerusalem without his suffering and death. That is a way of discipleship which Luke rejects. The tragedy of the Gospel is that the Messiah journeys to Jerusalem to be rejected by the Jewish people. When he *does* do something exceptional in the temple (19.45–6), this leads to the decision for his death (19.47). The progress of the Gospel shows that what the devil says is wrong. God does *not* spare Jesus (though doubtless he could have done); Jesus' repudiation of this temptation (4.12) is a way of saying that his installation as Messiah must take place through the cross. On the Mount of Olives, where Jesus wrestles with his impending death, he twice tells the disciples to pray lest they enter into temptation (22.40, 46). This looks back to the third temptation and reminds the readers to resist the temptation of removing suffering from their portrait of Christian discipleship.

The middle part of chapter 4 (4.14–30) is crucial for the plot. Jesus visits his home synagogue in Nazareth and is invited to read from the Bible, after which he offers an exegetical homily. The selected passage is from Isaiah 61 ('The Spirit of the Lord is upon me. . . . He has sent me to announce good news for the poor'). Jesus begins his homily by announcing: 'Today . . . in your hearing this text has come true' (4.21). The implication is that the prophecy is fulfilled both through the unique status of Jesus and more generally through the realization of Isaiah's eschatological vision, which has begun to happen. This part of chapter 4 is programmatic for Jesus' ministry. It constitutes his first explanation of what his mission is about.

The story has some internal difficulties which tease the reader into thought. The congregation initially receives Jesus' sermon with favour and marvels that it should come from 'Joseph's son' (4.22). In 4.23 Jesus seems to become cynical and says: 'No doubt you will quote to me the proverb, "Physician, heal yourself!" and say, "We have heard of all your doings at Capernaum; do the same here in your own home town."' Cynicism turns to hostility in 4.24–7. Jesus says that 'no prophet is recognized in his own country'. He follows this with the stories of Elijah and Elisha who were sent to people outside Israel. These words 'roused the whole congregation to fury' (4.28). They take Jesus to the brow of a hill to kill him (4.29) but he walks through the crowd and goes away (4.30).

The strangeness of the story makes the reader ask what is happening. At first sight, it is Jesus and not the townspeople who behaves badly. They welcome him; he insults them. Those commentators who argue otherwise see the question of 4.22b, 'Is this not Joseph's son?', as disparaging, as it is in the Marcan version of the story (Mark 6.1–6). But Luke significantly abbreviates the text of Mark and this interpretation is by no means obvious. The townspeople's reaction is given by 4.22a: 'there was general approval; they were astonished that words of such grace should fall from his lips'. This makes it unlikely that 4.22b is a sneer. It is *Jesus* who takes it as a sneer. He criticizes the people's rejection of himself and of all the prophets in Israel.

Evidently, we are dealing with an exchange where some of the logic is missing. What we know about Luke's careful manner of composition suggests that these elements are absent by design. The missing element is the statement that rejection has taken place already; Jesus *presupposes* rejection in what he says. This is why he speaks about his own rejection and about the Jewish rejection of the prophets. This presumed rejection leads, quite ironically, to an act of rejection at the end of the story. The people drive Jesus out of the town and try to hurl him over a cliff. The structure of the story leads it to confirm its own presuppositions.

Dawsey looks elsewhere in Luke to find this missing evidence for rejection.[3] He thinks that the parable of the great banquet in

14.21–2 contains allusions to this passage in its words, 'bring in the poor, the crippled, the blind, and the lame'. He also thinks that the rejection of John the Baptist – which Luke has described already in 3.19–20 – gives this story its logic (for it describes a prior act of rejection). We should add that the story almost forces the reader to look around for further material to interpret it since it is almost deliberately bizarre as it stands. It is programmatic of the ministry of Jesus, not just in what it records about his message, but also in what it implies about the course of his career.

The story further explains that the mission of Jesus is to those outside his own country. Jesus does not deny that his mission is to Israel but he says that 'no prophet is recognized in his own country' (4.24). This is paradigmatic of the plot since it includes the Gentiles in God's act of salvation. 4.25–7, which is unique to Luke, makes the point – on the basis of Hebrew Bible precedent – that the Christian preaching is quite legitimately addressed to people beyond the borders of Israel. This anticipates what will happen in Acts and indeed later in Luke (see 7.9). 4.25–7 provides Jesus' own authority for the spread of the gospel in this way.

The story closes with Jesus somehow evading the townspeople's attempts to kill him (4.28–30). The artificial construction of the story warns the reader that its conclusion will be as nuanced as the rest. The anger of the townspeople is understandable for Jesus has just insulted them. It is not clear, however, why they should want to *kill* him. This looks more like an attempt at lynching than a judicial execution. Those commentators who see here the preparations for stoning reconstruct a quasi-judicial meaning from the text. It is more likely that the people simply want to push Jesus over a cliff in demonstration of their anger. This conclusion resembles the story of the Gerasene demoniac in chapter 8. At the end of that story (8.34–8) the pigs rush over the cliff because they are demonized and Jesus is asked by the townspeople to go away. This is the complete opposite of what we find here. In chapter 4 no-one goes over the cliff and Jesus walks away of his own accord. The reader is left asking why Jesus walks away as he does. The answer is supplied by chapter 8. Those who go over the cliffs are the demonized in Luke. Jesus by contrast is possessed by the Spirit of God. That Jesus evades his pursuers is a demonstration of his Spirit-filled status which is the theme of the whole Gospel. He walks away from his would-be assassins for 'it is unthinkable for a prophet to meet his death anywhere but in Jerusalem' (13.33).

There is in this perhaps a deliberate contrast with the story of Stephen's death in Acts 7.54–60. Stephen is driven out of the city and stoned in the presence of witnesses (7.58). This is indeed a judicial execution. In Luke 4 Jesus is neither stoned nor killed; the attempt at lynching fails because the Spirit of God brings him through. He survives on the present occasion; but, like Stephen, he will eventually meet his death in the form of a judicial process.

The reader is thereby presented with a whole variety of themes in quite a short story. First of all Luke sets out his understanding of the mission of Jesus. This embodies the demonstration that eschatology is being fulfilled as is explained by the citation of Isaiah 61 in 4.18–19. This involves the parallel demonstration that Jesus is possessed by the Spirit of God in a context where such Spirit-possession is itself an eschatological sign. Thirdly, the story is a paradigm of the mission of Jesus because it anticipates the Messiah's rejection by the Jewish nation. Fourthly, we should notice that it explains the terms in which the miracles should be understood. Those who reject Jesus see them as 'doings' (4.23) when they are in fact signs of the kingdom of God, and evidence that the eschatological programme of 4.18–19 is being realized. It is significant that this story immediately follows the temptation story where Jesus' refusal to work the devil's miracles is narrated. Fifthly, the story anticipates the inclusion of the Gentiles in salvation through its reference to Elijah and Elisha. It closes by confirming the Spirit-filled status of Jesus. This provides the link with the next story which describes the first of the miracles of Jesus.

In 4.31–7 Jesus drives out the spirits in Capernaum. The first spirit to be despatched identifies him as 'the Holy One of God' (4.34) and asks whether he has 'come to destroy us'. For Luke, it is appropriate that a demon should recognize who Jesus is. The truth of the pronouncement is assured by the demon's supernatural nature. This identification is the negative counterpart of the earlier angelophanies. Jesus confirms it by casting the spirit out of the man. This proves that, as the Holy One of God, he has a higher prestige than the spirit. It is natural that the bystanders should ask the question, 'What is there in this man's words?' (4.36) and observe his authority over the unclean spirits. Their rhetorical question is answered by the pronouncement of the manifold spirits in 4.41. These assert that Jesus is 'the Son of God', to which the narrator adds that they know Jesus is the Messiah. The demons in Luke speak, ironically, with a Christian voice and confirm the truth of Jesus' messianic identity which the narrator mistakenly says is concealed in the Gospel (9.21).

The chapter closes with Jesus' statement that he must 'give the good news of the kingdom of God to the other towns also, for that is what I was sent to do' (4.43). This is the first use of the phrase 'kingdom of God' in Luke. I have suggested that the term is the rough equivalent of the phrase 'liberation of Jerusalem' (2.38) and bound up with the eschatological hopes of Hebrew writers. This prominent motif counters the suggestion that the world belongs to the devil which has been advanced and rejected by 4.6. For Jesus the kingdom is present but hidden as his ministry unfolds. In this reference it must certainly be present if it is to be preached in this way.

The placing of the first miracles at this point is by no means accidental. They follow the Nazareth episode where the meaning of Jesus' mission is disclosed. Despite the miracles, which reveal quite clearly who he is (at least to the demons), Jesus will be rejected by the Jews as he is by his own townspeople. The seeds of the tragedy are sown at an early point in the Gospel. But there is nothing in Luke to match the indication of Mark 3.6 that the moves to *kill* Jesus are taken at this early stage.

CHAPTER 5

The call of the first disciples is described in 5.1–11. It has the form of a miracle story but the statement of Jesus in 5.10, 'from now on you will be catching people', shows that this is not its only function. The miracle, which involves an unexpected catch of fish, makes the point that the fishermen will become workers for the kingdom of God. The performance of this miracle, which follows the reference to the kingdom as a present reality in 4.43, authenticates the authority of Jesus as he calls the disciples. Peter responds, 'Go, Lord, leave me, sinner that I am!' (5.8) and falls to his feet. Here, again at an early point in the Gospel, we find what is effectively the worship of Jesus with the use of the title 'Lord' and Peter's reverential falling before him. This reminds the reader that Jesus the Lucan character is also the heavenly Lord. Some scholars think that 5.1–11 is a post-resurrection story which has been imported into the body of the Gospel. The material does however have a purpose in this pre-Easter setting where it illuminates the double-edged nature of Luke's characterization of Jesus.

In 5.12 the narrator returns to the miracles of Jesus. Jesus heals a leper – someone who is held unclean by Jewish law (5.12–16). The certification of the cure by the priest (5.14) confirms the authenticity of the miracle. Here we find an early anticipation of the 'messianic secret' in the Gospel: 'Jesus then instructed him not to tell anybody' (5.14). This statement is assigned to the narrator; Jesus never forbids the promulgation of his Messiahship in Luke. The fact that Jesus instructs the man to consult the priest seems to go against what the narrator says at this point. The tension that exists in 5.14 should not be overlooked. It will be developed in chapter 9.

A new theme is introduced in connection with the miracles in 5.17–26. This is the issue of the forgiveness of sins which John had articulated in connection with his baptism of repentance in 3.3. The paralytic's friends lower him through the roof but instead of healing him Jesus says to the man: 'Your sins are forgiven you' (5.20). This statement doubtless reflects the ancient belief that illness and sinfulness are connected; but something more than that is meant here. The point of this story is that the forgiveness of sins is an eschatological function which Jesus discharges. The grounds for holding this view are to be sought in Jeremiah 31.34 whose context the longer text of 22.20 shows that Luke knew and referred to the ministry of Jesus. Forgiveness, as the Pharisees observe in 5.21, is a divine prerogative. Their criticism is that Jesus, even as a notable wonder-worker, was not worthy to act in the place of God by doing this. Jesus by contrast boldly declares that God's mercy to sinners, which Jewish sources such as *b. Rosh Hashanah* 16b–17a and *b. Pesahim* 54b reserve for the end-time, is available here and now. The miracle and the pronouncement are thereby related to the eschatological purpose which the Gospel articulates.

As a result of this saying, grumbling about blasphemy begins to surface. Such grumbling has a double edge. It implicitly criticizes the view that the eschatological benefits have become available with the mission of Jesus (as Luke believes that they had). It also criticizes Jesus' claim to act in God's name in making this declaration. This reaction to the miracle creates the need for a response. Jesus is only too happy to oblige by providing one.

In 5.23 Jesus asks a rhetorical question to which there is only one possible answer: 'Is it easier to say, "Your sins are forgiven you," or to say, "Stand up and walk"?' (5.23). Clearly, the former is true. This is the logic on which the story rests. The fact that Jesus then heals the man proves that 'the Son of Man has the right on earth to forgive sins' (5.24). The narrative conclusion – 'the things we have seen today are beyond belief!' (5.26) – shows the gulf in understanding that exists between the crowd and the readers. The crowd see the miracles but do not understand what they mean. The readers know what the miracles mean because they read from the perspective of faith that Jesus is Lord. Parts of the Gospel are directed against the readers, especially in the central section where their understanding of Jesus' Messiahship is criticized. The author begins by getting the readers on his side in contrasting their knowledge with that of the crowds. He will later use this empathy to criticize them.

This miracle is followed by the call of Levi (5.27–8). That becomes the occasion for some disputes and sayings of Jesus which take place in Levi's house (5.29–39). The Pharisees complain that Jesus 'eats and drinks with tax collectors and sinners' (5.30). Jesus replies that he has come to call 'sinners to repentance' (5.32). This picks up the thought of 5.24 and no doubt reflects Levi's vocation as a tax collector. The dispute is followed by the Pharisees' comparison between the behaviour of the disciples of John the Baptist and that of those of Jesus (5.33). They complain that John's disciples are devoted to prayer and to fasting but that Jesus' disciples revel much too much. Jesus states that his disciples eat and drink because the bridegroom is still with them (5.35). Fasting would be appropriate to the period when he had been taken away (5.35). Here, Jesus anticipates his rejection at the hands of the Jews.

The contrast between new and old in 5.36–9 is effectively a statement about the meaning of eschatology. Jesus says that a new patch should not be put onto an old garment, nor new wine into old skins. The implication is that something decisively new has arrived with his preaching. Readers know that this 'new something' is the eschatological age. The place of this saying, after the comparison between Jesus and John the Baptist, implies that even John belongs to the old order because he merely heralded the fulfilment like the other prophets. This passage looks forward to the enigmatic statement of 7.28 where Jesus says that the least in the kingdom of God is greater than John the Baptist.

CHAPTER 6

Chapter 6 is a collection of sayings with loose narrative links. The individual episodes are introduced imprecisely: 'one sabbath' (6.1);

'on another sabbath' (6.6); 'during this time' (6.12); and so on. This is the method that Luke will adopt in the central section of the Gospel. It implies that Luke's purpose is not the exact recollection of the occasion when something was said but the transmission of Jesus' words themselves. The episodes gain their force from their content which is woven into the wider narrative (the form of which is retained even though the links are loose).

The Jewish institution of the sabbath appears to be criticized in 6.1–5. We have seen that the focus of this passage really concerns the temple. Jesus' disciples do what is technically regarded as work and are criticized for this by the Pharisees. Jesus justifies their behaviour with reference to a Hebrew Bible story about David. David and his band ate the sacred bread from the temple. It is implied that, in the same way, Jesus the Messiah, as *Lord* of the sabbath, has authority over Jewish institutions. Luke removes Mark's additional comment, 'the sabbath was made for man, and not man for the sabbath' (Mark 2.27), and thus makes the dispute specifically concern the authority of Jesus. Several themes coalesce here. In the first place, Jesus' status as Messiah shows that a new order had arrived. Paul had taught that 'Christ is the end of the Law' (Romans 10.4). This is the view reflected here. Secondly, there is an implied view of the inviolability of the temple which hints, but does not say explicitly, that its functions could be challenged by someone with messianic authority. In this sense, the story antici-pates the cleansing of the temple in 19.45–6, for there Jesus does something unexpected in the temple. Finally, there is the also-implied view that the followers of Jesus can follow his attitude to the temple. This is what we find in Stephen's speech in Acts chapter 7 where the temple is roundly criticized.

The next incident is the healing of the man with the withered arm (6.6–11). This happens on the sabbath but again the issue is wider than a sabbath controversy. It concerns the nature of the mira-cles themselves. The scribes and Pharisees watch to see if Jesus will heal on the sabbath so that they can find a charge against him (6.7). Jesus 'knew what was in their minds' (6.8) and organizes events accordingly. He *does* perform the miracle (6.10) but only after asking a question which allows no easy answer: 'Is it permitted to do good or to do evil on the sabbath, to save life or to destroy it?' (6.9). The obvious implication is that the Son of Man, as Lord of the sabbath, can use the day of rest for a restorative purpose. Jesus duly heals the man and the Pharisees lick their wounds. It is said

ominously at the end of the story that: 'they totally failed to understand, and began to discuss with one another what they could do to
Jesus' (6.11). This marks the beginnings of a hostile interest in him
(but contrast Mark 3.6 again).

The next section describes the call of the Twelve (6.12–16). This
is a partial repetition of 5.1–11 which establishes the significance of
the Twelve as co-workers with Jesus. They are called 'apostles', the
title which features many times in Acts. It is worth noting that
there is full agreement among the Gospels about the number of the
Twelve but general disagreement as to their names. 'Judas, son of
James' is the unique feature of this list. The Twelve have an eschatological function in the Gospel as the designated leaders of the tribes
of Israel (22.30). This of course explains their number.

After this Jesus preaches and heals people who are suffering from
various diseases. The narrator says that people come from a wide
variety of places to hear Jesus ('from Jerusalem and all Judaea and
from the coastal region of Tyre and Sidon', 6.17). His popularity is
growing, despite what is said in 6.11. The general public may not
fully understand Jesus but they are grateful towards him and not
hostile. Such was his power that they have only to touch him to be
healed (6.19).

The second half of chapter 6 records Jesus' teaching to his disciples. This is addressed as much to the readers as to the original
characters. The first part of this section contains the Lucan version
of the Beatitudes (6.20–3). Luke differs from Matthew in including
woes as well as blessings. The meaning of the Beatitudes is given by
the first of them: 'Blessed are you who are in need; *the kingdom of
God is yours*'. Interpreters have often seized on the first phrase to
identify Luke's concern for the poor as the central feature of this
section, linking it appropriately with 4.18–19; but the second
phrase is the crucial one. The Beatitudes describe the kind of
behaviour that is appropriate to the kingdom of God. The people
described in 6.20–1 – the needy, the poor and the weeping – are
types like the stock characters whom Jesus heals in the Gospel. The
Beatitudes show that the kingdom of God involves a new perspective on society in which those who are downtrodden will be helped.
The fourth Beatitude ('Blessed are you when people hate you and
ostracize you . . . because of the Son of Man', 6.22) has an obvious
setting in the experience of early Christian churches (cf. 8.19–21).
6.23 links the rejection of Christians with the Jewish rejection of
the prophets.

In Chapter 5, I shall argue that the contrast envisaged here has a social and economic dimension. The preaching of Jesus is addressed to a situation characterized by 'dependency' in which a few people had the ability to exploit the majority, who lacked the power to resist them. Jesus' preaching embodies the conviction that the existing order needs to be changed. It articulates the conviction that such change is both possible and impending. This is why the Beatitudes are counterbalanced by the Woes in Luke (6.24–6). The Beatitudes are an expression of hope for the downtrodden and offer a new vision for society. The Woes are a warning of judgment for those who oppress the poor. We cannot read any of the Gospels without noting the social situation to which the preaching of Jesus is addressed. This is characterized both by inequality and by the conviction that things can be different. The Beatitudes express this belief in paradigm form.

The theme of the Woes (6.24–6) is again one of reversal, but viewed from the other side. Those who are currently rich are destined for a fall. This looks back to the theme of the *Magnificat* with its parallels in Jewish apocalyptic literature. We should not immediately conclude that some of Luke's readers were rich, although several of them may have been quite well placed to judge from the prosopography of other New Testament texts. The terms 'rich', 'hungry' and 'laugh' contrast with the portrait of the kingdom in 6.20–1 and warn readers that people can place themselves in such a position that they become strangers to the kingdom. The Woes are as much a call to self-examination among the readers as a more general prediction of judgment for outsiders. They warn that some may fail to enter the kingdom because they have moved out of sympathy with its basic aims.

The collection of material in 6.27–30 demands careful interpretation. At first sight it is a call for a ridiculous meekness: love for enemies, pacifism, even giving beyond the call of duty. The key to the passage is the recognition that hyperbole features here. Luke deliberately overstates his case to draw attention to the need for a more moderate action. 6.29 echoes the words of John the Baptist (3.11). It presents Jesus, like John, as teaching ethics of a kind appropriate to the belief that judgment is near (cf. especially 3.17). This is the theme also of 6.25 ('you will go hungry . . . you will mourn and weep') where the future judgment is based on the criteria of present status and response. Luke here advocates a generous form of behaviour under the belief that the kingdom of God is already present.

Ethical exhortation continues throughout the chapter. 6.31–6 says that people must treat others as they would like to be treated and adds to this the promise of eschatological reward. The implication is that Christians must be more virtuous than other people, evidently because the author is aware of the possibility that they, too, may fall under judgment. The motive presented for this in 6.35 ('you will have a rich reward') seems almost self-interested but there is a (not so) subtle blend of threat and promise in this chapter. Those who do what is virtuous will 'be sons of the Most High'. It is implied that those who do not will not.

There follows in 6.37–49 a collection of sayings with no obvious connection between them. Here are found such well-known parables as the mote and the speck (6.41–2) and the house built on sand (6.46–9). The passage begins with teaching about judging, condemning and forgiving (6.37–8). Not much distinguishes Jesus here, it must be said, from other ethical traditions (cf. *b. Megillah* 28a). The parable of the blind leading the blind (6.39) is combined with the statement that no pupil ranks above his teacher. The speck in the brother's eye is a warning against hypocrisy (6.41–2). 6.43–5 is a reminder that Christians must demonstrate behaviour which shows that they belong to the realm of salvation. The final saying (6.46–9) cautions that those who call Jesus 'Lord' – which means Christian readers – must do what he tells them (which no doubt means obeying the ethical principles enshrined in the chapter). This is illustrated by the parable of the house built on sand which contains an echo of the eschatological judgment in its final crash (6.49).

In 6.46 ('Why do you call me, "Lord, Lord . . . ?"') we find a clue to the focus of this ethical teaching. It is addressed to Christians who are in danger of not doing what Jesus tells them. For this reason basic teaching about humility and service is included to recall readers to a particular pattern of behaviour. The introduction of this teaching with the Beatitudes and Woes sets out the contrasting ethical possibilities with a stark realism. Those who look to their own comfort will be confounded at the return of Jesus. Those who looked to the interests of others will receive an eschatological reward. The final crash reinforces this warning and encourages readers to make changes in their lives. 'Obeying Jesus' in this context means doing what Luke tells the readers to do.

Most of the material in this section is not situation-specific. That is to say, it deals with general principles and not with precise individual situations. Part of the reason for this may be the desire to make Jesus say something that is relevant to many of the situations which people in the primitive church encountered. It also allows the interpretation and application of these ethical principles to be worked out by people in those different situations. One can imagine that this material probably served as the source for exegetical homilies in its earliest usage. Metacommentary on the words of Jesus is not just a modern phenomenon! The form of the material even suggests that it *depends* for its meaning on the provision of subsequent commentary. It is compressed and does not read easily when compared with Luke's pacier narrative. It requires careful unpacking and consideration to give meaning to short phrases such as 'Do not judge, and you will not be judged' (6.37). Luke nevertheless regarded this material as essential to his Gospel. Ethics features there because the 'pureness of the community' was a crucial factor for Christian bodies as they maintained high social boundaries in respect of outside groups in a polymorphous pagan world (cf. Ephesians 5.25–6). It is likely that the kind of ethics we find here – general principles for Christian behaviour – was developed precisely because people failed to live lives that matched the ideal in every respect. Such material was possibly developed in the course of catechesis and preaching, and attributed to Jesus to lend it authority.

CHAPTER 7

Chapter 7 relates the deeds and sayings of Jesus in the region of Capernaum. The function of the chapter is to recall what Jesus has said about his mission in chapter 4, especially in 4.18–19, and to demonstrate that the eschatological vision is indeed being realized. This is evident especially in the allusions here to the stories of Elijah and Elisha (cf. 4.25–7). The middle part of chapter 7 describes John's questioning of Jesus, answered by the miracles which are signs of the kingdom of God. This passage supplies the element of rejection that is missing from chapter 4 when the narrator comments: 'the Pharisees and lawyers, who had refused [John's] baptism, rejected God's purpose for themselves' (7.30).

The story of the Roman centurion with the sick servant is related in 7.1–10. Here we have an echo of the story about Elisha in chapter 4, for the centurion is of course a Gentile (although it is not said that the servant is a Gentile). The servant falls ill and the centurion asks Jesus for help through some 'Jewish elders' (7.3; presumably influential people in the synagogue). 7.4–5 develops the portrait of the centurion: 'he deserves this favour from you', the elders say, 'for he is a friend of our nation and it is he who built us our synagogue'. This brings the centurion close to the category represented by Cornelius whom Acts describes as a 'God-fearer' (e.g. Acts 10.2). He is an interested Gentile like those who convert to Christianity in Luke's second volume. The story has another feature which appears in 7.6–10. Not only does the centurion believe that Jesus can heal but he acknowledges his high status: 'I am not worthy to have you come under my roof' (7.6). More than once in Luke, Roman centurions pronounce the truth about Jesus; 23.47 is another example. 7.6 is not an explicit statement of Jesus' divinity but it does make the reader ask why a Gentile should address him in this way. The centurion expresses his sure belief that Jesus will heal his servant, producing his well-known military analogy (7.7–9). This leads Jesus to comment: 'not even in Israel have I found such faith' (7.9). That seems to be the point of the story. Luke, following Paul, tells his readers that Gentiles can participate in salvation on the basis of their faith in Jesus. When the messengers return home they find the servant restored to health (7.10). The working of the miracle is the proof that the Gentile has been included in this way. The benefits of the kingdom of God are thus shown to be extended beyond people in Israel. It is significant that the *Jewish elders* should plead for this extension.

Jesus proceeds to Nain where he sees a funeral procession (7.11–17). Luke has the art of presenting narrative details with simple poignancy: 'The dead man was the only son of his widowed mother' (7.12). The narrator continues: 'When the Lord saw her his heart went out to her, and he said, "Do not weep" ' (7.13). The title 'Lord' shows that this is the compassion of God himself who cares for the fatherless and widows in Jewish ethics (see e.g. Deuteronomy 10.18). This story recalls that of Elijah who was sent to the widow of Sarepta (4.26). Jesus touches the bier and tells the young man to get up (7.14). Jesus then restores him to his mother (7.15). 7.16 brings the sequence of miracles to a conclusion with the statement, attributed to the crowd, 'a great prophet has arisen among us' (7.16). We thus have two consecutive recollections of stories about Elijah and Elisha as if the allusions are not coincidental. The reader is purposefully taken back to chapter 4, where

Jesus' eschatological programme is announced, and shown that Isaiah's prophecy is being fulfilled.

The passage 7.18–28 about John the Baptist is crucial.[4] John is told about Jesus' miracles by his disciples. He sends them to ask Jesus whether he is 'the one who is to come' (7.19). This is the question of whether Jesus is the eschatological Elijah. Jesus gives no direct answer but performs further healings (7.21). Those healed include the blind and sufferers from many diseases. Jesus then gives John's disciples the following answer: 'Go and tell John what you have seen and heard: the blind regain their sight, the lame walk, lepers are made clean, the dead are raised to life, the poor are brought good news – and happy is he who does not find me an obstacle to faith' (7.22–3). This statement from Jesus confirms that the eschatological programme announced in chapter 4 is being realized. The reader quite rightly draws this inference from the narrative, and a further inference follows from it. Jesus is *not* Elijah (the herald) but the one whose ministry is synonymous with the arrival of the kingdom itself.

This reply problematizes the status of John the Baptist in Luke. Jesus makes the crowd ponder whom they went out to see (7.24–8). Jesus' own conclusion is that John is a prophet 'and far more than a prophet' (7.26). He cites Malachi 3.1 (in a form influenced by Exodus 23.20) to declare that John is the herald (7.27). In the terms established by Malachi this must mean that *John* is the prophet Elijah. Malachi says that Elijah will immediately precede 'the great and terrible day of the Lord' (Mal. 4.5). Jesus here presents John as Elijah. The context of this saying, however, which is constructed by the narrator, represents a development of that idea. It makes John the herald of *Jesus* and not of the kingdom as such. The narrator does not deny that the kingdom has been inaugurated with the ministry of Jesus but he concentrates on its 'unfulfilled' aspect to allow his second-generation readers to participate in the kingdom. There is a significant difference in outlook in this. Jesus teaches that the kingdom is present but hidden; the narrator argues that it has yet to be consummated in the future. Both of course are right, given that Jesus speaks about an unrealized and future aspect of the kingdom (chapter 21). The narrator's view is a reinterpretation of Jesus' understanding but not, it must be said, a fundamentally different eschatology.

This is the way in which 7.28 should be read. In 7.28 Jesus says: 'Among all who have been born, no one has been greater than John;

yet the least in the kingdom of God is greater than he'. Commentators have been scandalized by this passage because it seems to exclude John from the kingdom; but Luke does not in fact say that this is so. The statement concerns the presence of the kingdom among those who hear Jesus (cf. 17.21). John is removed from the scene in Luke before the baptism of Jesus (3.20) and so does not hear the preaching of the kingdom. As Jesus presents John, he is the last in the series of prophets who heralds 'the great and terrible day of the Lord'. 7.28 is a statement of narrative time-scale which draws attention to the fact that the last days have arrived. The passage comments on the great privilege of those who heard the preaching of the kingdom, and not initially on the inferior status of John.

The narrative conclusion to the story carefully delineates the supporters and opponents of Jesus. The people (including the tax collectors) 'acknowledged the goodness of God' because they had received John's baptism (7.29). The Pharisees and lawyers, who had refused John's baptism, 'rejected God's purpose for themselves' (7.30). This is a retrospective commentary on the effects of John's baptism. Many people accepted it. Some, however, rejected it. In the logic of 7.27–8, where John is Elijah and the kingdom is present already, the rejection of John signifies the rejection of Jesus and of the kingdom. This is the missing link which explains 4.21–30. Those mentioned by 7.30 are not the precise groups who are said to take the decision to kill Jesus in 19.47 ('the chief priests and the scribes, with the support of the leading citizens') but one wonders whether it is really correct to distinguish between the opponents of Jesus, for they represent a 'common type' in the Gospel. People fall into two camps in 7.29–30. The precise constitution of the opposing camp is subordinate to this broader distinction. This reference to John sets the Jewish rejection of Jesus in perspective and warns the reader of its inevitability.

To this is added, on the lips of Jesus, a commentary on his rejection. He says that it may be based on misunderstanding but that it is culpable none the less. 'How can I describe the people of this generation?', Jesus says in 7.31. They are like children who refuse to join in the game, even when it is changed to suit them (7.32). John the Baptist fasted and they held him possessed (7.33). The Son of Man comes eating and drinking and they call him a glutton who keeps bad company (7.34). The implication of the saying is not that 'you never can win', but that such people had always refused *all* of

God's advances, however they were expressed. This makes for a link with the saying about the bridegroom in 5.33–5 which confirms that the theme of rejection is high on the agenda of this passage. 7.35 summarizes what is said here: 'God's wisdom is proved right by all who are her children' (7.35). John and Jesus had both come with what Fitzmyer calls a 'critical, eschatological message'.[5] Although what they said might seem offensive, especially what Jesus says about the temple, it was validated by divine Wisdom and therefore must be true. The 'people of this generation' were not Wisdom's children at all because they had failed to recognize the divine moment when it came to them. This is what will be said more lucidly about the inhabitants of Jerusalem in 19.44.

The story of Jesus at dinner in the house of Simon the Pharisee is told in 7.36–50. This story has several parts. In 7.37–8 an immoral woman appears to anoint Jesus and to wash his feet with her tears. No reason is given for this but Simon instantly connects it with sexual misbehaviour: 'If this man were a real prophet, he would know who this woman is who is touching him, and what a bad character she is' (7.39). Simon – who appears in the story as sincere but misunderstanding – knows that the woman is a prostitute and suspects she is exercising her charms on Jesus. Jesus counters this conclusion with a parable (7.40–3). Two debtors are forgiven little and much. Jesus asks Simon which of the two owes the greater gratitude to the creditor. Simon replies, correctly, that it is the one who is forgiven more. Jesus then commends the woman's attitude (7.44). She has shown great affection for Jesus. This presents her as a penitent and not as a sinner: 'her great love proves that her many sins have been forgiven' (7.47). The woman has been included in the eschatological restoration because she accepts the forgiveness of sins, when (the virtuous) Simon failed to recognize his need for penitence (and is therefore by implication excluded from the restoration): 'where little has been forgiven little love is shown' (7.47). The story thus subverts the suggestion of 7.39 that Jesus has failed to recognize the woman's true character. He has, in fact, perceived much more than Simon. He sees the woman not simply as a prostitute but as a penitent. This means (as the reader duly concludes) that Jesus really is a prophet. His prophetic ability lets him look beyond superficial levels of meaning to see people's true character. The conclusion of the story makes Jesus pronounce the woman's sins forgiven (7.48) and to say that her faith has saved her (7.50). There is an obvious echo in this of 5.17–26 which makes the

point that class and gender distinctions are irrelevant to membership of the kingdom of God (cf. Gal. 3.28).

CHAPTER 8

At the beginning of chapter 8 Jesus tells the parable of the sower
(8.1–8, 11–15). I have suggested that this is in one sense a parable
about parables. It tells the reader how to approach Luke, and reiterates the warning of 6.46 that readers must do what Jesus (and of
course what Luke) says. Several classes of poor ground are described
but there is really only one distinction. This is between the ground
that bears fruit and that which does not. It is interesting that in
8.12 the first kind of poor ground is said to be that scavenged by
the devil. Although the devil might take some, and other pitfalls
arise, 'some of the seed fell into good soil, and grew, and yielded a
hundredfold' (8.8). In the contest between Jesus and Satan, the final
outcome is not in doubt (as the miracles constantly demonstrate).

The parable and its interpretation are separated by a statement by
Jesus about the meaning of the parables. The disciples ask Jesus what
the parable of the sower means. He tells them: 'it has been granted to
you to know the secrets of the kingdom of God; but the others have
only parables, so that they may look but see nothing, hear but understand nothing' (8.10). For Jesus, the kingdom of God is a present
reality, albeit an unseen one. This means that its secrets can be
disclosed to his followers. His statement indicates that the parables
have more than one level of perceptibility. Those outside the
kingdom hear the parables but fail to understand their meaning. This
represents a play on the meaning of the word, 'parable'. A parable is
only a parable for those who know what it means. In this context
these are those to whom Jesus tells the meaning. A parable becomes
an obstacle for those who do not know what it means (cf. 20.18).

The interlude confirms that Luke sees the sower as a parable
about parables. The poor ground corresponds to the ignorant
outsiders of 8.10. These 'look but see nothing'. This is because the
parables of Jesus have the kingdom as their basic theme. The
kingdom is present but hidden in Luke. Those who fail to understand the story fail to recognize that the kingdom has arrived.
When they are told about it they will not listen. There is a sense in
which Luke thinks that the behaviour of Christian disciples is the
visible fruit of the invisible kingdom. This is why the parable of
the sower is followed by the parable of the lampstand: 'those who

come in may see the light' (8.16). Luke's ethical instruction is intended to produce a series of signs which show that the kingdom has arrived. He says that readers must take care how they listen (8.18), for the future will bring an examination of how people have behaved (8.17).

In this context, where the kingdom makes its appeal, even family ties are irrelevant. 8.19–21 describes how Jesus' family come to hear him. Jesus seems at best ambivalent towards them. He comments enigmatically: 'my mother and my brothers are those who hear the word of God and act upon it' (8.21). The narrator says neither that Jesus refused to see them nor confirms that he actually did. Luke does however exclude Mark's statement that the family of Jesus thought he was mad (Mark 3.21). He relies on the device of hyperbole to supply the meaning of the statement. When compared with the demands of the kingdom, not even the most central of human relationships can intervene (cf. 21.16). This enigmatic statement probably represents a further repudiation of the culture of 'dependency' that pervaded first-century Palestine.

The rest of chapter 8 relates four miracles of Jesus. These raise the question of Jesus' identity to prepare for Peter's identification of him as Messiah in chapter 9. The first is a nature miracle (8.22–5). Jesus calms a storm and prevents the disciples' boat from sinking. The story is said to concern faith (8.25) which for Luke means faith in Jesus. The disciples ponder who Jesus is given that the wind and the waves obey him. It is surprising to find them apparently uncomprehending but the disciples are in fact prone to misunderstanding throughout the Gospel. The story itself contains information to answer the question which draws readers back to the Bible. In the Psalms *God* is the one who is said to still the storm and the waves (Psalm 107.29). This means that the miracles of Jesus disclose the action of God himself.

The boat journey brings the disciples to the territory of the Gerasenes (8.26). There Jesus meets a man who is possessed by demons (8.27). Like the other demonized in the Gospel, this man knows Jesus' identity and hails him as 'Son of the Most High God' (8.28). Jesus orders the demon to come out from the man (8.29). The story has an unexpected twist which means that it does not simply repeat the earlier examples. Jesus asks the demon its name and is told, 'Legion' because the man is possessed by many demons (8.30). He casts them into a herd of pigs who rush headlong over the cliffs to their death (8.32–3). The men in charge of the pigs see what happens and lose no time in telling it to their friends (8.34). They find the man clothed and in his right mind (8.35). The story contrasts with chapter 4 where Jesus fails to go over the cliff because he is the person imbued with the Spirit (4.29–30). The contrast with the earlier story is a striking (and probably a deliberate) one. The story ends with the whole population asking Jesus to go away (8.37) because he has perplexing powers (and no doubt because they were running short on pigs).

The third miracle is the raising of Jairus' daughter (8.40–2a, 49–56). Interspersed with this is the fourth miracle, the healing of the woman with haemorrhages (8.42b–48). There are obvious parallels between the story of Jairus' daughter and that of the centurion's servant in 7.1–10. Jairus is president of the synagogue. He, too, believes that Jesus can heal. The figure twelve, which is said to be the daughter's age, features also in the story of the woman with the haemorrhage. She had been ill for twelve years (8.43). The repetition means that the figure is foregrounded. It suggests that the healings symbolize the eschatological reconstitution of the twelve tribes which Luke thinks is happening in the ministry of Jesus (cf. 22.30).

CHAPTER 9

The Gospel's plot is developed in chapter 9. At the beginning of the chapter Jesus gives the Twelve power over demons (9.1) and sends them out 'to proclaim the kingdom of God and to heal the sick' (9.2). Here, he shares his ministry with the Twelve (just as in the church they hold authority during the absence of Jesus). 9.1–2 specifically links the disciples' authority over demons with their proclamation of the kingdom of God.

The description of the Twelve's simple lifestyle, which bears comparison with the instructions given to the seventy (seventy-two?) in chapter 10, probably reflects the experience of itinerant figures in the early Christian world. There is similar information in the late first century document called the *Didache* (11.3–6). The reason that the Twelve are to take nothing for their journey is because they are expected to receive support from the towns and villages that they visited. The fact that the commission is repeated in a different form in chapter 10 means that the command to evangelize stems from Jesus himself (cf. Matthew 28.20, which Luke omits at the end of his Gospel).

Interspersed between the commission and the return of the Twelve is the description of Herod's enquiries about Jesus (9.7–9). Herod wonders whether John or one of the prophets has been raised from the dead and whether Jesus is Elijah. The reader already knows that John, and not Jesus, is Elijah (7.27). This questioning of Jesus' identity prepares the way for Jesus himself to raise the issue later in the chapter. The reference to John's death, which is introduced almost incidentally by 9.9, means that the eschatological Elijah has perished like the prophets before him. This bodes ominously for the fate of Jesus and reminds the readers that Christian discipleship means an inevitable path of suffering.

On their return Jesus takes the Twelve aside for further teaching. He is surrounded by the crowds who hang on his words. The feeding of the five thousand is narrated in this context (9.10–17). This miracle presents Jesus as the source of nourishment. Readers would probably have made links with the Christian Eucharist (cf. John 6), but these are not made explicit in the text.

We now come to a crucial passage in the Gospel. It embodies an important disagreement between Jesus and the narrator concerning the identity of Jesus. Luke makes Jesus question the disciples about his identity (9.18–27). Jesus asks who people think that he is and is told variously John the Baptist, Elijah and a resurrected prophet (9.19). The narrator implicitly holds all these definitions wrong. Jesus then enquires who the disciples think that he is. Peter replies that he is God's Messiah (9.20). Jesus neither accepts nor rejects the title. We have seen that he will not call himself 'Messiah' until 24.26. 'Son of Man' is what he says he is beforehand. The narrator then appends his own commentary to this episode. He says that: '[Jesus] gave them strict orders not to tell this to anyone' (9.21). Here he forbids the promulgation of Jesus' Messiahship which Jesus himself never does at any point in the Gospel. Jesus' silence in 9.20 is a significant one because it makes readers ask why Jesus does not formally accept the title (which Luke has already told the readers is rightfully his). His reticence foregrounds the need for suffering and service among the disciples of Jesus. This is why, in 9.22, Jesus begins to speak about the suffering of the Son of Man.

The motif of secrecy is not without irony in 9.20–1. There *is* an element of concealment in the passage which the author uses against the narrator to expose his misunderstanding of the passion. The narrator says that Jesus keeps his Messiahship secret. This is his own interpretation which contrasts with what Jesus says (and does not say) about the issue. The irony is that the narrator unwittingly suppresses the suffering of Jesus in his attempt to conceal the Messiahship of Jesus. He makes Jesus forbid the promulgation of his Messiahship (9.21). Jesus then proceeds to explain precisely the kind of Messiah he is (9.22) so that the 'messianic secret' is controverted in his own direct speech. This is what the author allows to happen. It lets the author dialogue with the narrator (and thus with the readers) and to foreground the need for suffering as will be clearly explained in the connection between Messiahship and suffering made by 24.26. The irony rests in the fact that the narrator speaks against the words of Jesus and thereby shows that he does not understand what Jesus is saying. This makes readers ask who is telling the truth and what the disagreement signifies. The author by implication holds against the narrator his failure to recognize the connection between Messiahship and his suffering and thus presents the narrator to the perceptive reader as a whipping-boy whose misunderstanding must be avoided.

The suffering of the Son of Man will entail suffering for his followers, Jesus says in 9.23–7. Those who follow Jesus must follow the way of the cross (9.23). It is not certain what this means in practice but formal persecution of the Christians by the Romans was rare in the first century (being confined to the short Neronian *pogrom* of 64 CE). There is more evidence for it in second-century sources but these document the period after Luke was written. The primary reference of 9.23 is symbolic as the striking language indicates ('*day after day* he must take up his cross'). Walking with the cross meant bearing the stigma of a religion whose founder had been executed by the Romans and which constantly had to justify itself to the world for that reason. To this is linked the theme of service as several passages indicate. Bearing the stigma of the cross – and only that – will lead to acceptance by the Son of Man when he comes from heaven (9.26).

Jesus states that the Son of Man will come in the relatively near future: 'There are some of those standing here who will not taste death before they have seen the kingdom of God' (9.27). The direct and obvious meaning of this statement can hardly be circumvented. Jesus says that he will return before all the disciples are dead. Given that Luke was not written until *c.* 90 CE, and that the author retains this saying, it seems to be a prediction of eschatological imminence for Luke's readers. 9.27 reminds readers that they stand under the same eschatological conditions as when these words were first spoken. This is by no means conducive to the view that Luke relegates the climax of eschatology to the indefinite future. Readers must persevere with the path of suffering and service. They should 'hold [their] heads high, because [their] liberation is near' (21.28).

This important exchange is followed by the Transfiguration (9.28–36). Jesus takes Peter, James and John up the mountain and is transformed before them to resemble a heavenly being. The basis of the story lies in earlier Jewish visions of God and of angels. There is a tradition in Jewish apocalyptic literature, which derives from the theophany, that an angel appears in the likeness of God (cf. Daniel 10.5–6). It has been debated to what extent this represents a modification of Jewish monotheism. Certainly, the angel is never included in worship. But he is a significant member of the heavenly court who transcends the other angels. Reminiscent of Jewish angelology in this passage are the references to Jesus' face and his dazzling white garment (9.29). The Transfiguration reworks this strand of angelology to make Jesus a *second divine being* who is subordinate to God. This anticipates the status that he will acquire in the ascension and presents a vision of Jesus as he will be seen when he returns from heaven. The passage should be compared with Acts 7.56 where Stephen sees Jesus standing at the right hand of God, as if he has risen from his throne to return to earth.

Other heavenly characters feature in the Transfiguration. Moses and Elijah appear but then disappear. More than reason has been proposed to explain their presence. Many think that they represent the Law and the Prophets. It is difficult, however, to see why Elijah should have been chosen for this role when no biblical book is named after him. Moses is often regarded as a prophet in Jewish tradition (and why is there no representative of 'the Writings', the third division of the Hebrew Bible?). More convincing, perhaps, is the observation that both figures have eschatological significance in Jewish tradition. Elijah was expected to return at the end-time (Malachi 4.5). Jesus says that he has already done so in the person of John the Baptist (7.27). Moses typifies the 'prophet like Moses' whom Deuteronomy 18.15 predicts for the future (and whom Acts 3.22 identifies with Jesus). Luke implies that Moses and Elijah have come and gone and that the decisive eschatological figure is present. This is why Jesus is left alone on the stage to be identified by the heavenly voice: 'This is my Son, my Chosen; listen to him' (9.35). This is beyond doubt a messianic identification whose truth is assured by the heavenly pronouncement. The presence of the

Messiah on earth means that the eschatological age has arrived. The heavenly voice effectively controverts what the narrator says in 9.21. That Jesus is the Messiah is not a secret in Luke at all. It is proclaimed by the heavenly voice – the highest possible authority. There is thus more to the 'messianic secret' than meets the eye and I have explained this in terms of the narrator's suppression of the suffering motif which the author impresses on the readers.

The heavenly visitors discuss Jesus' 'departure' (9.31). This is the sequence of events he accomplishes in Jerusalem, primarily his death and resurrection (but also the ascension). The phrase contradicts the view that Luke has no 'theology of the cross'. It implies that the decisive eschatological events will be fulfilled *through the death of Jesus*. This is a major theme in the Gospel which emerges from the earliest chapters (not least from the third temptation). Given that Jesus sees his death as a 'new covenant' (22.20), this passage reinforces the belief that it has significance for the realization of the eschatological age.

The Transfiguration immediately precedes the final journey to Jerusalem (9.51). This is prefaced by four incidents. First of all, a man in the crowd tells Jesus that the disciples cannot cast out an evil spirit from his son (9.37–43). To this Jesus makes the comment: 'What an unbelieving and perverse generation!' (9.41). The recipients of this criticism are the disciples, for the man is willing to believe they can effect a cure. The words echo Deuteronomy 32.20 ('they are a subversive generation, children not to be trusted') where the speaker is God. 9.41 thus recalls the divine criticism of Israel to emphasize the lack of understanding even among the disciples. This is especially poignant, it must be said, at a time when three of them have just seen a vision of his heavenly glory.

Characteristically in Luke, an incident a few verses later looks back to this one. In 9.49–50 the disciples tell Jesus they have seen a man casting out demons 'in [his] name' and tried to stop him. Jesus rebukes them with the comment: 'Do not stop him, for he who is not against you is on your side' (9.50). This reply authenticates the results of faith in Jesus. Even those beyond the circle of the disciples can cast out demons because of the power associated with his name. Faith in Jesus is the critical thing by which the demonic world is subdued.

These two incidents are separated by two passages which emphasize the nature of Christian suffering and service (and which seem directed at the readers). In 9.44 Jesus tells the disciples that 'the Son of Man is to be given up into the power of men'. The narrator appends his own commentary to this statement. He says that the disciples do not understand what Jesus says because its meaning has been 'hidden from them so that they cannot grasp it' (9.45). This places them in the same category as the ignorant ones of 8.10. Given that the readers are the successors of the disciples, this is a criticism of their misunderstanding. They are reminded that Jesus only becomes Messiah through suffering. That is the path which they must follow.

This prediction of suffering is followed by a dispute among the disciples as to which of them is the greatest. This dispute appears to criticize presumption in the readers' community. Jesus takes a child and says that whoever receives a child receives him, 'for the least among you all is the greatest' (9.48). The connection with the previous passage lies in the link between discipleship and service. Readers are reminded that only this is the pattern of Christian discipleship.

A watershed in the plot is reached in 9.51: 'As the time approached when [Jesus] was to be taken up to heaven, he set his face resolutely towards Jerusalem.' In 9.52 Jesus sends messengers to the Samaritan villages through which he will pass. The Samaritans fail to welcome Jesus because he was journeying to Jerusalem. (9.53). This contrasts with the later story in Acts 8.6 where they pay close attention to Philip the deacon. The rejection of the messengers at this stage is symptomatic of the wider rejection of Jesus. It prompts James and John to ask whether they should call down fire from heaven to consume the Samaritans (9.54). That recalls Elijah's actions against the prophets of Baal in 2 Kings 1.10, 12 where fire is called down and consumes the false prophets. Jesus rebukes the disciples for their suggestion (9.55). This does not avert the Samaritans' punishment but it does postpone it until the eschatological future. Later in the Gospel Jesus will say that he has come to cast fire on earth but that it is not yet kindled (12.49). Judgment for Luke is a future certainty which is deferred until the kingdom's full manifestation.

The question of preparedness for the kingdom is discussed in 9.57–62. The section deals with objections to Christian discipleship. Hyperbole again features here. In 9.58 Jesus warns against the hope for a comfortable home with reference to his own example: 'the Son of Man has nowhere to lay his head'. The demands of the

Christian mission are such that they come above family ties: the dead must bury their own dead (9.60), so urgent is the task of preaching. Not even a fond farewell to one's family is allowed: no-one who is gripped by the message of the kingdom but turns to more mundane matters is fit for the kingdom (9.62). This passage is 'sandwiched' between two other stories which supply the context of its meaning. 9.52 describes the commission of messengers. 10.1–12 will describe the further commission of messengers. This confirms that reflection on the Christian mission undergirds 9.57–62. The theme of absolute devotion to Jesus finds its explanation in this context.

CHAPTER 10

The ministry of itinerant figures in early Christianity has again influenced 10.1–12. This passage describes the sending-out of messengers. Their number is given variously as 'seventy' and 'seventy-two' in the manuscripts. It is possible that, if Luke originally wrote 'seventy', he was thinking of the traditional number of the nations of the world each of which is assigned a representative. That would accord with the flow of thought in Acts which concludes with the Christian gospel being proclaimed in Rome. On the other hand 'seventy-two' is the harder reading. The variant is much discussed in the commentaries and I do not feel the need to resolve it here.

The missionaries are sent out by Jesus without financial support (10.4; cf. 9.3). Like the prophets of the *Didache* they must rely on hospitality from the towns and villages that they visit (10.7). Two different kinds of audience are envisaged for their preaching. Some people accept the message of the kingdom. Others reject it (cf. 8.4–8). The latter category put themselves in danger of judgment which is symbolized by the shaking-off of dust from the feet of the messengers (cf. Acts 13.51). The kingdom of God is a threatening thing for them because it will involve a fate worse than Sodom's (10.12), and of Tyre and Sidon (10.14). This will be the punishment of destruction by divine wrath. The significant thing is that this passage expects that the towns and villages will be judged according to their reaction to the *messengers* of Jesus. This devolves a considerable authority on the messengers on the grounds that they are emissaries of the Son of Man.

Before the return of the seventy (or seventy-two) is described,

Jesus gives the reason for this extension of his authority to the disciples: 'Whoever listens to you listens to me; whoever rejects you rejects me. And whoever rejects me rejects the One who sent me' (10.16). This reflects the Jewish view than an agent has his master's full authority. It makes the messengers speak with the authority of God. (There is a close parallel to this saying in John 13.20 which raises the question of the relations between Luke (and the other Synoptists) and the Fourth Gospel.)

The missionaries return to tell Jesus of their experiences (10.17). They report that even the demons submit to them (10.17; contrast this with 9.40). Their report is followed by Jesus' apocalyptic vision in which he sees Satan fall like lightning from heaven (10.18). This vision represents a commentary on his own ministry. Jesus holds that his mission involves Satan's overthrow which takes place as he speaks. That Satan has fallen from heaven does not of course exclude the possibility that he continues to be active on earth. Indeed, it is evident from 22.3 that he is active there. 10.18 is an apocalyptic vision which projects into the ministry of Jesus what now pertains in heaven and will be realized on earth in the future: the complete sovereignty of God which is the state of being that Luke calls the kingdom of God. To this extent it makes the future hope a present reality.

The disciples' authority is further expressed in the strange comment about snakes and scorpions in 10.19. These are here equated with 'all the forces of the enemy', recalling perhaps the story of the fall in Genesis (Genesis chapter 3). If Genesis is in view, it is possible that Luke thinks of Genesis 3.15 where the serpent is told that humankind will 'strike at [his] head'. This implies that, in the Christian mission, the old enemy is finally being defeated. In Acts Paul successfully handles a snake (Acts 28.3–6) so that Jesus' words are fulfilled in Luke's second volume.

Apocalyptic categories undergird 10.20: 'Do not rejoice that the spirits submit to you, but that your names are enrolled in heaven.' The thought is not that the disciples will pass to a heavenly existence after death but that their names have been inscribed in the heavenly ledgers which will ensure their safety at the final and earthly judgment. 10.21–2 continues the atmosphere of heavenly revelation in words that again have affinities with John's Gospel (chapter 17): 'No-one knows who the Son is but the Father, or who the Father is but the Son, and those to whom the Son chooses to reveal him.' The section concludes with the statement of Jesus that 'many prophets and kings' desired to see and hear what the disciples did (10.23–4) but that they had not done so. This indicates quite clearly that Israel's hopes are in process of fulfilment as Jesus journeys towards Jerusalem.

The parable of the good Samaritan is Jesus' response to a test-question from a lawyer (10.25–37). The lawyer asks what he must do to gain eternal life. He is told, on the basis of the Ten Commandments, to love God and love his neighbour with full sincerity (10.27). The parable answers his supplementary question, 'Who is my neighbour?' (10.29). Its purpose is not so much to offer a legal ruling about the identity of neighbours, including ethnic neighbours, as to expose the hardness of heart which had created certain restrictive attitudes towards neighbours. Of those who see the wounded man, only the Samaritan helps him. *He* is the neighbour, despite the traditional hostility between Jews and Samaritans. The narrator's attitude to the Samaritans has changed from chapter 9. In Acts chapter 8, Samaritans are among the first to embrace the Christian gospel. The parable of the good Samaritan places the Samaritans in the readers' minds and encourages them to reflect on where they fit into the wider purposes of God.

The story of Martha and Mary (10.38–42) highlights the importance of attentiveness to Jesus. The reader has a considerable sympathy for Martha, distracted as she is by her many tasks (10.40). Jesus apparently rebukes her (10.41) but the rebuke calls to mind the language of 9.57–62. That language is hyperbole which overstates a contrast in order to reinforce it. The crucial thing is listening to Jesus which over-rides all other responsibilities. This story presents female disciples in the same terms as male disciples when it criticizes Martha for fulfilling the traditional role of serving those who sit at table. It reminds readers to consider the teaching of Jesus. This prepares the way for probably the best-known teaching of all.

CHAPTER 11

The Lord's Prayer follows the story of Martha and Mary in 11.1–43. It begins a section about prayer, doubtless because it is the archetypal way in which the primitive Christian communities prayed. The Lord's Prayer is attributed to Jesus to give it authority. It begins with a blessing on the name of God and a prayer for the coming of the kingdom (11.2). One can imagine the early

Christians praying like this whenever they met for worship. Luke thinks the kingdom is already present in the ministry of Jesus and tells the readers to pray for its full and final manifestation. The prayer continues with the request for daily bread (11.3). It moves from there to penitence (11.4) and concludes with a petition that Christians may not be 'put to the test' (11.4). This is perhaps the process of inward temptation rather than the final, eschatological trial.

Jesus continues with stories about the need for persistence in prayer (11.5–10) and the goodness of God in providing the Holy Spirit (11.11–13). This teaching gains its logic from the fact that prayer for the coming of the kingdom precedes all other forms of intercession (11.2). Persistence in prayer for the kingdom must have been an important item of teaching in early Christian churches as the return of Jesus tarried. Jesus seems to imply that (only) the persistent would be answered. This reminds readers to pray hard for the things that they most desired (including the eschatological hopes to which Luke refers).

The next saying (11.11–13) softens this portrait by explaining that God is not an ill-tempered old grudge who must be persuaded by repeated insinuation. 11.13 even recognizes the limitations of human language for describing the generosity of God. If human beings can give good things to their children, then God will do more so. The kingdom will come because that is what God wills for his children!

There is a return to the theme of the miracles in 11.14–20. Its context is a dispute about the authority by which Jesus acts. He is accused of driving out the demons (*the* basic miracle in Luke) by the power of the chief demon, Beelzebul (11.19). The narrator adds that people demand a sign from heaven to test him (11.16). The dispute means that Jesus is under scrutiny. He replies with a saying aimed at his detractors. If Satan is divided against himself, Jesus says, his kingdom must surely fall (11.18). Jesus adds that it is not by Beelzebul that he casts out the demons but by the 'finger of God' (11.20). This phrase alludes to the Pentateuch (Exodus 8.19; Deuteronomy 9.10) in a biblical demonstration that Jesus embodies the full power and activity of God: 'if it is by the finger of God that I drive out the demons, then be sure that the kingdom of God has already come upon you'. This strong claim is reinforced by the saying about the Stronger Man who carries off the Strong Man's armour for spoil (11.21–2). The implication is that, with the arrival of Jesus, Satan's rule is coming to an end.

The two striking features of this exchange are the demand for a sign and Jesus' reference to the kingdom of God as a present reality. That people demand a sign proves they are unable to understand Jesus and his ministry. Jesus in fact picks up the demand for a sign in 11.29–32. Here, we must note that the misunderstanding represented by the request (11.16) is matched by the popular misunderstanding about why Jesus casts out the demons (11.15). It is the inability to accept that the eschatological age has begun. The accusation of 11.15 is not just that Jesus is in league with demons but more directly that his miracles have no eschatological meaning. This is the same tendency to look for 'doings' that is criticized among the Nazarenes in 4.23. It sees the miracles as 'wonders', to be sure, but not as 'signs' of the kingdom. This inability to understand the miracles is the fundamental inability to see that the kingdom is present and that Jesus is its critical figure.

The next part of chapter 11 contains an amalgam of sayings, possibly derived from a source. 11.24–6 broadly follows the Beelzebul controversy. It makes the point that a person ('a house'), when cleansed from a demon, must be filled by something else – clearly, by the Spirit of God – otherwise the demon will return with seven worse fiends and that person's plight will be worse than before. This saying must have found a ready context in early Christianity with its interest in demon- and Spirit-possession which is exemplified many times in Acts. The 'physical' sense of possession is very striking in this passage.

A woman cries out to Jesus: 'Happy the womb that carried you' (11.27–8). Jesus replied that happy are those who hear and keep the word of God. This recalls earlier passages in the Gospel, notably the parable of the sower (especially 8.15) and of course 8.21 ('My mother and my brothers are those who hear the word of God and act upon it'). The repetition of this theme in different contexts reinforces the message in the minds of the readers.

There is a return to the theme of judgment in 11.29–32 (cf. 10.12–15). Jesus picks up the narrator's statement of 11.16 that the crowd demand a sign. Jesus says that no sign will be given save 'the sign of Jonah' (11.30). The primary reference is probably to the preaching of Jonah which is mentioned in 11.32; but the Matthaean parallel (Matthew 12.38–42) understands 'the sign of Jonah' as the resurrection, the point of comparison being Jonah's well-known sojourn in the belly of the whale. Matthew's appears to be a secondary interpretation, however ingenious it may be. The significance of preaching in this context is shown by the reference to the Queen of the South in 11.31: she came to hear Solomon, which leads Jesus to say of himself, 'and what is here is greater than Solomon' (11.31) 'and Jonah' (11.32). Jesus is the more important figure because, in his ministry, the kingdom of God is being made present and the hopes of Israel realized. The sign of Jonah is followed by the sayings about the lamp and the lampstand (11.33–5; cf. 8.16) which remind readers not to be furtive about their Christian commitment.

The rest of chapter 11 inveighs against the Pharisees and the lawyers (11.37–54). The narrative link is vague; a dinner party at the house of a Pharisee (11.37). Jesus is rebuked for not washing before the meal (11.38). He replies with a diatribe – by no means complimentary to his host – that the Pharisees are filthy within despite their concern for ritual purity. 11.42 says they pay tithes but neglect the weightier matters of justice and the love of God. It is also said that they love public acclamation (11.43), that they are unmarked graves (11.44) and load people with intolerable burdens (11.46). They build monuments to the prophets (11.47) but this merely testifies to the fact that they supported those who killed them: 'they committed the murders and you provide the monuments' (11.48). This leads to a saying attributed to the Wisdom of God: 'I will send them prophets and messengers; and some of these they will persecute and kill' (11.49). That saying connects prophecy with suffering (Jesus himself is often called a prophet in Luke). Jesus continues by warning of their impending punishment: 'this generation will have to answer for the blood of all the prophets shed since the foundation of the world' (11.50). The thought is that the present generation will suffer because they are the eschatological community. The chapter closes with criticism aimed at the lawyers (11.52) and the statement that the scribes and the Pharisees try to trick Jesus with questions (11.53–4).

This portrait seems a harsh one but it is by no means so harsh as Matthew's portrait of the Pharisees (see Matthew chapter 23). Luke tones down Matthew's material considerably. One wonders in fact whether the invective (11.37–46) is used to introduce the statement about the murder of the prophets which occupies the central part of the diatribe. This is addressed not to the Pharisees but to 'this generation' as a whole (11.50). 11.50 holds the Jewish nation collectively responsible for the fate of the prophets and implies that their rejection of Jesus will bring eschatological retribution (cf. 20.14–16). We must also note passages in Luke where the Pharisees are presented in a quite different light (see 7.36–50; 13.31) so that Luke's portrait of them is by no means harsh and monolithic.

CHAPTER 12

The first section of chapter 12 also inveighs against the Pharisees (12.1–3). Jesus warns against their leaven, by which he means the leaven of hypocrisy. The nature of their hypocrisy is given by 11.37–43 which criticizes their concern for outward appearance but not inward purity. This saying is followed by the familiar warning, 'there is nothing covered up that will not be uncovered' (12.2). This suggests that it too has a traditional nature and that Luke does not so much inveigh against the Pharisees as offer a general warning of the type we have met already in 8.16–17.

The rest of the chapter contains a further collection of sayings. These are placed together, often with no obvious connection. Those who argue for a sayings-source such as Q find their most convincing evidence here. The material makes a number of basic points about God. We read here both of his judgment (12.4–5, 8–10, 13–21) and of his providential care for his people (12.6–7, 11–12, 22–34). Much of this material has an eschatological reference. This is true of the saying about the Son of Man in 12.8–40 and especially true of the parables of the wedding and the burglar in 12.35–40 which end with the conclusion (which is clearly applicable to the readers): 'Hold yourselves in readiness, because the Son of Man will come at the time you least expect him' (12.40).

One wonders about how such material was used in the churches which read Luke. The sayings are general and not situation-specific. This suggests that they were used as the spur for preaching. They encourage particular patterns of behaviour, not least eschatological preparedness. We can reconstruct a broad picture of Luke's demands by examining the material more closely.

The thought of 9.26, that whoever acknowledges Jesus will be acknowledged by the Son of Man before the angels, but that whoever disowns Jesus will be disowned by the heavenly mediator, is repeated in 12.8–9. This leads to the difficult saying about blasphemy against the Holy Spirit in 12.10. Jesus says that blasphemy against the Son of Man can be forgiven but that blasphemy against the Holy Spirit will never be forgiven. 'Slandering the Holy Spirit' presumably means denying that the Spirit is bringing in the kingdom of God (and thus that he is present in the ministry of Jesus and the early Christians). 'Blasphemy against the Son of Man' probably denotes that misunderstanding of Jesus – revealed throughout the Gospel – which is the precursor to faith and which for that reason may not be finally culpable. The converse is that a person ceases to be forgivable when he sets himself against God's kingdom and refuses to accept that God is working through Jesus. This I think is the difference between the two forms of blasphemy. 12.11–12 elaborates the reference to the Spirit by promising that he will provide Christians with suitable words when they are brought to trial for their faith. This extends the possibility of 'blaspheming the Spirit' to the situation in which Luke's readers find themselves, much as other passages make the disciples co-workers in the mission of Jesus.

The next section concerns the place of property in the mind-set of the Christian (12.13–34). The introduction is a request from someone in the crowd to arbitrate in a family dispute (12.13). This Jesus refuses to do (12.14). There is a note of irony in his comment, 'Who set me over you to judge or arbitrate?' (12.14) for Luke reserves Jesus' role as judge until his return from heaven (9.26; 12.9). There follows the parable of the rich man with the barn (12.16–21). This tells of the person who builds bigger barns to store his grain but loses his life on the same day. On one level this parable conveys the sense of moderation in ambition; but it offers eschatological paraenesis as well as proverbial wisdom. The reason that the man is foolish is because he has failed to perceive that his time is near. The parable prepares the way for the eschatological teaching imparted later in the chapter, especially the parable of the burgular, which recommends vigilance in the face of the end (12.39–40).

The parable of the rich man is appended with commentary. Jesus says that Christians are worth more than birds and that God will take care of them (12.22–6). They are in consequence not to set their minds on matters of food and drink (12.29–30) but on the kingdom of God (12.31). One detects here a further note of hyperbole. 12.32–4 tells readers to sell their possessions and give to the poor. The command for absolute poverty implants the need for relative poverty in the minds of the readers.

Then, 12.35 moves the discussion explicitly to eschatology.

Christians must be 'ready for action' with their 'robes hitched up' and their lamps alight. Jesus tells the parable of the wedding party in which the servants are uncertain about when their master will come (12.36). The meaning of the parable is that uncertainty about the return of Jesus does not mean that he will not return (cf. the parable of the absent king in chapter 19). He may come in the middle of the night, or just before dawn (12.38). The point is that at any rate he will come. This warning is given also by the parable of the burglar (12.39–40). If the householder had known when the burglar was coming, he would have prevented the burglary (12.39). Luke's teaching about the future teaching is summarized in the conclusion of this section: 'Hold yourselves in readiness, because the Son of Man will come at the time you least expect him' (12.40). The clear implication is that Jesus may return at any time. Luke offers no support for the view that the return has been postponed to the indefinite future. Uncertainty prevails. The only certainty is that Jesus will indeed return.

The significance of the parable is reinforced by Peter's question in 12.41: 'Lord, do you intend this parable specially for us or is it for everyone?' Jesus responds with another parable (12.42–6). This deals with the question of stewardship and how an absent master's property should be managed. The steward who is found trustworthy will be set over all the property but the reckless steward will be punished when the master returns. Every reader is a steward. Through the Gospel, Jesus speaks even to those who were not born when he died. 'The master will arrive on a day when the servant does not expect him, at a time he has not been told' (12.46). Those who are found wanting will be punished. 12.47–8 offers some casuistry about the punishment. The servant who did not know what was required will be punished less severely than the servant who did. One wonders how precisely Luke expected this to happen; but he offers a commonsense approach to the problem that reflects the usual conventions of justice.

12.49–53 is striking. Jesus says that he has come to set fire to the earth (12.49), that he has a baptism to undergo (12.50) and that he has come to bring dissension to the earth, not peace (12.51). The notion of setting fire recalls the request of James and John in 9.54. This passage answers what was left incomplete there. Luke says that Jesus will indeed bring fire on earth but that he will not do so until the final judgment. The 'baptism' of 12.50 is his death. This brings about the dissension mentioned in 12.51–3 where family members are set against each other, for discipleship to Jesus causes social divisions in the Jewish and Hellenistic world. The statement that Jesus has not come to 'establish peace on earth' (12.51) contrasts with what is said about the dawn of peace in the Infancy Narrative (e.g. 1.79; 2.14) and makes Christian discipleship no comfortable thing.

Chapter 12 ends with two eschatological warnings (12.54–6, 57–9). The first uses natural phenomena to predict that the end is near: 'you know how to interpret the appearance of earth and sky, but cannot interpret this fateful hour' (12.56). 12.57–9 adds a warning about punishment. People should settle their affairs on the way to court, otherwise they may find themselves in jail. They will not be let out until they have paid the very last penny (12.59). The meaning of this saying appears to be that people should settle their accounts with God (and with each other) before the last assize in order to escape the just punishment for their misdeeds. Luke has several other examples of such 'worldly wisdom' which give his Gospel a distinctive character (see especially 16.1–8).

CHAPTER 13

Chapter 13 is again an important one in terms of the Gospel's plot. It opens with a story about Pilate who had mingled the blood of some Galileans with their sacrifices (i.e. killed them, 13.1–3). The point of the story is that those whom he treated unjustly were not greater sinners than anyone else. Luke rejects the conclusion that misfortune is necessarily a punishment for wrongdoing. His argument is reinforced by another example in 13.4: a natural disaster in which eighteen people were killed when a tower collapsed in Siloam. These people again are not said to be punished for specific misbehaviour. They were just unfortunate to be in the wrong place at the wrong time. Jesus concludes that *all* sin will be punished and that the view which holds that only really bad sinners suffer is wrong (13.5).

The theme of judgment is continued in the parable of the fig tree (13.6–9). Jesus tells the story of a tree which had failed to produce fruit for three consecutive years. The owner is minded to destroy it but is advised by the vine-dresser to leave it a further year for tending. If it fails to produce fruit then, the vine-dresser says that it can be destroyed. The parable reminds readers to take stock of their behaviour while time remains. It hints that judgment is not far away.

The reader has almost lost sight of the miracles of Jesus in this wealth of teaching. Luke now describes how Jesus cures a woman who had been possessed by a spirit for eighteen years (13.10–17). The president of the synagogue is indignant that Jesus should heal her on the sabbath. Jesus replies by appealing to the Jewish principle of care for animals which over-rides the demands of the sabbath. This is used as an argument *a fortiori* to support Jesus' intervention on behalf of the woman who is both a human being and what he calls a 'daughter of Abraham' (13.16). The conclusion of the miracle shows the confusion that surrounds Jesus because of his teaching and behaviour: his opponents were covered with confusion but the people delighted with his deeds (13.17). We should remember that the formal moves to kill Jesus will not be taken until 19.47.

Two further parables of the kingdom are recorded in 13.18–21. The parables of the mustard seed and leaven show that the kingdom is growing and that it will soon be mature. For the kingdom to be growing means of course that it exists and is present already. This is a major theme in Luke. 13.19 comments on the spectacular results that will emerge from such hidden origins. It is a warning to readers not to mistake the delay in the kingdom's manifestation as a sign that the kingdom will not appear. For this reason (13.22–4) people must strive to 'enter through the narrow door'. The door is called 'narrow' because there were so many obstacles to being a Christian in the first century CE.

In 13.25–30 Jesus speaks directly to the readers. He tells a parable in which someone knocks on the door of a house but is refused admission because his identity is unknown to the householder. Those who are refused entry protest: 'We used to eat and drink with you, and you taught in our streets' (13.26). The scarcely veiled eucharistic reference in this verse shows that Christian protestors must be meant. The offence of the protestors is not described but evidently they are guilty of failing to do what Jesus has commanded (cf. 6.46). Luke warns that even the followers of Jesus may fail to meet the standards needed for final entry into the kingdom. He says that these people will wail and grind when they see the blessed ones at the eschatological banquet (13.28–9). Those invited to the banquet include people from all corners of the earth (Gentiles clearly among them) and sit at table with the patriarchs. There is a clue to the nature of the wrongdoing in 13.30 which encapsulates a wider theme in the Gospel: 'Some who are now last

will be first, and some who are first will be last.' This is the call for
humility and service as we have seen. The passage suggests that
some of Luke's readers were not doing all that they might to foster
the needs of others.

Some Pharisees warn Jesus that Herod wants to kill him
(13.31–3). Here, they are presented in a good light, unlike their
portrayal in chapters 11–12. The reference to Herod provides the
introduction for a critical speech by Jesus: 'Go and tell that fox,
Listen: today and tomorrow I shall be driving out demons and
working cures; on the third day I reach my goal. However, I must
go on my way today and tomorrow, because it is unthinkable for a
prophet to meet his death anywhere but in Jerusalem' (13.32–3).

The basis of this speech, with its reference to 'three days', is a
vaticinium ex eventu (or prophecy compiled in the light of events)
which assigns to Jesus knowledge that presents him in control of
the situation because of his foreknowledge of it (cf. 9.22). Jesus says
that his goal is Jerusalem (cf. 9.51 and the Infancy Narrative). This
is a declaration of intention as well as a geographical indicator. Jesus
says that 'it is unthinkable for a prophet to meet his death anywhere
but in Jerusalem'. He aligns himself with the tradition of prophetic
rejection in Israel and states with grim humour that in Jerusalem he
must die because this is where all the prophets have perished.
13.34a is a lament over Jerusalem which calls the city: 'the city that
murders the prophets and stones the messengers sent to her'. There
is good precedent for this statement in the Hebrew prophetic
denunciations of the Jewish capital (see e.g. Jeremiah 4.14; 6.8;
13.27).

The second half of 13.34 reflects Christian sadness (and the
problem posed for evangelism) by the fact that the Jewish nation
had rejected the Messiah when he came to her: 'How often have I
longed to gather your children, as a hen gathers her brood under her
wings; but you would not let me.' This statement makes the goal of
Jesus' journey to Jerusalem the regathering of the twelve tribes
which I have suggested must be seen in company with 22.30 where
Jesus states that the Twelve will sit on thrones and judge the tribes
of Israel. The idea is that Jesus' journey to Jerusalem helps to make
Israel what the Bible intends it should be. In his ministry the
restoration has already begun. The leaders of the tribes are in place
and the Messiah is centre stage. Jesus longs for the kingdom to be
fully realized. The tragedy is that the tribes of Israel will choose to
reject him. But the plot accommodates such exigencies. Luke knows

that, through the death of Jesus, God will indeed effect the reconstitution of Israel for Jesus' death had effected a *new* covenant
(22.20). The plot is full of paradoxes. The Jewish rejection of Jesus,
lamented in 13.34, is made the means by which the restoration is
secured.

The chapter concludes with a saying about the temple: 'There is
your temple, forsaken by God' (13.35). I have argued that this
represents a denunciation by Jesus of the present temple in the hope
that the eschatological temple will be revealed by God. Jesus is not
just the critic of the present temple and the prophet of the new
temple but also the corner-stone of the new temple according to
20.17. The full significance of that criticism will be revealed as the
Gospel unfolds.

The second half of 13.35 incorporates a *double entendre*. Jesus
says: 'I tell you, you will not see me until the time comes when
you say, "Blessings on him who comes in the name of the Lord."'
This saying looks forward to the triumphal entry (19.28–40). The
words 'blessings on him' are a messianic acclamation. They derive
from Psalm 118.26, which was used by pilgrims as they travelled
to Jerusalem, and refer in their original setting to the Jewish
king. Jesus tells Jerusalem that, when he enters the capital, its
inhabitants will acclaim him as Messiah. The description of Jesus'
arrival in Jerusalem both fulfils and questions this prediction.
The people do acclaim Jesus in 19.36 – but not much later they
turn against him (23.13) so that their acclamation is at best a
temporary one.

This makes it likely that there is a hint in 13.35b of Jesus'
further visitation of Jerusalem when he will be universally acknowledged as the Messiah. This will be at the moment of his return from
heaven (cf. 9.26). The thought stands close to Revelation 1.7a:
'Look, he is coming with the clouds; *everyone* shall *see* him, including
those who pierced him'. It would be wrong to exclude this shade of
meaning from the passage. Jesus predicts his return from heaven in
Luke.

CHAPTER 14

The end of chapter 13, 13.32–5, is a 'purple passage' among an almost
rambling collection of sayings and miracles. The looser style is
resumed in chapter 14 where we find further development of themes
already presented, especially the Gospel's interest in eschatology.

The chapter opens with another healing miracle (14.1–6). The reader knows by now that the Pharisees will be watching Jesus (14.3) and that Jesus generally heals on the sabbath. The Pharisees fall silent before his question of whether or not it is right for him to do this (14.3). Jesus repeats the question of whether it is lawful to help an ox on the sabbath. He draws the unspoken conclusion, as before, that it is permissible to help humans for the same reason (14.5). The Pharisees can find no answer to this argument (14.6).

The next section is arranged around the theme of feasting. Jesus notices guests trying to secure places of honour at a dinner-party and tells the parable of the wedding feast (14.7–11). This explains that those who humble themselves will be honoured by the host and vice versa. It develops the already-established theme of humility in Luke. The conclusion of the parable (14.12–14) shows the humble behaviour Luke wants his readers to adopt. 14.13 resembles 4.18–19 in its description of who should be invited to a banquet ('the poor, the crippled, the lame, and the blind'). The imprecise language permits a variety of interpretations. General and generous hospitality is certainly one of them. The eucharistic is another. Luke says that those who should be most honoured on this occasion in the Christian community are those who might otherwise be despised or rejected. Perhaps this is a criticism of social distinctions in the readers' community. We know from 1 Corinthians 11.17–22 that the eucharist was the subject of abuse in some churches. Perhaps the practices found there, where some – evidently the less powerful – went hungry explains why Luke writes as he does. But we do not know enough about the actual circumstances of the readers to speak with certainty on this point.

The parable of the great feast which the guests refuse to attend is narrated in 14.15–24. It is clear from the introduction that this parable concerns the feast that will inaugurate the kingdom of God (cf. 13.29). The refusal of the guests makes the master of the house send out his servants to invite 'the poor, the crippled, the blind, and the lame' (14.21). This phrase picks up 14.13 and of course 4.18–19. These people are included and the others excluded. Those who refuse present a variety of excuses. These are deliberately lame to emphasize their stupidity and blatant rejection. The parable ends with the statement that 'not one of those who were invited shall taste my banquet' (14.24). This is a commentary on the future rejection by God of those who now reject what God is doing through Jesus. It reminds the reader of what Jesus has said about future judgment in 13.25–30.

This parable is followed by further warnings about the cost of discipleship. 14.26 repeats in a more intense form the thought of 12.49–53 that discipleship means the loss of family ties. Luke says that people must *hate* their families to be disciples of Jesus. 14.28 is a call to count the cost of discipleship which 14.33 relates to the Christian attitude towards possessions. Those who are not prepared to forsake everything cannot be disciples of Jesus. This warning is reinforced in 14.34–5 by the saying about salt which makes anything but total commitment without value (and destined for rejection). One can only conclude from this passage that the actuality fell short of the ideal in many cases.

CHAPTER 15

Chapter 15 contains some well-known parables of Jesus. It opens with the lost sheep (15.1–7) and the lost coin (15.8–10). These assert, notionally against the Pharisees and the scribes, that God is concerned as much with the lost as with the righteous and that he will go to great lengths to find them. Luke states that God does not want anyone to miss out. This is the other face of eschatological punishment in the Gospel.

These parables are followed by the parable of the prodigal son (15.11–32). This is much longer but develops the same theme. Its message is that even the person who deliberately rejects can be forgiven if he repents. This well-known parable describes how the profligate son wastes his inheritance while his brother works solidly and virtuously with his father. The younger brother runs out of money and tries to return as a labourer but is greeted and restored by the father. This causes much anxiety to the older brother who complains that his loyalty had been in vain. The interest in recent interpretation of this parable has fallen on the second half where the brother is rebuked although he has done nothing wrong.[6] The parable reminds readers that some of those who now reject the Gospel (including no doubt Jews) will be included in the kingdom. This must cause rejoicing and not anger among those who have borne the cross for longer. There remains the warning of chapter 13 that some of those who are now included may exclude themselves from the kingdom by reason of their behaviour. The kingdom's boundaries are not fixed. Luke's God is a God of continual surprises.

CHAPTER 16

The beginning of chapter 16 narrates one of the most extraordinary parables in the Gospels. Here we find Jesus commending someone whose behaviour is shrewd but not strictly honest. The parable describes how a steward, asked by his master to provide an account of his dealings, persuades the master's debtors to provide bills which show lesser amounts in the hope that one of them will employ him if his present employer sacks him. The parable ends with the master commending the steward for a reason that is not easy to discern. We can hardly suppose that the master commends the steward for defrauding him! Perhaps this is because the dues are finally being paid, albeit at a lower level.

The narrator adds the worldly-wise comment that 'in dealing with their own kind the children of this world are more astute than the children of light' (16.8). This parable cannot be told *against* such an attitude (as some commentators would prefer) because 16.9 says that readers must 'use their worldly wealth to win friends for [themselves]' so that when money is a thing of the past they may be received into an eternal home. This saying advocates the generosity extolled earlier in the Gospel and adds to it the promise of eschatological reward. It is striking that the example used to support this demand should be that of the likeable rogue. This is a particular feature of Luke's narrative style with its eye for the unusual if not the comical. The unlikely hero of the parable continues to make a bold impression on the Christian imagination.

The parable is followed by two further interpretations (16.10–13). These are probably examples of the way in which the parable was understood before the writing of the Gospel. The fact that we have *three* such interpretations shows that Luke had great difficulty with the parable, as do many commentators today. 16.10–12 says that those who are trustworthy in small matters will be trustworthy in great ones and vice versa. Jesus uses this maxim to contrast trustworthiness about 'the wealth of this world' and 'the wealth that is real' (clearly the riches of the kingdom of God). (This is a virtue which, it must be said, it is by no means obvious that the parable actually supports.) 16.13 says that no-one can trust two masters and contrasts God and Money in this respect.

The Pharisees scoff at Jesus because, as the narrator says against them, they 'loved money' (16.14). Luke is once again harsh in his treatment of the Pharisees: 'You are the people who impress others with your righteousness; but God sees through you.' This saying is followed by a collection of other sayings. 16.16 reiterates the place of John the Baptist in the economy of salvation: 'The law and the prophets were until John: since then, the good news of the kingdom is proclaimed, and everybody forces a way in.' This statement presents the ministry of Jesus as a new age because the kingdom of God has now arrived. John is ranked with earlier Judaism because he (merely) heralded the kingdom. It is not implied here that John is *excluded* from the kingdom (cf. 7.28). He is presented as a transitional point in the history of salvation. John the Baptist remains a significant figure for Luke and it is the narrator, not the implied author, who modifies his position in respect of Jesus. 16.16b states that people are so determined to enter the kingdom that they force their way in. Matthew has a much more difficult version of this saying: 'Since the time of John the Baptist the kingdom of Heaven has been subjected to violence and violent men are taking it by force' (Matthew 11.12). Luke apparently reworks Matthew to remove the reference to the violent people.

It *could* be taken that 16.16 implies that the kingdom has made the Law redundant for Christians but Luke swiftly counters this impression in what follows. 16.17 says that heaven and earth will more easily pass away than one letter of the Law lose its force. This categorical statement introduces the saying about divorce which follows in 16.18. Here Jesus offers a more rigorous rule than the Torah. Jewish law permitted divorce and remarriage provided that the correct procedure was followed (see Deuteronomy 24.1–4). Jesus does not criticize divorce as such but he does criticize remarriage after divorce which he calls adultery. To preserve the flow of thought between 16.16 and 16.18 we must assume that Jesus here *intensifies* the Mosaic commandment to demonstrate its abiding validity. Unless 16.17 is set aside (for which the text provides no evidence) Jesus does not forbid divorce as such (despite what is sometimes said in the commentaries). His prohibition of remarriage seems to be an eschatological intensification of Moses which works from the premise that the kingdom is nigh (cf. 1 Corinthians 7.10–11). It is Matthew who restricts divorce when he allows it for sexual immorality alone (Matthew 5.32), as did the Shammaites against the Hillelites.

The parable of Dives and Lazarus (16.19–31) contrasts the state of rich and poor at present and in the afterlife. Lazarus, the poor man, goes to Abraham's bosom after death and the rich man has torment in Hades. It is not said that this distinction results from their social status but it is at least implied that it reflects their behaviour. Hades in 16.23 is the intermediate state of the dead and not the place of final punishment (cf. 16.9). This is true also of 'Abraham's bosom' (where the language is unusual and is not otherwise found in Luke). The parable clearly articulates the resurrection hope on which Luke's Gospel depends (16.31). The rich man asks that Lazarus bring a message about judgment to his brothers (16.27–8). This request is refused on the grounds that the brothers have Moses and the prophets and that, if they will not believe these, they are unlikely to believe even if someone were to rise from the dead (16.29–31). The point of this rebuttal is that Moses and the prophets, when properly understood, speak about judgment (and thus about Jesus) and that those who ignore them will not heed the Christian preaching of judgment. The passage establishes a continuity between the Hebrew Bible and the preaching of Jesus. The Jewish scriptures have abiding validity because they bear testimony to the Christian dispensation.

CHAPTER 17

Chapter 17 continues the by now familiar mix of sayings, narrative and parables. It opens with Jesus speaking about the causes of stumbling (17.1–3a). He says that woe betide anyone who makes 'one of these little ones' stumble. The 'little ones' are probably children (cf. 9.47–8) but the term is used also for the disciples in Matthew (10.42). This saying is accompanied by teaching about forgiveness in which it is said that a brother must be forgiven each time that he asks for forgiveness, even up to seven times a day (17.3b–4). Here we find the beginnings of a penitential system which recognizes that a single forgiveness may not be enough.

The next saying is a request for faith by the disciples, to which Jesus replies that faith as small as a mustard-seed is enough to accomplish great tasks (17.5–6; cf. 13.19). We are reminded here of the seed growing secretly which is a parable of the kingdom of God (13.18–19). Next, the parable of the dutiful servant (17.7–10) who is told to wait at table and who eats his meal only after his master has finished. Luke uses this parable to tell readers that, in their Christian service, they are doing a duty and not something exceptionally virtuous. Here is another clue to reconstruct the identity of the implied readers and the message the author wants them to hear.

They are people who need reminding about service and who may have presumed on their status to deny the rights of others.

Jesus enters a village and is met by ten men with leprosy (17.11–19). He tells them to show themselves to the priest, the traditional certification of a cure (cf. 5.14). As they do so they are healed. Only one returns to thank Jesus. He is a Samaritan (cf. 10.33). Jesus marvels that a foreigner should thank him in this way. This implies that the Jewish lepers have failed to appreciate what was done for them. The conclusion of the miracle states that the man's faith has made him whole (17.19; cf. 7.50). This story is an excellent example of the use of repetition in Luke's narrative method. It recalls several earlier healing stories to reinforce the importance of faith in the performance of the miracle. Luke says that all people come to Jesus on the basis of faith regardless of ethnic origin. This is evidence that Luke was written for readers for whom this point was relevant (and thus presumably for Gentile Christians).

The Pharisees appear again (17.20–1). They ask Jesus when the kingdom of God will come, to which he replies that its arrival cannot be discerned by observation. This is because 'the kingdom of God is among you!' (17.21). Some commentators, observing that the Greek word translated 'among' can also mean 'within', suggest that Luke presents the kingdom as an internal and primarily an ethical concern. The rest of Luke makes this conclusion unlikely. Jesus constantly speaks about the kingdom as an external and eschatological reality that is already present in his ministry. It would be surprising if his view were changed here without textual indication. The most obvious reason that the kingdom cannot be discerned by human observation is because it is here already. There is perhaps also the hint that the attempt to place a precise time-scale on the return of Jesus is futile because the completion of the kingdom is equally indiscernible.

The next section explicitly discusses this problem (17.22–5). Jesus says that the disciples will long to 'see one of the days of the Son of Man' but that they will not see it (17.23; cf. 21.9). This explains that the delayed return of Jesus does not mean that the eschatological hope is redundant. People will say 'here it is' and 'there it is' but they will be wrong (17.23). But for sure, at an inde-terminable time, 'like a lightning flash, that lights up the earth from end to end, will the Son of Man be in his day' (17.24). The Son of Man will suddenly appear from heaven and then he will be perceived by all. Before this he must 'endure much suffering and be rejected by this generation' (17.25; cf. the imprecision of 9.44). Here, Luke prescribes certain eschatological conditions as he will do in chapter 21. Significantly, only in fact the prediction of 17.24 ('like a lightning flash . . . ') of the list presented here remains to be fulfilled. This implies that the Son of Man might arrive at any moment so that the theme of eschatological imminence is implicitly foregrounded here.

The rest of the chapter offers more eschatological teaching. 17.26–7 compares the 'days of the Son of Man' to the time of Noah. People ate, drank and married – but were suddenly covered by the Flood. So it will be when the Son of Man appears. 17.28–9 reinforces this warning with the example of Lot. People behaved as they pleased until fire and brimstone fell from heaven. Luke uses this biblical material in a typological way to insist that the same things will happen when the Son of Man is revealed. The present continuity of the world order must not lull readers into a false sense of security that the judgment will not happen (cf. Jude 5–6; 2 Peter 2.3–9). There *will* be a time of punishment when, it is implied by the biblical analogies, those who are found wanting will be destroyed.

The nature of the eschatological punishment is described in pictorial form by 17.31–7. It will occur suddenly while everyday things are being done (17.31–3). Two people will be lying in bed or grinding corn. One will be taken and the other left (17.34–6). This process seems arbitrary but that is not the principal point of the allusion. The thrust is that the judgment will intervene suddenly into everyday life. This passage is a good example of what first-century Christianity believed about the suddenness of the return of Jesus from heaven and the all-embracing nature of its effects. They really did believe that judgment was a threatening thing. The chapter closes menacingly with the saying, 'Where the carcass is, there will the vultures gather' (17.37). The judgment will show no mercy, as Luke has implied already (see especially 13.25–30).

CHAPTER 18

Chapter 18 is a collection of sayings, parables and miracles. It begins with the parable of the insistent woman who pesters the judge until she is given justice (18.1–8; cf. 11.5–10). On the face of it this parable concerns prayer, but the conclusion reveals a close link with the preceding material about eschatology ('But when the Son of Man comes, will he find faith on earth?', 18.8). This phrase takes the reader back to the second petition of the Lord's Prayer (11.2) which is a prayer for the coming of the kingdom.

There follows the parable of the Pharisee and the tax collector (18.9–14). Both men go to the temple to pray. The Pharisee thanks God for his righteousness. The tax collector can scarcely apologize for his sin. Jesus says that it is the tax collector and not the Pharisee who goes home justified (18.14). The parable demonstrates the virtue of humility which is always linked with the (eschatological) offer of forgiveness in Luke.

To this is linked to the story of Jesus blessing babies (18.15–17). The disciples try to prevent this but are rebuked because 'whoever does not accept the kingdom of God like a child will never enter it' (18.17). This again is a call for an unhesitating acceptance. It agrees with the attitude of the tax collector in the preceding parable and shows the radical humility needed to enter the kingdom.

The next parable tells the story of the rich young ruler (18.18–26). This sincere young man wants to gain 'eternal life' (18.18). Jesus tells him to keep the Ten Commandments. He replies that he has always done this. Jesus then tells him to sell all that he has and give to the poor. His heart sinks 'for he was a very rich man' (18.23). This leads to the statement that it is hard for rich people to enter the kingdom (18.23) and the equally enigmatic 'what is impossible for men is possible for God' in response to the disciples' question about who can be saved (18.26). The passage must be seen in the context of the Christian ethical tradition (inherited from Judaism) where the love of money was regarded as a vice (see 1 Timothy 6.10). Peter asks about the disciples (18.28–30). He is assured that those who had left homes and families will be 'repaid many times over in this age, and in the age to come have eternal life' (18.30). It is rather difficult to know what is meant by the statement about repayment 'in this age' but this is perhaps bound up with Jesus' transformative view of the present order which we shall consider in Chapter 5. The saying embodies the suggestion that effort will be rewarded and not subsumed by the totalistic demands of an overlord. Luke leaves the saying unappended by commentary as if he, like us, found difficulties with it.

Jesus now for the third time predicts his suffering in Jerusalem (18.31–4). The prediction again has the air of deliberateness: 'We are now going up to Jerusalem; and everything that was written by the prophets will find its fulfilment in the Son of Man' (18.31). Luke does not say *which* prophets he has in mind nor *how* their prophecy will be fulfilled in the death of Jesus. Perhaps the combined witness of the prophets is meant and a christological interpretation of them implied. 18.32–3 continues to present Jesus in control of the situation. 18.34 says of his followers that 'they did not understand this at all or grasp what he was talking about; its meaning was concealed from them'. There is an element of irony here which matches that in chapter 9. Readers know that Jesus suffered and died in Jerusalem. They have knowledge which transcends that of the original characters whose misunderstanding of Jesus is a constant theme in Luke. Yet the narrator's comment is also made against the readers (evidently unbeknown to the narrator, who to this extent speaks against himself). Luke subtly indicates that there is an aspect of the passion of Jesus which *they* have failed to understand. This is that Christian discipleship means the service of others and that only this pattern conforms to the career of Jesus (cf. 9.23).

The passion predictions thus work on more than one level in Luke. They predict what will happen to Jesus and expose the disciples' misunderstanding of this event. But they also speak directly to the readers and remind them there is something which *they* need to learn from the knowledge which the author shares with them. The concluding statement, 'its meaning was concealed from them', is a warning to readers not to fall into the same trap as the characters who fail to understand the meaning of the suffering of Jesus.

As Jesus approaches Jericho a blind beggar calls out to him, 'Son of David, have pity on me' (18.35–43). The crowd tell him to be quiet but the man persists in his request. Jesus orders that he be fetched. His sight is restored. Jesus refers the miracle to the man's faith (18.42). That the blind man calls Jesus here 'Son of David' anticipates the important statement by Jesus about David's Son and Lord which follows in 20.41–4.

CHAPTER 19

Chapter 19 begins the moves towards the death of Jesus. It opens with the story of Zacchaeus, the little tax collector who climbs the tree to see Jesus (19.1–10). Jesus calls him down and says that he will stay at his house. People complain that Jesus is the guest of a sinner but the request makes a profound impression on Zacchaeus.

He offers to give half his possessions to the poor and to repay four-fold everyone whom he has defrauded (19.8). Jesus appends the comment: 'Today salvation has come to this house – for this man too is a son of Abraham' (19.9). This statement acknowledges that salvation, like the kingdom of God, is a present reality. There is perhaps a deliberate interplay between the phrase 'son of Abraham' here (cf. 13.16) and 'Son of David' in 18.37–8. The point is that not all Jews reject Jesus, as is demonstrated by the 'fruits' which Zacchaeus bore (cf. 3.9).

The next section (19.11–27) is again significant for the plot. It is the parable of the absent king which the narrator introduces in the following way: '[Jesus] went on to tell them a parable, because he was now close to Jerusalem and they thought the kingdom of God might dawn at any moment' (19.11). The narrator here denies that the kingdom of God will appear when Jesus gets to Jerusalem. Readers already know that the kingdom of God is present but hidden (17.20–1 *et al.*). 19.11 must therefore involve the denial that Jesus' arrival in Jerusalem will mean the *full revelation* of the kingdom of God (which the Gospel implies will involve the restoration of the twelve tribes and the replacement of the present temple). This is because the dawning of the kingdom is connected with the return of Jesus 'as king' (19.15) and it is clear in Luke that, although Jesus dies as king of the Jews, he is not universally perceived as Messiah. 19.11 anticipates Jesus' future rule when this earlier misunderstanding and rejection would be overcome.

This parable is certainly related to the theme of the return of Jesus, as its introduction indicates. The chieftain is called 'a man of noble birth' before his departure. He goes on a long journey 'to have himself appointed king and then return' (19.12). The parallels with Jesus are impossible to miss. It is through his death that Jesus thinks that he passes to his Messiahship so that his installation as Messiah, as Luke understands it, takes place in the heavenly world ('abroad'). This is why the ascension is such an important theme in Luke (cf. Acts 2.36). The parable is addressed to the servants of Jesus in the period of his absence. The nobleman gives them a sum of money to invest while he is away (19.13). 19.14 mentions rejection of Jesus: 'His fellow-citizens hated him and sent a delegation after him to say, "We do not want this man as our king"' (cf. 23.2 where the Jewish leaders tell Pilate that Jesus 'claimed to be Messiah, a king'). The man however returns as king to call his servants to account (19.15). Those who have done well are rewarded. The over-cautious investor, who has done nothing with his money, is punished and his sum given to the person who produced the best result. The parable ends with the comment that: 'everyone who has will be given more; but whoever has nothing will forfeit even what he has' (19.26). It is addressed to people who need reminding that the owner's continuing absence means neither that he will fail to return nor that his return will prove easy for those who had failed to do what they should (witness the constant links between eschatology and ethics in Luke).

After this parable 'Jesus set out on the ascent to Jerusalem' (19.28). This sets the scene for the triumphal entry (19.28–40; cf. 13.35). Technically, Jesus does not enter the city until 19.45. What is described here is the ascent or approach to Jerusalem. The centre-piece of the story is the description of Jesus riding on a colt (19.35). It seems likely that this recalls Zechariah 9.9 ('See, your king is coming to you, his cause won, his victory gained, humble, and mounted on a donkey, on a colt, the foal of a donkey'). Matthew (21.4–5) explicitly links the colt with that passage. We can hardly deny that Luke is aware of this identification even if he does not cite Zechariah. The implied link makes Jesus' arrival a messianic one for Zechariah uses the words 'your king' in his description (cf. Luke 19.38). Jesus for Luke approaches Jerusalem as king. The disciples acknowledge this in 19.38: 'Blessed is he who comes *as king* in the name of the Lord! Peace in heaven, glory in highest heaven!' The phrase 'as king' is added to the citation to emphasize it in the wake of 13.35b. The addition of the words, 'Peace in heaven, glory in highest heaven' (19.38b), recalls the angelic chorus of 2.14 which follows the identification of Jesus as Messiah in 2.11 to place this point beyond doubt. The peculiar story about how Jesus knew where the colt was tethered, and gave instructions for its collection, demonstrates his authority over events which will be a major theme of the trial narrative (19.28–34).

The triumphal entry does not meet with universal approval. In 19.39 some Pharisees tell Jesus to restrain his disciples. He replies: 'If my disciples are silent the stones will shout aloud' (19.40). This saying alludes to Habakkuk 2.11 ('the stones will cry out from the wall, and from the timbers a beam will answer them'). It implies that, if people fail to understand the true significance of what they see, the very stones would proclaim it. This anticipates 20.17 where Jesus is made the corner-stone of the new temple.

Jesus' first sight of Jerusalem and how he weeps over the city is described in 19.41–4 (cf. 13.34). 19.42–3 implies that, if Jerusalem had known the way that led to peace (cf. 1.79; 2.14), no disaster such as 70 CE would have overtaken it. As it was, Jerusalem had opened the door to her own destruction (19.43–4). Her destroyers 'will not leave one stone standing on another'. Jesus says this is because Jerusalem has failed to 'recognize the time of God's visitation' (19.44). This makes the events of 70 CE a divine punishment for the Jewish rejection of Jesus (cf. 21.20). We have seen that the saying must be carefully distinguished from what Jesus says about the destruction of the temple (13.35; 21.6), which is far from punitive in character. The passage implies that the divine punishment of Jerusalem was complete from the perspective of Luke's readers. The destruction of the temple, by contrast, is still a future event.

In 19.45–6 Jesus enters Jerusalem and goes immediately to the temple. There follows the cleansing of the temple. Jesus drives the traders from the temple with the words, 'Scripture says, "My house shall be a house of prayer", but you have made it a bandits' cave' (19.46). In Chapter 2 I explained that this incident is essentially ambiguous and that its meaning must be reconstructed from the text by the reader. It *might* mean that Jesus is purifying the temple by driving out the corrupt traders. It more likely has an eschatological significance in the words used in 19.46, which recall the prophecies of Isaiah and Jeremiah. On this view Jesus criticizes those who place their confidence in the present temple and anticipates the time when purified worship will be offered in the new temple. When 19.45–6 is read in the light of 13.35 and 20.17, it seems that Jesus may be giving a symbolic demonstration of the present temple's destruction in order that it can be replaced with the eschatological temple by God. But the cleansing of the temple is an enigmatic story in Luke and it would be unwise to ignore the different shades of meaning that can be gleaned from it.

This incident, and the teaching which follows, leads directly to the decision that Jesus must die: 'Day by day he taught in the temple. The chief priests and scribes, with the support of the leading citizens, wanted to bring about his death' (19.47). Luke does not tell us the offensive content of Jesus' preaching but the parable of the vineyard implies that the cause of offence is his criticism of the present temple and its guardians. The narrative certainly suggests that the teaching is related in some way to what Jesus does in the temple in 19.45–6 as if both his teaching and his behaviour are responsible for the events that lead to his death.

CHAPTER 20

Chapter 20 describes four test-questions put to Jesus and his successful handling of them. 20.1–8 concerns the authority of Jesus (immediately after his action in the temple). The same people who decide on his death in 19.47 ask him about his authority in 20.2. Jesus replies with a question about the authority of John the Baptist. Was John's baptism from God or from men?, he asks (20.4). Jesus holds the trump cards in this exchange. His question turns the focus of the dispute and confounds his opponents (20.5–6). They recognize that, if they say John's baptism was from God, this will highlight their disbelief of John. But if they answer that it came from men, that will outrage the people who revered John as a prophet (20.6). These are the (only) options which the story permits. The interlocutors reply that they cannot answer Jesus' question (20.7). This allows Jesus in turn not to answer theirs (20.8). The implication of the story is that Jesus' authority, like John's, comes from God. The reader infers this conclusion from the text. The statement that Jesus confounds his opponents is reinforced by the structure of the story which shows they are unable to criticize him.

The parable of the vineyard (20.9–16a) also demonstrates the authority of Jesus. Jesus explains how a man let out his vineyard to tenants and sent his messengers to collect the tithe. All the servants are mistreated and the rent refused. Finally, the owner sends his son in the belief that he will command respect from the tenants. This proves not to be the case. The tenants kill the son and think they will thereby gain the vineyard for themselves. Their act, however, brings swift retribution from the owner. He comes in person to kill the tenants and to let the vineyard out to others.

We saw in Chapter 2 that this parable makes good sense if it is seen as a parable about the temple. This interpretation avoids some of the exegetical problems which arise when the vineyard is referred to Israel. In this case the parable refers directly back to 19.45–7. The messengers are the prophets. The final messenger is 'the beloved Son' (20.13), i.e. the Messiah. The tenants decide to kill the Son because he represents a threat to the temple to which they cling. They think that they will thereby secure the future of the present temple. Ironically, in doing this, they secure the destruction of the holy city, as Luke explains in 19.41–4, and prevent the appearance of the eschatological temple. Luke goes on to assert that

God will still introduce the eschatological temple of which the main corner-stone is Jesus himself (20.17). The death of Jesus, paradoxically, had aided and not thwarted the divine purpose in this way.

The parable ends with the scriptural citation: 'The stone which the builders rejected has become the main corner-stone. . . . Everyone who falls on that stone will be dashed to pieces; anyone on whom it falls will be crushed' (20.17–18). Its source is a fusion of Psalms 118.22 and Isaiah 8.14–15 concerning the Lord of hosts: 'The stone which the builders rejected has become the main corner-stone. He will become a snare, an obstacle, and a rock against which the two houses of Israel will strike and stumble. . . . Many will stumble and fall and suffer injury' (Isaiah 8). The corner-stone in Jewish buildings was the main stone which held the edifice together. The citation states that Jesus, although rejected by the Jews, has become the key to God's dealings with the nation. If the parable of the vineyard refers to the earthly temple, to which the Jewish authorities vainly cling, it is natural that 20.17 should refer to Jesus as the corner-stone of the eschatological temple. The two temples starkly contrast with each other. Beneath the *contretemps* between Jesus and the authorities lies the evanescence of the present temple and the promise of its eschatological replacement. If this reading of 20.17 is correct, the corner-stone of the eschatological temple, like the kingdom of God, is present already and standing on the site of the present temple. The Jews stumble on Jesus when they fail to perceive his true significance. This means that they put themselves in a position where they are unable to receive the eschatological benefits.

This is why, in 20.18–19, it is said that the scribes and chief priests want to seize Jesus straight away. They perceived that the parable is told against them: 'but they were afraid because of the people' (20.19). The repetition of the threat to kill Jesus confirms that 19.45–6 and the parable of the vineyard have the same theme. 20.20 describes the strategy which his opponents adopt to trap Jesus. They send 'agents in the guise of honest men' to seize on some word of his which can be used as a pretext to hand him to the Romans. These agents ask whether or not it is lawful to pay taxes to the Romans (20.21–6). Jesus asks whose inscription is on the local coinage. On being told, 'Caesar's', he replies: 'Pay to Caesar what belongs to Caesar, and to God what belongs to God' (20.25). This is essentially a compromise ethic, evidently because Jesus believes that a complete reordering of society is imminent and that the reordering is God's task and not his. Jesus also breaks down the binary opposition between God and Caesar and rejects the possibility that the question can easily be posed in such polarized terms (in a way that is most significant for subsequent Christian ethical reflection).

Next the Sadducees step forward with a question (20.27–38). It is a complicated one about the resurrection. It depends on the principle, set down in Deuteronomy 25.5 and Genesis 38.8, that a widow may not marry outside her husband's family and that a brother must do his duty to his sister-in-law if a man dies childless (the so-called principle of 'levirate marriage'). The Sadducees posit a case in which a man dies childless. His seven brothers step forward in turn but none produces an heir. Whose wife, they ask, will the woman be in the resurrection? (20.33). The question is a nuanced one because the Sadducees did not believe in the resurrection. The question is thus as much about the plausibility of belief in the resurrection (which for Luke means first and foremost the resurrection of Jesus) as about legal principles. Jesus upholds the validity of belief in the resurrection – the reader knows this already from 16.31 – but characteristically turns the situation back on his questioners. He states that marital relations will be irrelevant in the resurrection life and adds the comment that the resurrected will be like angels (20.36). This presents the resurrection as a completely different order of existence and implies that sexual relations, and possibly even gender differentials, will be superseded at that time. Belief in the resurrection is supported from scriptural evidence so that Jesus pronounces the Sadducees' view invalid exegetically. It is not said how this view of the resurrection coheres with the wider picture of the kingdom of God. We should doubtless exercise the greatest caution in attempting to deduce a clear understanding from this passage.

The role of questioner now shifts to Jesus. Nobody 'dared to put any further question to him' (20.40) – clearly because they had been unable to catch him out – but Jesus asks them a question about the status of the Messiah (20.41–4). How can people say the Messiah is David's Son, he asks, when David calls him 'Lord' (in the text of Psalm 110.1)? Luke again teases with parallelism. Jesus is like David (this has been said in 6.3) but unlike David (here). The point at stake is that Jesus as Messiah is not only descended from David but also David's Lord because he is a divine being. Jesus again avoids calling *himself* Messiah, which he will not do until 24.26, but he does criticize the view that the Messiah is (merely) a human being. The Messiah for Luke is the resurrected and enthroned Jesus who will soon return to earth.

The second half of the citation of Psalm 110.1 (20.43) hints that Jesus will remain enthroned in heaven until his enemies have been made his footstool. Here, Luke provides an explanation of sorts for his delayed return. In Luke's view God's kingdom is progressively displacing the kingdom of Satan. Part of this task for Luke involves the carrying of the Gospel throughout the Gentile world. This is why it is important that Paul should preach the Gospel in Rome. That Rome is evangelized at the end of Acts is a sign, alongside others in the Gospel, that the situation anticipated by 20.43 is nearing fulfilment. We should link this with Acts 7.56 where Jesus rises from his throne as if to emphasize the nearness of his return.

The chapter concludes by criticizing the scribes (20.45–7). The scribes (but never the Pharisees; cf. 13.31) take an active part in the moves against Jesus. They are presented here as pompous, unscrupulous people who will most certainly be judged for their wrongdoing.

CHAPTER 21

Chapter 21 contains further eschatological teaching on the part of Jesus. This part of the Gospel has sometimes been called 'The Synoptic Apocalypse' but it does not display many typical features of an apocalypse and for that reason it is better called an 'eschatological discourse'. This discourse presents the signs of the end – most of which in Luke's view have been accomplished – and anticipates the sudden appearance of the Son of Man from heaven (21.27) to effect the 'liberation' of Israel (21.28; cf. 2.38). The emphasis on fulfilment is the crucial feature of this chapter. It offers reassurance about the coming of the Son of Man – the yet-to-be-fulfilled aspect of eschatology – and presents other information almost as a guarantee that this event will happen.

The chapter is introduced by the story of the widow's mite (21.1–4). This has relevance because it is a story about the temple and because it contrasts with the attitude of the scribes ('they eat up the property of widows') whom Luke has just criticized. In 21.5 some people are talking about the temple and admiring its stones and ornaments. Jesus warns of a time when the stones of the temple will be thrown to the ground (21.6). This provides the cue for the disciples to ask when this will be, which in turn provides the rather artificial introduction to the rest of the chapter. I argued in Chapter 2 that 21.6 must be identified with 21.27 as an indication of what will happen at the climax of the eschatological process.

As with Paul's teaching in 2 Thessalonians chapter 2, which (if genuine) was written a generation earlier than Luke, the purpose of Luke 21 is to specify the events that precede the end. The Thessalonian correspondence was written to people who thought the consummation of eschatology imminent; Luke is written for readers for whom its delay is a worrying thing. There is some evidence of a progress of thought in Luke 21 but it is wrong to expect a full consistency of the material. Luke does not so much provide a systematic scheme of eschatology as specify events in a quite symbolic way. The message of the chapter is that the Son of Man will return (21.27) despite the substantial period which has intervened.

The first stage in the eschatological process is described by 21.12–19. Jesus says that Christians will be handed over to synagogues and thrown into prison, even hauled before kings and governors for their faith in him (21.12). Yet they will be given the words to speak on these occasions (21.13–15). This happens because Christian faith means the disruption of family ties, including the betrayal of one family member by another (21.16; cf. 12.49–53). The Christians will be universally hated for their beliefs (21.17) but not a hair of their heads would be harmed (21.18). If they stand fast they will gain life (21.19). Much of what is said here is fulfilled in Acts. In Acts Christians are hauled before the Jewish authorities (e.g. Acts 4.5–12). On more than one occasion Paul makes his case before a Roman official (see Acts 24; 25), and before King Agrippa (Acts 26). The Holy Spirit speaks through the mouth of Peter (Acts 4.8), and the other apostles. The statement about not a hair of their heads being harmed is repeated in Acts 27.34. These parallels with Acts, which demonstrate that what Jesus says has come true, show that the theme of eschatological fulfilment is on Luke's mind in his work.

The next stage in the eschatological process is given by 21.8–11. This passage predicts the advent of false Messiahs (21.8) and mentions rumours of warfare and their fulfilment (21.9–10). Jesus says that there will be earthquakes, famines and plagues in many places (21.11). This information is sufficiently general to permit of many applications. There were indeed other messianic claimants in the first century (see Acts 5.36–7). The First Jewish Revolt, which culminated in the Roman destruction of Jerusalem in 70 CE, was certainly an act of warfare. The reference to earthquakes, famines and plagues (21.11) can be paralleled in a variety of prophetic and apocalyptic literature, so that Luke's language is quite traditional at this point. He is harnessing wider material to support his own distinctive portrait of the end.

At some point in the process – and the time-scale lacks precision – Jerusalem will be encircled by armies and the time of her devastation arrive (21.20). This material is peculiar to the Lucan version of the eschatological discourse. The prediction lends a note of inevitability to what happened in 70 CE. This was past history for the readers; 21.20 (along with earlier passages) is a clear reference to the Roman destruction of Jerusalem. It sets the Gospel after that date. For Luke, 70 CE signified the 'time of retribution when all that stands written is to be fulfilled' (21.22). The author sees this event as divinely willed punishment for the Jewish rejection of Jesus. In the terms set out by 13.34 the punishment was due also for their murder of the prophets; 21.22 looks back in a general sense to Hebrew prophecy and calls to mind its wide-ranging criticism of the Jewish nation. This was the time when 'this generation [answered] for the blood of all the prophets shed since the foundation of the world' (11.50). Luke adds that Jerusalem will be 'trampled underfoot by the Gentiles' until the Gentiles have run their course (21.24). Everything up to this point in chapter 21 is past history for the readers. The passage states, quite strikingly, that the punishment of Judaism has already been completed. The way is now open for her eschatological reconstitution which is the major theme of the Gospel.

Genuine prediction of the future begins in 21.25–7. The discernible shift from historical review to actual prophecy at this point indicates that the only events yet to be fulfilled in the chapter's scheme of things are the specific events of the end. Jesus says that portents will appear in the heavens (21.25) and that the celestial powers will be shaken (21.26). Then people will see the Son of Man coming in a cloud with power and great glory (21.27). The direction of his movement will be from heaven to earth (and not towards the Ancient of Days in heaven, as it is in Daniel 7.13–14, which resources this passage). The fact that the Son of Man comes 'with power and great glory' means that he acts with the authority of God himself in effecting the eschatological climax.

His coming will be for judgment. It is implied that the kingdom of God will be made fully present at that time.

The chapter concludes (21.28–32) with a series of sayings about the nearness of the end. 21.28 says that, when 'all of this begins to happen, stand upright and hold your heads high, because your liberation is near'. The word 'liberation' recalls 2.38; the passage implies that Israel's restoration is near. 21.29–31 records the parable of the fig tree. Jesus says that the budding of the tree means that summer is nigh (21.30). This interpretation of this parable leads to the conclusion that 'the kingdom of God is near' (21.31). Jesus adds that 'the present generation will live to see it all' (21.32; cf. 9.27). Luke would surely have removed this passage had he not thought the imminent climax of eschatology a realistic possibility. It does appear to place a temporal limitation on the kingdom's full appearance (particularly when we consider that Luke was not written until perhaps *c.* 90 CE). 21.33 enigmatically anticipates the renewal of the created order in language that is not dissimilar to Revelation 21 (cf. Romans 8.18–25). Jesus uses the statement 'heaven and earth will pass away' to make the point that his words are absolutely true.

The chapter closes with ethical exhortation which is directly related to the eschatological promise (21.34–6). This passage shows affinities to other New Testament paraenesis (e.g. 1 Thessalonians 5.1–12). That encourages the conclusion that Luke is drawing on a wider exhortatory pattern. Luke tells his readers to be alert in view of the imminent end. They must pray for the strength to pass through the trials and to stand 'in the presence of the Son of Man' (21.36). This is the moment to which Luke's eschatology looks forward.

CHAPTER 22

Chapter 22 tells the story of the Last Supper (22.1–37). From now on the narrative is more connected than in the central section of the Gospel. Many people think that this is because Luke is drawing on a source or sources at this point but this hypothesis must not be allowed to obscure Luke's creativity as an Evangelist. Since his account of the trial is significantly different from Mark and Matthew's, and then again from John's, we have no exact way of telling how far Luke used sources and where his own insertions lie. Luke's trial narrative shows that he is capable of writing a story which reads interestingly and well. This is the criterion by which his narrative ability should be judged.

Chapter 22 opens with the statement that the Passover is drawing near and that the chief priests and scribes are trying to do away with Jesus (22.2). 22.3 states that 'Satan entered into Judas'. This brings the battle between the kingdoms of God and Satan to its climax as Satan tries to do away with the representative of the former. This passage sets the drama which follows in a particular light. The conspiracy between the Jews and the Romans against Jesus is at one and the same time the battle-ground between God and Satan. This explains why Jesus is consistently in control of the situation, against the flow of the story. This is because he is the divine representative who acts with the power of God. There is a substantial irony in the fact that Jesus is crucified, and Satan ostensibly wins, but that Jesus is shown to be the Lord and Messiah so that his death is not at all the defeat that it seems. Luke makes it a necessary stage in the eschatological process so that the tragedy has an unexpected outcome.

Judas goes to the chief priests and temple guards to discuss how to betray Jesus (22.3–6). The story implies that Judas is needed to enable the arrest of Jesus apart from the crowds who idolized him (see 22.6). It has been suggested that this may not have been his function in the actual (i.e. historical) betrayal of Jesus.[7]

The preparations for the Passover are described in 22.7–13. They recall the triumphal entry. Once again the disciples are met by a stranger who provides something of use to Jesus. Jesus' knowledge again confirms that he is fully in control of the situation. Commentators have discussed at length the question of whether the Last Supper is a Passover meal. Luke certainly says that it is (22.7, 15). This allows him to present the death of Jesus in sacrificial terms according to the symbolism of the festival. The Passover looks back to the time when the people of Israel were miraculously delivered from Egypt. Luke identifies Jesus with the sacrificial lamb when he makes the bread and the wine symbolize his own body and blood.

The Passover serves as the occasion for Jesus to tell the disciples about his death. 22.16 sets the meaning on the meal: 'Never again shall I eat it [i.e. the bread] until the time when it finds its fulfilment in the kingdom of God.' This makes the Last Supper also symbolize the kingdom's inaugural banquet. It looks forward to the time when the kingdom will be fully present, following the return of Jesus from heaven, and Jesus will preside over the banquet as Lord and Messiah.

The textual tradition of Luke 22 raises a major problem. We have

seen that the manuscripts have both a 'longer' and a 'shorter' text in
22.19(–20). The 'shorter text' (followed by the REB) makes Jesus
say only 'this is my body'. The 'longer text' (given here by the
NRSV) reads: '"This is my body which is given for you. Do this in
remembrance of me." And he did the same thing with the cup after
supper, saying, "This cup that is poured out for you is the new
covenant in my blood." ' The difference between the two versions is
that the longer text introduces two cups at supper (22.17, 20) and
specifically makes Jesus say that his death is a covenantal sacrifice.
The mature Joachim Jeremias (who changed his mind on the issue)
argues persuasively that the longer text should be preferred on the
grounds that a scribe may have omitted the sacred words of institution when copying Luke for a pagan reader. *All* the Greek
manuscripts bar one (the so-called Codex Bezae) read the longer
text, as do the other versions and the early Fathers who used Luke.
It would be foolish to ignore this substantial evidence. The longer
text adds a more explicit covenantal overtone to the death of Jesus
than would otherwise be found in Luke. On this view Jesus calls his
death a 'new covenant'. This contrasts with the 'old covenant' of
Judaism, as has been suggested earlier by 16.16, and presents
Christianity as continuous with Judaism in the sense that it has a
covenant but also discontinuous because that covenant is a new one.

The background of this passage deserves brief exploration. All
Christian theology about the new covenant looks back to Jeremiah
31.31–4: 'The days are coming, says the Lord, when I shall establish
a new covenant with the people of Israel and Judah. . . . I shall set
my law within them, writing it on their hearts; I shall be their God,
and they will be my people. . . . I shall forgive their wrongdoing,
and their sin I shall call to mind no more.' Luke has a predilection
for Jeremiah as we have seen already. Here he uses a passage which
indicates that the time of the new covenant has arrived. This new
covenant has been ratified in the death of Jesus. His death is in this
sense a covenantal sacrifice. From Jeremiah derives the conviction
that the forgiveness of sins has become a reality in the eschatological
age. The fact that sins are forgiven by Jesus and the disciples in the
Gospel is an eschatological sign which demonstrates the nature of
the Christian movement.

It is not therefore true, in the light of this passage, to say that
Luke has no theology of the death of Jesus. The covenantal motif
makes the point that his death has effected eschatological salvation.
Luke presents his death as a covenantal sacrifice which reveals him

as Lord and Messiah and results in the forgiveness of sins. There are signs here of a dependence on various aspects of Pauline theology.

In 22.21–3 Jesus says that his betrayer is at table. This causes the disciples to ponder the traitor's identity. After this a (somewhat artificial) dispute arises among the disciples as to which of them is the greatest (22.24–7). Jesus addresses this by saying that the greatest must be like the servant, adding the words, 'I am among you like a servant' (22.27). This repeats the ethical instruction proffered earlier in the Gospel (9.48) and draws attention to the theme of suffering and service which we have seen is crucial in the Gospel.

There follows a significant passage in which Jesus comments on the nature of the eschatological age (22.28–30). Jesus tells the Twelve that he entrusts to them the kingdom with which his Father has entrusted him (22.29). The passage shows that the Twelve have an important role in the kingdom: 'In my kingdom you shall eat and drink at my table and sit on thrones as judges of the twelve tribes of Israel' (22.30; Matthew 19.28). Luke, unlike Matthew, places this saying in the context of the Last Supper and connects it with the eschatological banquet. This highlights the role of the disciples when the kingdom finally comes. The seating arrangement resembles a council of war in which Jesus sits attended by his lieutenants. The disciples are said to assist in the judgment of Israel. They apparently have the status of heads or presidents of the tribes of Israel. Their presence with Jesus at the Last Supper symbolizes the fact that the restoration of Israel will indeed happen given that the leaders of the tribes have been appointed and are in place in the church.

In 22.31–4 Jesus tells Peter that Satan has asked to sift the disciples but that he has prayed for Peter that his faith may not fail. Despite Peter's assertion that he will go with Jesus to prison Jesus says that he will soon deny him three times. This prophecy is fulfilled not much later when Peter denies Jesus in the High Priest's courtyard. Peter's statement about going to prison for Jesus, however, is fulfilled in Acts 5.17–26 so that Luke's view of Peter does have a forward-looking aspect. Peter certainly substantially changes in character after Pentecost. Satan may be 'sifting' Peter at this point in the Gospel but his deflection of the apostle in Luke's scheme is a momentary one.

The two earlier mission charges are recalled in 22.35–8. Previously, the disciples were sent out without support. Now, Jesus says they must take their purse and their pack, even buy a sword.

The disciples reply that they have two swords. Jesus says this is enough. Some commentators interpret this as misunderstanding on the part of the disciples and grim humour from Jesus; but underneath the passage may lie the genuine historical reminiscence that Jesus and his band were lightly armed. Presumably this was needed for personal safety by anyone who ventured beyond the city walls (as the disciples do in 22.39). There is no suggestion that two swords are adequate to ward off the arrest party as 22.50–1 will show.

In 22.39 Jesus goes to the Mount of Olives and removes himself to pray. He asks that the cup (of suffering) be removed from him but that God's will be done (22.40–2). 22.43–4 (the angel's appearance from heaven and the description of Jesus' sweat resembling blood) are omitted by many manuscripts. The textual support for them is less strong than for the longer text of 22.19–20 (and the issue is consequently more difficult to judge). The passage nevertheless indicates the depth of anguish that was felt by Jesus on this occasion. This was no doubt compounded when he returned to find the disciples asleep (22.45–6).

The arrest party now arrive, headed by Judas (22.47–8). Judas tries to kiss Jesus. The disciples put up notional resistance in which a servant of the High Priest has his ear cut off but is healed by Jesus (22.49–51). Jesus makes the point, related to the earlier narrative, that they are taking him by stealth when they had ample opportunity to arrest him publicly in the temple (22.52–3), which implies an act of cowardice.

Jesus is taken to the home of the High Priest (22.54). The narrator's interest switches to Peter. Peter sits warming himself in the courtyard. Three times he denies that he is one of Jesus' followers. On the third occasion, after the cock crows, the narrator says starkly: 'the Lord turned and looked at Peter' (22.61). Peter goes out and weeps bitterly that Jesus' prediction about him has come true.

In 22.53–65 the mockery of Jesus by his guards is described. The crucial issue is the prophetic status of Jesus: 'If you are a prophet, tell us who hit you' (22.64). Readers know that Jesus is a prophet (e.g. 4.24; 7.39). The irony rests on the fact that Jesus refuses to authenticate this status which the readers know that he enjoys and which the soldiers unwittingly pronounce. The prisoner is in control of the situation. He confounds his unwitting persecutors by his superior knowledge which the author shares with the readers.

The 'trial' of Jesus before the Jewish Council is described in

22.67–71. In Luke this has the nature of an inquisition and not of a trial as such. No formal charges are levied or witnesses summoned. The purpose of the meeting is to find concrete evidence whereby Jesus can be brought before the Romans. The authorities begin by asking Jesus whether he is the Messiah. Readers again know that he is the Messiah but Jesus makes no answer to the question. This is because he will only call himself Messiah after his passion (24.26). The exchange which follows teases the reader into asking why Jesus is reluctant to acknowledge the truth about his identity. The answer is that Luke is foregrounding a particular understanding of Messiahship in which this position is achieved only through the cross.

Jesus tells his accusers that, if he tells them the truth, they will not believe him (22.67). He then proceeds to tell them the truth: 'From now on, the Son of Man will be seated at the right hand of Almighty God' (22.69). This is much more than they had asked; and, as Jesus predicts, they fail to believe him. They even pronounce the truth in order to reject it: 'You are the Son of God, then?' (22.70). Jesus once more replies ambiguously: 'It is you who say I am' (22.70). The assembly assumes that Jesus has replied in the affirmative and conclude they have all the evidence that they need. This is an example of double irony in the Gospel because the accusers (correctly) assume that Jesus thinks that he is the Messiah but (incorrectly) assume that he is an impostor in making this claim.

It is impossible to read this report without recognizing that it is written from a Christian point of view. The irony is that the High Priest, whose task it is to identify the Messiah, fails to do so. The chapter closes with the Jewish conclusion: 'We have heard this evidence from his own lips' (22.71). This, too, is ironic, for the authorities fail to understand the significance of what they have heard in this way. Because of their lack of understanding, Jesus is handed over to the Romans, and the will of God furthered in the unfolding succession of paradoxes.

CHAPTER 23

In chapter 23 the assembly brings Jesus before Pilate. They claim that 'we found this man subverting our nation, opposing the payment of taxes to Caesar, and claiming to be Messiah, a king' (23.1). The reader knows that all these charges are untrue. Jesus did not sanction the withholding of taxes and in the Gospel he has never claimed to be the Messiah. The reference to 'subverting our nation' probably refers back to his action in the temple. If it does it shows that the Jewish authorities have misunderstood the true significance of this event by seeing it only as a threat against the present temple (and ignoring its eschatological consequences). The charges laid against Jesus emphasize the point that his condemnation is unjust.

Pilate asks Jesus whether he is the king of the Jews. Jesus replies, 'the words are yours' (23.3). Pilate then adjudicates that Jesus has no case to answer (23.4) but the chief priests and the crowd assert, 'His teaching is causing unrest among the people all over Judaea. It started from Galilee and now has spread here' (23.5). This makes Pilate refer the case to Herod Antipas who is in Jerusalem at the time (23.6–12). The trial before Herod is not mentioned in the other Gospels. For this reason many scholars have questioned its historicity.[8] Luke includes it to emphasize the point that Jesus is innocent: Herod questions Jesus at length but receives no reply (23.9). This leads to repeated mockery of him (23.11). But Herod does nothing to condemn Jesus so that Pilate must conduct further investigation himself in 23.13–25.

The presentation of Pilate in 23.13–25 is of a governor who finds Jesus innocent but who bows to mob rule and delivers Jesus to the will of the Jews. We do not know the precise extent to which this portrait is historical but it is virtually certain that the Jews did not possess the right to conduct executions at the time (see John 18.31). This meant that the death penalty had to be sanctioned and carried out by the Romans. Although the Jews, or some Jews, doubtless agitated against Jesus the Romans may not have needed much persuasion to kill someone whom the authorities said was a threat to stability. One can hardly read the trial narrative without asking historical questions of this kind. They follow naturally from the literary questions. In Luke the Roman part in the crucifixion is suppressed and *the Jews* lead Jesus away for execution (23.26).

In 23.13–25 Pilate states that Jesus is innocent of all charges and offers to release Barabbas. Those addressed in this way are 'the chief priests, councillors, and people'. This implies that all the inhabitants of Jerusalem call for Jesus' blood. This is not just misunderstanding by a few but rejection by one and all. Barabbas is introduced obliquely, quite unlike the version of events in the other Gospels. Mark's comment that 'at the festival season, the governor used to release one prisoner requested by the people' (Mark 15.6) is omitted by Luke. This heightens the impression of mob violence for the willingness to condemn an innocent man is matched by the (unexplained) demand to release a guilty one. Reason goes out of the narrative in 23.13–25. Pilate tries vainly to persuade the crowd but weakly yields to their demand. 23.24 confirms that the death of Jesus has almost the character of a lynching in Luke: 'He released the man who had been put in prison for insurrection and murder, and gave Jesus over to their will.'

The Jews lead away for execution. They make Simon of Cyrene carry his cross (23.26). Jesus then makes another lament over Jerusalem which explains the tragedy of his passion (23.27–31). The women who follow Jesus mourn and lament for him (23.27). Jesus tells them to weep for themselves for the days are coming when people will envy the barren and pray to be covered by the mountains (23.29–30). This links the death of Jesus with the Roman destruction of Jerusalem and confirms that Luke understands 70 CE as punishment for the Jewish rejection of Jesus.

The crucifixion is described in 23.32–48. Jesus prays for his persecutors, saying that 'they do not know what they are doing' (23.34). He even asks God to forgive them. 23.34b–38 describes how people taunted Jesus that he saved others but that he cannot save himself. This again is ironic given what Jesus says about his fate on the Mount of Olives. There is another ironic moment of disclosure in 23.38 when the *titulus* is placed on the cross. It reads: 'This is the king of the Jews.' This tells the readers what they already know and what the crowds fail to recognize. Jesus *is* the Messiah. He is killed for what he is. The messianic secret is especially controverted at this point in the Gospel.

The words of the two criminals crucified with Jesus are recorded in 23.39–43. The first cries in desperation, 'Save yourself, and us!' (23.39). The second is more reflective. Acknowledging his own crime, he pronounces on the innocence of Jesus (23.41) and asks that Jesus will remember him when he comes to his throne (23.42). Jesus promises that that day he will be with him in Paradise (23.43). Paradise in this context denotes the intermediate place of the dead (cf. 16.23).

The death of Jesus is narrated in 23.44–7. Darkness falls over the whole land between noon and three o'clock (23.44). The curtain of the temple is torn in two further symbolizing the building's destruction (23.45). This again makes an interesting parallel with the thought of Hebrews where Jesus enters the heavenly sanctuary at the moment of his death on the cross (Hebr. 10.19–20). Jesus commends his spirit into God's hands, using the words of an evening prayer (23.46). At the moment of Jesus' death, the narrator states that the Roman centurion pronounces him innocent beyond all doubt (23.47). The crowd go home, beating their breasts at the execution (23.48).

The passage 23.50–4 explains that Jesus is buried in the tomb owned by Joseph of Arimathea. The women observe the location of the tomb and go home to prepare their spices. They rest on the sabbath to prevent the impurity that would be caused by contact with a corpse (23.55–6).

CHAPTER 24

On the first day of the week (i.e. Sunday) the women come to the tomb with their spices (24.1). They find the stone rolled away (24.2) and cannot see the body of Jesus inside it (24.3). Two men in dazzling garments – clearly angels – appear (24.3). They ask the women why they seek the living among the dead (24.5) and remind them that Jesus predicted his own resurrection when he was in Galilee (24.6–7). The women remember the words of Jesus and go to tell the Eleven what they have seen (24.8–11).

There follows in 24.11 a significant statement in the search for what the resurrection means. The narrator says of the disciples, when they heard the report of the women, that 'the story appeared to them to be nonsense, and they would not believe them'. With this should be compared the narrator's comment in 23.55–6 that the women go home to prepare spices and do not think to break the sabbath legislation. Their preparations for embalming show that they expected to find a corpse. It was the vision of the heavenly visitors which convinces the women that Jesus has been raised. The same is true of the disciples who did not believe when told about the empty tomb. They were not expecting the resurrection, either. It is the vision of the heavenly Jesus which convinces them that he had been raised. The risen Jesus is a heavenly being who appears to the disciples in chapter 24.

With 24.13–35 we reach the Gospel's dénouement. Luke records the story of the disciples as they journey to Emmaus. They are joined by a stranger, Jesus himself, of whom the narrator says, 'something prevented them from recognizing him' (24.16). The narrator does not say why this is but the possibility is that elements drawn from Jewish angelology undergird the story and that Jesus, as a heavenly visitor, appears to the disciples in something other than his crucified form. This is what the deutero-Marcan version of the story says explicitly (Mark 16.15). Had Jesus appeared to them as a broken victim of torture, they would certainly have recognized him. The disciples tell Jesus about their failed hopes that he would liberate Israel (24.21) and about the reports of his resurrection (24.23–4). Jesus' reply in 24.25–7 sets the Gospel in perspective: 'Was not the Messiah bound to suffer in this way before entering upon his glory?' (24.26). At this climactic moment Jesus calls himself Messiah and says that suffering is a necessary part of his messianic office. This is both a retrospective commentary on his refusal to use the 'Messiah' title so far in the Gospel and a promise that his death has not invalidated the eschatological restoration, but has helped to secure it. This is because the suffering Messiah, in the language of 22.20, has effected the new covenant and entered on his heavenly position from which, it is implied by 9.26 and chapter 22, he will return to preside over the kingdom of God.

Jesus vanishes at the moment that he is recognized (24.30). There is doubtless a eucharistic symbolism in the fact that Jesus makes himself known in the breaking of bread. The Emmaus disciples return to Jerusalem to tell the others what they have seen (24.33–5). As the disciples mull things over, Jesus appears again (24.36–49). As if to prove that he is not a ghost, he eats some fish (24.41–2). 'Ghost' in this context signifies a spirit of a dead person who belongs to the intermediate region. For Luke, Jesus is not a dead spirit but the risen Lord. He had passed to the heavenly world and shares the glory of God.

In 24.44–9 what Jesus told the Emmaus disciples is confirmed: 'everything written about me . . . is bound to be fulfilled'. This is an explicit acknowledgement on the part of Jesus that he is the Messiah. In 24.46 Jesus adds that 'scripture foretells the sufferings of the Messiah and his rising from the dead on the third day' and says that scripture 'declares that in his name repentance bringing the forgiveness of sins is to be proclaimed to all nations beginning from Jerusalem' (24.47). Forgiveness is an eschatological commodity; Jesus says here that the Gentiles are included in it.

Luke alone of the Evangelists narrates the ascension. Jesus is taken up to heaven at the end of the Gospel. We know from 22.69 that this is for him to be enthroned at the right hand of God (cf.

Acts 2.33). The disciples return to Jerusalem with great joy 'and spen[d] all their time in the temple praising God'. This is no doubt because the temple is expected to be the centre of the eschatological climax. The disciples return to the place which symbolizes the future full appearance of the kingdom of God.

Chapter 4

Alternative readings of Luke

INTRODUCTION

This reading of Luke presents the story as a description of Jesus' journey from Galilee to Jerusalem, with its implications for eschatology, and emphasized the theme of the temple as one that does much to hold the Gospel together. As I explained earlier, it would be wrong to pretend that any single reading offers a final or definitive perspective on Luke. To demonstrate this point, I now want to offer two further readings of the text, one written from a deconstructive stance and the other from a feminist perspective. Neither again offers a final perspective on Luke: nor indeed will one person's deconstructive or feminist reading necessarily be shared by anyone else! But the further attempt at reading is useful because it draws attention to the need for a variety of approaches to text and highlights the fact that interpretation must be a corporate exercise, which is not the prerogative of a single method or scholar.

A DECONSTRUCTIVE READING

Deconstruction has enjoyed a mixed reception in scholarship (not least in biblical scholarship). It has been called 'nihilistic', 'dehumanizing', 'unethical', 'virulently anti-Christian' and 'particularly hostile to religious ideas and people'. These criticisms have been surveyed in a paper by David Clines who responds to them in a characteristically robust manner.[1] Clines follows Derrida in observing that *all* texts are capable of deconstruction because they contain binary oppositions which can be shown to be open to question. The ethics of a deconstructive approach, Clines argues, lies in its commitment to the truth: 'I think that wanting to know is not just idle intellectual curiosity, but a kind of ethical courage, like wanting to know the worst from my doctor. I cannot bear to be kept in the dark about something that is the case, and I think it my duty to let other people in on secrets – especially secrets that important people would like to stay secrets.'[2] Clines emphasizes the point that deconstruction, far from being brought to the text from outside, happens when a text is read and works from the information that lies within the text. It is thus an internal activity in which the reader responds to textual signs and not an alien importation with nihilistic tendencies.

I begin my deconstructive reading by identifying some themes which are set in a 'binary opposition' of this kind. This will be a selective and far from an exhaustive list. The first consideration is the tension that exists between the presence and the absence of Jesus in the Gospel. Jesus inhabits Luke as a character in the story. Luke ends with the ascension where Jesus is taken off to heaven to be enthroned as a heavenly being (cf. 22.69). Jesus in Luke is thus a character who disappears. His absence gives the story its meaning: Jesus for the readers is the Lord who journeys from earth to heaven (9.51). The heavenly Lord makes his presence felt whenever Jesus the character is mentioned. His enthronement is a symbol that he is waiting to return to earth to effect the visible climax of the kingdom of God (22.69; cf. Acts 7.56).

Jesus in this sense is both present and absent for the readers. He is present in the text and present through his Spirit in every act of worship whenever the Gospel is read. Yet the presence of Jesus also draws attention to his continued absence because he has yet to return from heaven to act as the eschatological judge (9.26).

Part of the Gospel's function is to make the absent Jesus present by the repetition of his life and words. The very fact that the Gospel is written down (supplementing the oral tradition) is a sign of his significant absence. The return of Jesus will over-ride the need for authority to which the Gospel responds. In this sense the written record anticipates the eschatological manifestation of Jesus as Lord. In the meantime the Gospel offers a constant representation of him. It makes Jesus present but at the same time draws attention to the as-yet unfulfilled aspect of Christian eschatology.

So the absent Jesus is always present (through the reading of the Gospel) and the present Jesus is always absent (because of his delayed return). This means that the binary opposition between presence and absence breaks down completely. The two are not opposites at all. Each of them informs the other. The ascension is a pictorial demonstration of this. It is both a symbol of the absence of Jesus and a symbol of his future return (see Acts 1.11). At his return, it is implied, absence will yield before presence and the eschatological hopes which the Gospel creates will be satisfied.

We should ask what Luke gains by placing this deconstructible tension in his Gospel. It is deeply embedded and serves perhaps as the Gospel's most significant contrast. It is bound up with the question of Luke's response to the delay in eschatology which we shall examine in the next chapter. It makes the point that Jesus is *never* fully absent because he is present in the text and present through his Spirit in worship. Those who are feeling the weariness of the delay can take comfort from the fact that many of the eschatological events have already been accomplished. The kingdom is present already (17.21) and day by day people are entering it (even as late as Acts 28.24). Chapter 21 especially comments on the fufilment of eschatology. At the same time the contrast is a means of sustaining hope while the Lord tarries. What is now perceived is not the final state of the kingdom as Luke envisages it. The return of Jesus will initiate an act of judgment (9.26) when the causes of oppression will be removed from the kingdom. The absence of Jesus is a sign that the kingdom will appear and that Luke's hopes for liberation will be realized.

This Lucan tension mirrors the general pattern of New Testament eschatology. Even in 1 Thessalonians 4 – the earliest Christian literary evidence we have – Paul is obliged to defend the eschatological hope against those who think it should have been realized already. Frustratingly, we lack the full evidence to know what Paul had preached about the return of Jesus. But if he found himself confounded by his own words – or a contortion of his words – when writing to the Thessalonians, it is likely that he preached an imminent eschatology in which Jesus' sojourn in heaven was made a temporary visit. Paul's mature treatment of eschatology contains the view that God has delayed the climax to facilitate the conversion of Israel (Romans 9–11). The (much later) 2 Peter 3.9 presents an explanation of a similar kind which explains the delay with reference to God's patience. In Ephesians 2.6 we find the view that the church has been enthroned with Christ in the heavenly places. This offers reassurance about the eschatological benefits despite the fact that Jesus has not returned.

None of these texts has abandoned the view that Jesus will return from heaven. Both the late Paul (Philippians 3.20–1) and the book of Revelation (22.20) insist that he will return. Luke's 'now and not yet' must be seen against this wider background so that its impact is neither unduly emphasized or improperly minimized. The crucial question is whether Luke has given up believing that Jesus will return in the immediate future and what happens to a reading of the Gospel if this view is taken. My reading of the text concludes that Luke has *not* taken this course of action and that his Gospel contains signs of a potentially imminent climax in eschatology. I shall examine this matter in the next chapter. It shows that the ambivalence between the presence and absence of Jesus is not exclusively a Lucan device (although it is undoubtedly emphasized in the Gospel).

A further deconstructible element is the uncertainty surrounding the question of whether or not Jesus is the liberator of Israel in Luke. The Infancy Narrative introduces this theme into the Gospel. Simeon is called one who 'watched and waited for the restoration of Israel' (2.25); Anna, someone who 'talked about the child to all who were looking for the liberation of Jerusalem' (2.38). But this is not what Jesus says about his destiny. On his lips 'the Son of Man has to endure great sufferings, and to be rejected by the elders, chief priests, and scribes, to be put to death, and to be raised again on the third day' (9.22). When he speaks about the role of Jerusalem it is in very different tones: 'I must go on my way today and tomorrow, because it is unthinkable for a prophet to meet his death anywhere but in Jerusalem' (13.33). This conflict of expectations is picked up by the Emmaus disciples in the Gospel's dénouement: 'Our chief priests and rulers handed him over to be sentenced to death, and crucified him. But we had been hoping that he was to be the liberator of Israel' (24.21). To which Jesus replies in his most significant sentence: 'Was not the Messiah *bound* to suffer in this way before entering upon his glory?' (24.26).

Perhaps the most striking feature of the speeches made by Simeon and Anna is that they fail to define what is meant by the concept of 'liberation' in the Gospel. The *Nunc Dimittis*, however, shows that neither character works with an innocent understanding. 2.26–7 introduces the canticle by mentioning three important themes in the Gospel: Spirit, Messiah and temple. The *Nunc Dimittis* supplies the framework in which these must be understood. The coming of Jesus is said to introduce a deliverance which will 'bring revelation to the Gentiles and glory to your people Israel' (2.32). Intertextuality plays its part in the creation of meaning in this statement. The primary reference is to Isaiah 49.6: 'I shall appoint you a light to the nations so that my salvation may reach earth's farthest bounds.' There is also an implied allusion to Isaiah 46.13: 'In Zion I shall grant deliverance for Israel my glory'. This Hebrew background prevents the view that any narrowly political understanding of 'liberation' is involved in Luke. This cannot be so, for the people who under those circumstances are the oppressors (the Gentiles) are *included* in the act of liberation. At stake is a much more comprehensive understanding of 'liberation' which has eschatological overtones. It is the decisive liberation of God which will be totalistic in its effects and which for this reason can be introduced only by divine intervention and not through human action.

This means that we must carefully examine the concept of 'reversal' in Luke. The belief that the hungry will be fed and the mighty punished, exemplified by the Beatitudes and Woes, is central to the Gospel. Luke's biblical heritage leads him to conclude that the biblical promises about Israel and the social convictions of the Hebrew Bible will both be fulfilled. The Bible has much to say about the proper treatment of the poor and reminds those in authority of their obligations in this respect. Luke's understanding of 'liberation' picks up this theme of social justice and applies it to the existing order which was characterized by the experience of patriarchy and dependency. 'Liberation' for Luke is thus both a religious and a social phenomenon. It anticipates a process which began with the preaching of Jesus whereby the rules that governed society and kept things as they were would be changed with the full emergence of the kingdom of God.

The question of how Jesus is the 'liberator' is the subject of a binary opposition in Luke. On the one hand Simeon and Anna identify him as such. There is no suggestion that anyone else is the liberator of Israel. On the other Jesus is not (yet) the liberator as Luke tells his story. This last point is demonstrated vividly by 19.45–6. Jesus makes a lot of noise in the temple – but nothing actually happens when he does. 19.11 even warns the reader that nothing will happen when it says that the kingdom of God will not appear when Jesus reaches Jerusalem. This is what happens (or does not happen) for the judge is taken prisoner at the end of the story and put to death by the Romans. The kingdom is not fully present at the end of Luke. It is not even present at the end of Acts where Paul's preaching of the kingdom (Acts 28.31) draws attention to the fact that it is not fully present.

Yet for Luke this 'yet-to-be-accomplished' aspect of the liberation has an 'already accomplished' aspect. Jesus says so in 22.20
where he calls the cup 'the new covenant, sealed by my blood'. The
tension between Jesus as the liberator of Israel and the Jesus who
dies is a purposeful one in the Gospel. For it is through the death of
Jesus, quite paradoxically, that his act of liberation is secured. The
implication of 24.25–7, where Jesus tells the Emmaus disciples
about the need for the Messiah's suffering, is that the promised
liberation has not failed but that it has been achieved in an unexpected way. This is through the Messiah's death which is followed
by his resurrection and heavenly exaltation. The fact that Jesus is for
Luke a heavenly being explains the unfulfilled aspect of eschatology
along the lines of the 'presence–absence' opposition which I have
deconstructed already. Eschatology remains incomplete because of
the absence of Jesus in heaven. It will however find its goal in his
return from heaven when his presence will be a permanent one and
the kingdom be fully present.

We must also consider the binary opposition between 'rich' and
'poor' and suchlike terms which feature especially in the Beatitudes
and Woes in chapter 6. The Beatitudes describe the kind of people
who belong to the kingdom and those who can expect punishment
at the Eschaton. The latter are said to be the rich and prosperous
whose happy time is now. This opposition reflects the Palestinian
culture of 'dependency' which allowed a small minority to wield
power and influence over the vast majority of people. One of the
features of the Gospel is that it transfers the preaching of Jesus from
its original life-setting in the Palestinian agrarian economy to an
implied setting in the social situation of Christians in the
Hellenistic cities of the Roman Empire. This means that Luke
apparently finds difficulty with some of the source material –
notably, perhaps, with the command to 'hate' one's family – which
he reinterprets to suit this new situation.

Part of Luke's reinterpretation is his deconstruction elsewhere in
the Gospel of the binary oppositions which are erected in chapter 6.
This is evident in his wider view of riches and in his view about the
accessibility of the kingdom without qualification to all. For Luke,
riches have positive value if they are distributed according to the
demands of charity (16.9). Luke also cautions that those who belong
to the kingdom – which he says in chapter 6 are 'the poor' – may
find themselves ostracized from it because of their behaviour
(13.25). The rich *can* thus enter the kingdom and the poor and

needy *may* be excluded from it. This material offers a fascinating new perspective on the Beatitudes. It is not true to say that the kingdom belongs only to the poor and the deprived in Luke. These qualities may be appropriate to the kingdom but they are not a prosopographic portrait of the kingdom's constituency. Similarly, it is not riches in the bald sense but the *use* of riches that places a person 'inside' or 'outside' of the kingdom of God.

We may perhaps not doubt that such bald oppositions are an authentic part of what Jesus actually preached. The historical Jesus probably used them to let his audience practise their powers of deconstruction. Many aspects of his preaching cry out for deconstruction because he spoke in polarized terms and without a full consistency. This is an inevitable feature of the parable. Luke handles such material in a distinctive way. He preserves the binary oppositions in chapter 6 but provides material elsewhere in the Gospel to help the reader break them down. This both allows for the perhaps rather mixed constituency of the Lucan churches and throws issues of ethical concern and decision into the arena of debate. The rich can choose not to be rich by giving their money away. This is what Jesus tells the Rich Young Ruler in chapter 18. But the deconstruction also tells the rich that they do not *need* to be bankrupt to enter the kingdom. Similarly, the poor are told that any presumption on their poverty may lead them to be debarred from the kingdom despite their status and profession. They, too, must act ethically by doing what Jesus tells them. The basis of the deconstruction is the demand for mutuality where both giving and receiving are significant concepts. In this sense the poor must behave in precisely the same way as the rich. They must give and forgive if they want to be treated like this themselves.

We might even say that Luke's ethical teaching is founded on a deconstruction. The basis of the argument is that the poor must behave like the rich and the rich must behave like the poor. This is the pattern of suffering and service which is emphasized throughout the Gospel. Only by doing this can people be members of the kingdom. The Beatitudes and Woes are a spur to thought about what constitutes the kingdom's standards. They should not be read without consideration of what Luke says elsewhere in his Gospel; and they certainly do not advocate a particular view about the social constituency of the Lucan churches.

Finally, the theme of the temple in Luke. Here, too, there is an interesting deconstructibility. Luke knows of two temples: the present temple and the eschatological temple. These temples are apparently opposed to each other in Jesus' prophetic denunciation of the first (13.35) and symbolic anticipation of the second (20.17). Yet this opposition breaks down when we recognize that the denunciation of the present temple is undertaken by the person who is the corner-stone of the eschatological temple. The truth of 13.35 – that the present temple is *currently* forsaken by God – is authenticated by the fact that the eschatological corner-stone is already in place and that he is even the speaker in this verse. Not only so but the chief corner-stone conducts his preaching ministry on the site of the present temple (chapters 20–1). It is in the temple that Jesus warns that 'not one stone (*sc.* of the present temple) will be left upon another' (21.6). This passage is the fulfilment of 20.18 where it is said that 'everyone who falls on that stone will be dashed to pieces'. Luke loved this contrast between the two temples to judge from its prominence in the Gospel. The significance of the deconstructible opposition is that the readers do not have to wait for the eschatological temple to be built at some point in the future. God has *already* constructed the temple. It is currently in heaven and exists, with characteristic apocalyptic ambivalence, as a significant factor in the readers' imagination. The present temple is not the true or future temple; but the future temple (like the kingdom) is none the less fully present in the drama of the Gospel despite its perceptible absence.

A FEMINIST READING

From deconstruction we move to feminism (but without presenting the two as binary opposites!). The meaning and interpretation of 'feminism' has provoked a controversy similar to that thrown up by deconstruction. One person's feminism, so it seems, is someone else's patriarchy. The women's movement has unsurprisingly progressed since its first emergence in the 1960s. We need to be clear about what might emerge from a feminist reading of Luke.

Such a reading begins from the observation that Luke is a narrative. A feminist reading asks about the portrayal of the women characters in the story.[3] Are they real women or merely a male author's or narrator's androcentric view of women? Does the story serve women's interests or do the women by contrast serve the men? These questions are important ones because of the familiar scholarly view that Luke as an author is especially interested in women. This makes it all the more urgent to ask whether Luke's women are real women or merely subordinate characters in the male author's drama of salvation. To answer this question means that we must examine all the characters in Luke. Are there implied distinctions between the men and women or are the two portrayed in similar terms? And how realistic is the characterization in any event? This research will supply the information that lets us answer to the first question concerning Luke's portrayal of his women characters.

The first woman we encounter is Elizabeth (chapter 1). She appears in tandem with Zechariah and becomes the mother of John the Baptist. Elizabeth fulfils the traditional role of wife and mother in a patriarchal culture. She features as a minor character in a story that concerns men. We are told, first of all, that she is of priestly descent (1.5) and secondly that she is barren (1.7). Her usefulness as a character is here defined by her (in)ability to produce children. When she does conceive, this is referred specifically to the intervention of God (1.13). No genuine account is provided of her feelings at any time (did she *enjoy* the sex which conceived the Baptist?). During her pregnancy Elizabeth lives in seclusion so that no-one can see she is pregnant (1.24–5). This is presumably to avoid the ridicule associated with conception in old age. But it also makes Elizabeth disguise her natural status as a mother as if this is somehow uninteresting or unimportant.

Next on the scene is Mary. Mary, too, is a mother. She is the mother of Jesus. The status of the son determines the status of the mother. The fact that Mary's son is superior to Elizabeth's explains the fact that Elizabeth treats Mary as superior (1.43). Mary's supreme status in the Gospel is defined by the fact that she is the mother of the Messiah. Luke's presentation of the birth of Jesus further illustrates the point we have seen with Elizabeth, that his interest in Mary as mother is with the status and function of her son and not with her own feelings nor with her ability to shape her son's personality and future as every mother does.

In this sense the *Magnificat*, which is ostensibly a hymn about Mary, is in fact a hymn about Jesus: 'From this day forward all generations will count me blessed, for the Mighty God has done great things for me' (1.48–9). The goodness of God for Luke lies in the provision of Jesus and not with the high estimation of Mary as such. Luke's interest in Mary's motherhood lies firmly in the provision of eschatological salvation. Mary's status as a woman is a secondary consideration.

These remarks must be counterbalanced by consideration of what Luke appears to be doing in the Infancy Narrative. We have seen that the shift from Attic to biblical Greek in 1.5 indicates that the Hebrew Bible is essential for the story that Luke tells. In this context Luke makes a deliberate allusion to earlier miraculous conceptions, notably those of Samuel and Samson.[4] The patriarchal portrait of Elizabeth and Mary must be evaluated in this context. Intertextuality forms the basis of the picture. The two Lucan mothers recall the two Hebrew mothers. This explains the emphasis which the story places on the themes of barrenness and divine intervention. Only if the rest of the Gospel continues this kind of portrait can we conclude that Luke thinks about women in this way. The evidence shows that in fact he does not.

The next woman whom we meet is Anna (chapter 2). Anna appears in tandem with Simeon as a prophetess of the restoration of Israel. She fits a well-known holy type: Anna is a godly widow who is known for her prayer and devotion (2.36). Luke introduces two prophets at this stage in deference to the fact that in Jewish Law there must be more than one witness. It is significant that Luke should make the witnesses a man and a woman. This implies that their testimony is of equal value. It suggests a particular view of gender distinctions in the Gospel. Even when writing in his biblical vein Luke is prepared to place a woman on an equal footing with a man in terms of the provision of witness to Jesus the Messiah. That this happens in the Infancy Narrative suggests that the patriarchal aura is qualified there.

Women are among those whom Jesus heals in his ministry. One such person is the woman who has the issue of blood in 8.43–8. It is certainly true that she suffers from a woman's complaint but the way in which Jesus deals with her seems hardly different from the way that he treats male sufferers in the Gospel. The woman shows the faith that Jesus will heal her by touching the hem of his garment (8.44). Jesus says that this has made her whole (8.48). It is not said that the woman's sins are forgiven but this is a feature of other miracle stories that involve both men (5.20) and women (7.47).

The last of these passages – the story of the allegedly immoral woman in 7.36–50 – is interesting for what it reveals about the different characters involved. First of all we meet Simon, the Pharisee who invites Jesus to dinner (7.33). The woman enters in 7.37. She is described as 'living an immoral life in the town'. The woman brings myrrh and anoints Jesus' feet with her kisses and tears (7.38). Simon immediately suspects the worst: the woman sees Jesus as a potential client (7.39). He thinks that Jesus should have more insight into her character. Irony is a significant feature of this story. Jesus *knows* what Simon is thinking (7.40). He tells the parable of the debtors to rebuke him. The parable leads to the conclusion that the woman's many sins have been forgiven (7.47). It thereby subverts the expectations which the narrative constructs. Simon thinks that, if Jesus is a prophet, he must know that the woman is a prostitute. The narrator indicates that, because Jesus is a prophet, he can see that the woman is a penitent despite the fact that he knows she is a prostitute. This amounts to a reinterpretation of the familiar biblical image of the prostitute. That the woman is a prostitute is not denied by the story but the important thing about her is that she recognizes her need of forgiveness and comes to Jesus as the person who can help her. She is not presented as a greater sinner than anyone else – such an interpretation is implicitly criticized by 13.1–5 – but as someone who acknowledges her need for forgiveness. She is therefore not rejected as a prostitute but welcomed as a penitent (which is how everybody comes to Jesus as Luke understands it). The implication of the story is that the virtuous Simon, who has failed to recognize his need of forgiveness, comes off worse than the woman because, in criticizing her, he has failed to recognize the dilemma of his own condition.

There is a brief reference to women at the beginning of chapter 8. Jesus goes from village to village accompanied by the Twelve, 'proclaiming the good news of the kingdom of God' (8.1). His band is accompanied by 'a number of women who had been set free from evil spirits and infirmities' (8.2). At first sight this reference seems patronizing: it implies that the men follow Jesus (*sc.* because Jesus had called them) but that the women follow Jesus because Jesus has healed them from various complaints. But this initial impression that they are camp-followers must be resisted. The passage makes the point that Jesus is followed by men *and* by women. Healings in Luke are not so much signs of personal weakness as a demonstration of people's willingness to receive the kingdom of God, and thus a positive thing. This positive attitude towards women as disciples is continued in the second half of 8.3: 'these women provided for them out of their own resources'. This verse states that the women not only received the kingdom of God but also gave what they had to secure the success of its preaching. This is more than the men are said to do. One must conclude that Luke thinks of men and women as disciples of Jesus on equal terms and that he even emphasizes the role of women as those who make the preaching possible through their generosity. This foregrounds the significance of women in a context where this might not be expected.

From here, we turn to the story of Martha and Mary (10.38–42). Martha is introduced first. She welcomes Jesus (10.38) but is 'distracted by her many tasks' (10.40), so much so that she asks Jesus to tell Mary to help her. Mary, by contrast, 'seated herself at the Lord's feet and stayed there listening to his words' (10.39). Jesus rather surprisingly rebukes Martha: 'Martha, Martha, you are fretting and fussing about so many things; only one thing is necessary. Mary has chosen what is best; it shall not be taken away from her' (10.41–2). It is by no means accidental that the two characters in this story are women. The fact that they are sisters emphasizes the contrast between them. Martha does what any woman in the ancient world was expected to do. She provides for the visitor and gets on with the chores. Mary adopts an unusual position: she reclines with Jesus, probably at table, and talks with him. This is the traditional role of the man. Here, Luke subverts the gender distinction by praising Mary for doing what a woman would not normally do: reclining at a table and talking on equal terms with a man. The criticism of Martha is overtly a criticism of those who are too busy to listen to Jesus. But it is more than this. It is also a criticism of the system which casts women in this role and probably of the way in which some women were being treated in the readers' churches. This story in particular counterbalances the much more patriarchal portrayal of women in the Infancy Narrative. It represents a breaking-down of the binary opposition between male and female by allowing the emphasis to fall on personhood in discipleship to Jesus, and not on gender.

In 11.27 a woman calls out to Jesus from the crowd. She does here exactly what the (male) blind beggar will do later in 18.35–43.

Chapter 20 contains the test question from the Sadducees about levirate marriage and the resurrection (20.27–38). Jesus denies that the woman will belong to any particular brother in the resurrection age. He justifies this conclusion with reference to the angelomorphic status of the resurrected: 'those who have been judged worthy of a place in the other world, and of the resurrection from the dead, do not marry, for they are no longer subject to death. They are like angels; they are children of God' (20.35–6). This represents the denial that sexual relations will be appropriate in the resurrection age. By implication, it also means that gender differentials will lose their force at that time. In that case, we possibly find a scheme in which the hope for the coming of the kingdom is connected with the overcoming of gender differentials between men and women. That might explain why Luke speaks as he does of the equality between men and women as disciples of Jesus in the Gospel. It is because the kingdom of God is present already (17.20–1), albeit hidden (13.21), that its standards impinge on the present as people respond to Jesus. Luke advocates an equality between the sexes which reflects this fact and agrees with what Paul said about this issue in Galatians 3.28. We are hard pressed not to conclude that the need for equality is an issue which looms large in the pages of the Gospel, evidently because women were disenfranchised in the circles for which the Gospel was written.

Women play a significant role in the crucifixion and resurrection narratives. As Jesus is led away for execution, 'great numbers of people followed, among them many women who mourned and lamented over him' (23.27). Jesus warns them to weep for themselves because the day of judgment is impending. It is the women, and not the men, who are said here to regret the sentencing of Jesus. There is a substantial irony in this. The male characters in the trial, who had the power to spare Jesus, did not do so. The disciples deserted Jesus in his tragic hour. The female characters, who were not involved as protagonists, have the insight to recognize the true pathos and tragedy of the situation. To this extent they are more insightful than the men.

Women are the first to discover the empty tomb of Jesus (24.1–9). As at the beginning of the Gospel women witness an angelophany which discloses to them authoritative truth: 'Remember how he told you . . . that the Son of Man must be given into the power of sinful men and be crucified' (24.6–7). The women then 'recalled his words' (24.8) and go to tell the disciples what they had seen. The disciples, however, refuse to believe them: 'the story appeared to them to be nonsense' (24.11). Here again the women are portrayed as insightful and the male disciples as disbelieving.

We must now consider the relative qualities of the men and women characters in the Gospel. I have said earlier that most Lucan characters are 'stocks' who allow the spotlight to fall on Jesus. If it is true that Luke's women are stock characters, this is true also of

Luke's men. We know more about Peter than the other disciples and have only brief snippets about these others, such as James and John. But even Peter is the narrator's tool. He is presented both as impulsively enthusiastic (9.20) but also as wilfully rejecting (22.54–62). The men whom Jesus heals are 'types' who demonstrate that Isaiah 61 is being fulfilled. Women are no more or less 'types' than these male minor characters. This is well illustrated by the story of the allegedly immoral woman where both the woman and Simon the Pharisee are judged according to the nature of their responses to Jesus.

This conclusion certainly qualifies what we can say about Luke's portrayal of women as real women. The women may not be fully 'real' but they are no more or less real women than the men are real men. The lack of detailed characterization makes this conclusion inevitable. It is not to be seen as a repudiation of women as such but as a general feature of the way that Luke tells his story. It is definitely to be noted that the patriarchalism of the Infancy Narrative is more than overcome by the positive portrayal of women in the body of the Gospel, especially in chapters 8 and 10.

Chapter 5

The themes of Luke's Gospel

We shall now study the 'themes' of Luke's Gospel or at least some of them. This material is what many commentators would call the 'theology' of Luke but I shall avoid that term here in deference to my narrative approach.[1] Our reading of Luke has thrown up areas where the Gospel uses themes that have a wider currency in the primitive Christian world – and passages where problems exist. These deserve to be examined more fully to make sure that we have not missed any of Luke's carefully constructed nuances.

SEEING IS BELIEVING

One characteristic Lucan theme is the frequent use of the verb 'to see'. There is a good example of this in the story of the shepherds which forms part of the Infancy Narrative. The shepherds say that they will go to *see* the nativity (2.15). The narrator adds that, when they have seen it, they report their angelic vision to the main characters (2.17). This exchange comes at an important point in the Gospel when Jesus is first introduced. It shows that the concept of 'seeing' has a great force in Luke's work. This impression is confirmed by later evidence. Luke 3.6 expresses the hope that all flesh will 'see' the salvation of God. Moreover, the comment placed by Jesus on his parables in 8.10 contrasts 'looking' and seeing' ('the others have only parables, so that they may look but see nothing') to state that those beyond the circle of the disciples cannot understand the meaning of Jesus and his message. Many other examples could be produced of this use of the verb. This Lucan usage draws the reader into the narrative and involves him or her in the unfolding story of Jesus.

This is analogous to what happened to them in their corporate lives as Christians as the Gospel is read in the context of worship. What takes place on the narrative level supports the conviction that Jesus is present as the Lord through his Spirit when they worship. Luke's concept of 'seeing' allows the readers to share, at the narrator's invitation, the privileged position of the original disciples – and to have even greater insight because, through the narrator's guidance, they know the full facts about Jesus so that the original characters' misunderstandings are avoided. This perhaps compensates for the fact that Luke, as opposed to John (1 John 1.1) and probably the other Evangelists (Mark 14.51–2; Matthew 9.9), was not an eyewitness of the events that he records (see especially Luke 1.2). He is sensitive to the needs of others who stand in a similar position.

Stephen Moore is right to say that to this extent Luke's Gospel embodies an epistemology.[2] By this he means that behind the Gospel (and Acts) stands a theory of knowledge through which readers are reinforced in their understanding. What passes for 'truth' is encoded for them in the text in the insistence that Jesus – the hero crucified by the Romans – provides salvation and is a divine being in his own right. The epistemology pivots on the 'seeing' terminology. Those who 'see' the events of the Gospel encounter, not just this story from the past, but their heavenly Saviour who is present in the church. The description of the absent Jesus, symbolized by the ascension, is paradoxically an assertion that Jesus is ever and more universally present because he is a heavenly being. Acts shows that the work of the Spirit is still not complete given that Jesus has yet to return from heaven. This is significant if the sudden ending of Acts is deliberate and Paul is left proclaiming the facts about Jesus quite openly under house arrest in Rome (Acts 28.30–1). That would make the point that the preaching had as yet no end (whatever happened to Paul) because of the continuing absence in heaven of the Proclaimed. The conclusion of the Gospel is equally 'open' to the extent that it removes Jesus from the scene but promises the Holy Spirit to continue his work (24.51, 49). 'Seeing' the narrative Jesus brings this dimension into play and makes the act of reading far from a monochrome experience.

LUCAN ESCHATOLOGY

At this point we must consider Conzelmann's thesis that Luke has relegated the return of Jesus from heaven to the distant future and substituted for it the period of the church which is currently defined by persecution.[3]

The hope that Jesus will return from heaven was the mainstay of Christian eschatology throughout the first century. Jesus himself had expected the kingdom of God in the relatively near future (9.27). He evidently saw himself as the Messiah (9.20–1) and the members of his inner circle as the leaders-elect of the transformed Israel (see 22.30b). 1 Thessalonians 3.13 (cf. 2 Thessalonians 1.7) shows that the hope for his return was firmly established by the middle of the first century when Paul (who cites an earlier formula) anticipates that Jesus will come 'with all those who are his own'. The belief that earth will be the place of salvation is found in Christian literature as diverse as Romans 8.18–25 and Revelation 20.4. It represents the absolute bedrock of the primitive Christian eschatology.

To consider Conzelmann's theory we must first of all recognize that the delayed return of Jesus is a problem for *all* New Testament literature and not just for later documents like Luke. It is reflected in the strong assertion of Revelation 22.20 ('I am coming soon!' – 90–95 CE) but also in the discussion of death which Paul undertook some forty years earlier (1 Thessalonians 4.13–18). That the sense of delay was felt so early shows the imminent character of the Christian eschatological hope. Robert Jewett has described the Thessalonian community as containing some in a state of millenarian frenzy who had even given up their jobs in expectation of the imminent end.[4] Paul answers them by saying that the end is not yet and that human death (which the church has begun to experience) is not a barrier to participation in the kingdom. To say that many Christians, as Paul did, recognized the difficulties of eschatological fervour is by no means to concede that first-century Christianity progressively abandoned its hope for the return of Jesus. We can see this from Paul's last letter, Philippians (3.20–1 – 'from heaven we expect our deliverer to come') and from Revelation ('I am coming soon'; 22.20). No text gives a positive indication that the hope was abandoned in the first century.

Conzelmann's persecution hypothesis needs careful handling in its bald form. There is very little evidence that the Christians were persecuted by the Romans in the first century – not even towards the end of the reign of Domitian when Luke was written. The absence of any determinative evidence for a Domitianic persecution in the book of Revelation (a contemporary text) must be mentioned here. Acts, it is true, documents a series of Jewish moves against the Christians but these have the nature of local reprisals and not of persecutions as such. The Christians were certainly misunderstood and even held in suspicion by people not of their religious persuasion. The Jews disliked them because they proclaimed a crucified Messiah (Galatians 3.13). The Romans failed to understand them at all. But one should not mistake social isolationism and the misunderstanding which this provoked for persecution. Nor should one ignore the fact that the fervent eschatology which inspired early Christianity was generally matched by a social conservatism that viewed the existing order with a resigned acceptance under the belief that its eschatological replacement was the task of God alone.

I have held 19.11, and the parable of the absent king which it introduces, to be a crucial passage for Lucan eschatology. Luke certainly acknowledges a delay in the return of Jesus but this is counterbalanced by the assurance of the master's return which is the real theme of the parable. I think it is also counterbalanced by the distance between 19.11 as originally spoken and the time the parable is presented to readers some sixty years later. It seems that in 19.11 Luke is not so much advocating a further and protracted delay to his readers as explaining the (by now quite substantial) delay that had occurred already. 19.12 calls the nobleman's journey a long one but insists he will return when he has been appointed king. It is surely implied that the 'long journey' is nearing its end given that half a century or more has elapsed since the parable was spoken. Only the hypothesis of a proximate consummation of eschatology explains the urgency of the warning about judgment which dominates the second half of the parable. Readers are told to consider how they live as if they do not have much time for repentance. The ethical exhortation is underscored by eschatology. The eschatology gains its force from the reference to the 'long journey' in 19.12 which I have interpreted retrospectively with reference to the period between the historical Jesus and the reading of the Gospel.

We should also examine the progress of thought in chapter 21. My exegesis of this chapter made two related points. First of all, the reference to the destruction of the temple in 21.6 must be distinguished from that to the destruction of Jerusalem in 21.20. 21.6 comes last in the eschatological sequence and is preceded in time by 21.20. The distinction is between the destruction of Jerusalem by the Romans (70 CE) and the replacement of the temple by God (at the eschatological climax). Secondly, it is remarkable how little of Luke's eschatological prediction remains to be fulfilled. Only 21.6 and the actual climax of 21.27–8 are still-future events. Everything else has been fulfilled already. The implication of 21.27–8, which describes the Son of Man's arrival, is that his appearance will mean the replacement of the present temple and the full emergence of the kingdom of God. The wording of 21.28, 32 is most significant for understanding Luke's eschatology. In 21.28, Luke says that 'when all this *begins* to happen . . . your liberation is near'. Not only have these events begun to happen, as the readers perceive them, but many of them have been fulfilled already.

To this Luke adds, in repetition of 9.27, that 'the present generation will live to see it all' (21.32). This again is indicative of eschatological imminence. One wonders how many of the Twelve were still alive *c.* 90 CE. It is by no means impossible that some were. But it is most unlikely that all or perhaps even many of them had survived that long; and the life expectancy of the remaining apostles cannot be regarded as substantial. This gives an urgency to 21.32 if the words are taken at their full force. Jesus tells the Twelve that some of them will live to see his return. Luke includes this saying in the Gospel when he could easily have removed it. This by implication sets an urgency on the return of Jesus and militates against Conzelmann's view that Luke thought it would be substantially delayed. Although Luke does not say when the return will happen, he does acknowledge that the conditions are ripe for it.

A further consideration supports this conclusion. We have seen that Luke includes the Gentiles in salvation on the basis of their faith in Jesus. We have yet to consider the relation of Gentiles to Jews in the Gospel but it is true to say Luke thinks that they form part of the covenant people of God. Acts closes with the Gospel being preached in Rome and with the salvation of God offered to the Gentiles there (Acts 28.31). This statement cannot be evaluated apart from the Jewish material we examined in Chapter 2 which makes the salvation of the Gentiles a feature of the eschatological age. In this light Acts 21.28 looks like a declaration of eschatological fulfilment: 'Therefore take note that this salvation of God has been sent to the Gentiles; the Gentiles will listen'. The inclusion of the Gentiles is what Judaism expected about the end-times. Acts states that this has taken place already so that again belief in eschatological fulfilment emerges from Luke's work.

In this light it is worth observing that Luke's ethics, on which

Conzelmann set great store for his theory of delay, frequently (but not always) have an eschatological foundation. The sayings about food and clothing in 12.22–31 are examples of this. Jesus tells the disciples that God will supply their everyday necessities. He links this to the command to worry about more important things: 'set your minds on the kingdom, and the rest will come to you as well' (12.31). The demand to follow the kingdom is articulated within the framework of the 'now and not yet'. Luke's ethics are, absolutely and entirely, the ethics of the kingdom of God. The kingdom supplies the framework in which they are to be understood. The forward-looking aspect of the kingdom expects there will be a judgment for those who set themselves against its ideals (9.26). Although Luke's ethics, like the rest of his Gospel, are neutral in their time-scale of the end, the mere fact that Luke prescribes ethical regulations is not necessarily a sign he thinks that the return of Jesus will be delayed. His ethics must be interpreted in the broader light of the Gospel's eschatology which, as we have seen, does not lack an imminent aspect.

THE KINGDOM OF GOD

At the heart of Luke's eschatology stands the concept of the kingdom of God. This phrase is used some thirty-one times in the Gospel (and 'kingdom' rather more so). It denotes the full reign of God over Israel which is symbolized by the new covenant (22.20) and enshrined in the Jesus movement with its new understanding of social relations. For Luke the kingdom of God is present in the ministry of Jesus (17.20–1) but it will not become fully visible until the climax of eschatology. The kingdom's present invisibility is symbolized by the rejection of Jesus, the prophet of the kingdom. Luke thinks the kingdom will become fully manifest when Jesus returns as Lord and Messiah from heaven (21.31). The kingdom, like Jesus himself, will then make a decisive impact on those who have rejected it.

The phrase, 'the kingdom of God' has an extensive background in Jewish and Christian literature. The related term 'the kingdom of YHWH' is used in 1 Chronicles 28.5. The notion that God is the king (*the* king, not *a* king) is a commonplace of Hebrew literature. The notion of God's kingship, combined with the often beleaguered attitude of the Hebrew people, meant that the concept of the divine kingdom embraced much more than hopes about the survival of

Israel as such. If Yahweh is king, it must be true to say that there is no people or territory from which his sovereignty is withheld. Thus Psalm 47.2 calls him the 'great King *over all the earth*'. This idea is sustained and developed in the apocalyptic literature (e.g. *1 Enoch*. 84.2). It is significant that it features also in the *non*-apocalyptic literature of Judaism so that it cannot be held to be merely the fantasy of groups who deny the value of the present world in the hope that a better world will emerge. Thus *Psalms of Solomon* 17.3 say that 'the kingdom of our God is forever *over* the nations in judgment'; and *Testament of Moses* 10.1, that 'God's kingdom will appear throughout his whole creation'. Israel's God is the universal king and the only king (hence the appearance of universalist ideas in Jewish eschatology).

In Judaism around the time of Christian origins there was a conflict of opinion as to whether the kingdom of God had a legitimate political dimension. The view that it did is found for instance in the Qumran *War Scroll* which includes a passage (probably) anticipating the earthly rule of God's people Israel over the nations (1QM 12.7–15).[5] In rabbinic literature, however, the concept of the kingship of God is introduced in essentially non-political terms. The rabbis often say that one should 'take the yoke of the kingdom upon oneself'. By this they mean the reading and keeping of the Torah. Perhaps this difference of opinion reflects the crisis of confidence for Judaism caused by the destruction of its national sanctuary in 70 CE. The Qumran community evidently disappeared around this time. The rabbinic literature was written after it. A new situation inevitably brought different attitudes with it.

The 'kingdom of God' is certainly an eschatological concept in the Gospels. It designates God's final rule over all people when Israel would be purified and the Gentiles included in salvation. In the light of this Jewish background it is easy to see why Luke should insist that the Gentiles belong to the salvific order. To exclude them would be to deny that God's kingly rule extends over the whole earth, which is effectively to deny the full sovereignty of Israel's God. Luke's God is king over all people. The ministry and the death of Jesus are the events through which the demonstration of God's kingship will be secured.

For Luke, like all the New Testament writers, the 'kingdom of God' is an earthly phenomenon. It represents a transformed version of the present order. This process of transformation is already happening but its effects have yet to become universally obvious.

We cannot read Luke without recognizing that the kingdom means both continuity but also discontinuity with the way things are at present. The discontinuity means that the present must be judged by an invisible standard which will be demonstrated only in the future when the kingdom is fully present.

Luke's understanding of the kingdom is thus an eschatological one but it also has moral, social and economic implications. This book would be incomplete without consideration of the question of why Luke writes as he does about the kingdom of God. This is to raise a question which concerns the ambitions of the historical Jesus. Seminal research has been undertaken in this area by Richard A. Horsley who describes the situation of social unrest in which the Jesus movement came to birth.[6] Horsley shows there was a fundamental conflict in first-century Palestinian Judaism between the ruling groups on the one hand and the bulk of the people on the other.[7] Both groups shared essentially the same set of traditions and religious assumptions but the power of the rulers meant that they were in a position to exploit the peasants who lacked the necessary resources to resist them. This resulted in a considerable social unrest. Horsley notes that 'peasant revolts may have been infrequent among other precommercial agrarian empires, but they were strikingly frequent in Jewish Palestine'.[8] This was because of the inequalities between rich and poor which were so sharply focussed there at the time. Those in authority extracted tithes, tributes and taxes from the peasants. Loan-sharks were a familiar feature of Palestinian agrarian life in the first century. When stocks of corn and oil ran out people were forced to borrow from the sharks at exorbitant rates of interest. This is no doubt the background to the parable of the crafty steward in 16.5–7 who reduces the interest on a loan to secure an actual return. Horsley shows that the Palestinian social system was entirely based on the phenomenon of indebtedness: 'The vast majority of Palestinian Jewish people would have been peasants living in villages and working the land to support the Temple, priests, Herodian régime(s), and Roman tribute as well as their own families.'[9] 'Indebtedness' denotes the way in which those without were forced to rely on others for their daily necessities; and where those who had shared their resources only at a price.

Against this background, perhaps not unsurprisingly, a number of popular prophetic movements emerged in first-century Palestine. The Jesus movement was one of these. Despite the fact that (classical) prophecy is often thought to have ceased with Malachi, the appearance of people like John the Baptist, Jesus, and Jesus son of Ananias shows that *popular* prophecy was very much alive and well in the first century CE. Jesus son of Ananias is remembered for predicting the imminent destruction of Jerusalem (see Josephus, *War*, 6.300–1). Horsley notes three types of 'popular prophetic movement' in the first century CE.[10] The revolts in three Jewish districts of Palestine after the death of Herod and the movement headed by Simon bar Giora in 68–70 CE were led by people who were popularly acclaimed '*kings*'. Secondly, the large popular movements which occurred in the middle of the century in Judaea were headed by self-styled '*prophets*' (see Acts 5.36). Thirdly, there were *the Zealots* who tried to restore a legitimate and popular hierocracy in 68 CE. These movements exercised a great influence in the popular culture of the time.

This wide-ranging evidence provides an explanation for some of the titles accorded Jesus in Luke – 'Messiah', 'king' and 'prophet' among them. Whatever else they do, these titles indicate that a subversion of sorts is taking place within the social order. To call oneself 'a prophet' at a time when it was widely held that prophecy had ceased was to draw attention to the message which a self-styled prophet proclaimed. The message of these prophets, as of Jesus himself, concerned the hope for social transformation and the reshaping of attitudes which was needed for this to happen. Even more striking is the self-designation 'king'. Kings hold power and authority. For a peasant to call himself 'king' makes a striking claim to status. The incongruity between the title and the person's actual status draws attention to the demands that are associated with the proclamation of kingship. We should never forget that the titles of Jesus in the Gospels have a social significance as well as a place in the history of ideas. It does not, of course, matter that in some cases (as again with Jesus) the protest stands its distance from all forms of violence (see Josephus, *War*, 6.283–5). The articulation of the protest, in a situation which does not encourage this, is the critical thing.

This information prompts further consideration of the message proclaimed by Luke's Jesus. It has often been observed that 'reversal' is a prominent theme in the Gospel. Two examples of it are the words of the *Magnificat* in 1.51–3 and the Beatitudes and Woes in chapter 6. Both passages anticipate the overthrow of the rich and mighty and the enfranchisement of those who are deprived. In the latter passage Luke makes Jesus effectively announce that the rules that govern Galilean society are being rewritten. An alternative perspective is offered which benefits the disenfranchised. The kingdom of God belongs to the poor (6.20) which, in concrete social terms, means the majority of people as distinguished from the powerful oligarchy. The kingdom as Jesus proclaims it embodies the theme of reversal. Its charter is expressed by 6.21: 'Blessed are you who now go hungry; you will be satisfied.' Hunger was a by-product of the Palestinian economic system with its culture of dependency. Jesus articulates the vision of a new social order which gives expression to the belief that things can be different.

In this context we should evaluate Jesus' statements about 'hating your family' (e.g. 14.26). These depend for their effect on hyperbole. They represent a repudiation of authority in favour of a new understanding in which the dominant earthly 'father' is absent and his place taken by God, the heavenly Father. Patriarchy was the central feature of life in first-century Palestine.[11] Each village was composed of several extended families. This had clear implications for social arrangements like marriage and employment (cf. 15.11–32). The fact that each villager was more or less 'on the same level' as every other meant there was little collective ability to resist the small number of people who had the power to tithe and to tax them. Oppressive taxation wore down not just individuals and families but whole communities too. By saying that his followers should '*hate* their families', but that they will receive many blessings in the present age (18.30), Jesus is effectively saying that the rules which permitted exploitation and oppression have been altered in favour of a new way of life which depends on different structures of authority. Luke invites people to live out the implications of this new vision of mutuality and to proceed on the basis of equality (cf. Galatians 3.28). The Gospel preserves the vision of Jesus and communicates it to the Hellenistic cities with their (rather different) set of social relations and assumptions. Part of the reader's response is to make the link between what Jesus says and the way in which their own lives are lived. One wonders how great a process of interpretation must have taken place to make the teaching of Jesus relevant to their new situation.

What is said about mutuality in Luke is continued in Acts (we must observe). The early Christian communities were known for their mutual provision of help for their members.[12] Acts 4.32 states that the Jerusalem community held its property in common, for which there are parallels in the literature of the Essene community at Qumran. This mutuality, which involved the common ownership of property, is matched by the New Testament view of the church as a pure community where high social boundaries were maintained in respect of other people and where the threat of exclusion was used to justify the strong sense of solidarity that pertained among the baptized (cf. 13.25–30). The statement about the 'hiddenness' of the kingdom in Luke (17.20–1) is a way of explaining to readers how they should regard Jesus' message of social transformation. The kingdom might not be making an immediate and visible impact on society but this did not mean it was either absent or deficient. Likewise, its invisibility does not invalidate the demand to behave in a mutual way. Like the mustard seed the kingdom of God will one day be openly perceived and humankind in general will conform to the new vision articulated by Jesus, much as they now adhere to the old patriarchal system. This future hope is expressed under the traditional Jewish image of the messianic kingdom.

This understanding of Jesus and his preaching makes possible a new reading of the Lord's Prayer as a passage that enshrines the counter-cultural standards of the kingdom of God. The Christians first of all call God 'our Father'. This is an implicit rejection of patriarchy whereby most people in Palestine were dependent for their subsistence on a better-placed person or people. Jesus proposes a different understanding of society where mutuality and not dependency is the key. 'Thy kingdom come' is both the formal expression of this ideal and – we must not overlook the point – a prayer for future divine intervention that will make the new standards fully operative. 'Give us each day our daily bread' is a prayer for sustenance whose full meaning is given by the phrase that follows. 'Forgive us our sins . . . as we forgive all who have done us wrong' represents a repudiation of the debt system where huge profits were made at the expense of those who could ill afford to pay the interest. It is a further declaration of mutuality in which the reception of forgiveness is accompanied by the demand to display it. Perhaps, in this context, the final 'do not put us to the test' has the almost sinister sense of a prayer for deliverance from open revolt: the final recourse of relatively deprived people when all other forms of negotiation break down. Luke reminds his readers of what had happened when revolt broke out in 70 CE (21.20). He is adamant that all future change must be introduced by the Son of Man and not by human intervention (9.26).

The people who follow Jesus are drawn mainly from the peasant class. They include fishermen, local craftspeople and the like. These people would have shared the lot of the poor I have just described. Indebtedness must have been a constant problem for them. Indeed, it is only against such a background that the binary oppositions of the Gospel — rich/poor, blessings/woes, king/subject — find their real meaning. Horsley suggests that:

> The communities of the Jesus movement thought of themselves as a new social order. This was variously symbolized as 'the kingdom of God', or as an alternative new 'temple', but one 'not made with hands' of which Jesus was the foundational corner-stone (Mark 14:58; 12:10), or as the restored 'Israel' indicated in the miracle stories or represented by the Twelve (Mark 5–8; 3:14; 6:7 etc.), who would be 'liberating' or 'saving' the twelve tribes (Matthew 19:28/Luke 22:28–30).[13]

It is typical of many so-called 'millenarian movements' that the impending change is described only allusively in the Gospel. Luke includes many parables of the kingdom but he does not provide a detailed brochure of what the kingdom will be like. There is more than one reason for this (perhaps rather surprising) absence of information. In the first place articulation of the demand for change is generally more important for millenarian prophets than providing a catalogue of the projected benefits. This is because the crucial thing in such movements is the achievement of enough cohesion to articulate dissatisfaction in a society which does not encourage protest. Luke advocates the vision of the kingdom as something being realized. He draws attention to the need for change in his succession of binary opposites. The vision of the future, and not its actual blueprint, inspires him.

The second reason for the absence of detailed information lies in the early Christian belief that the future lies in the plan and intention of God. This means that it cannot be second-guessed by human beings. Luke continues to advocate belief in the return of Jesus and constructs a scheme of eschatology in which this is seen as the decisive event. It doubtless seemed presumptuous to speculate in detail on what God's intervention would bring. Luke retains a properly biblical emphasis on judgment but follows the Hebrew writers in his reluctance to force God's hand by saying how God will act. At present, the disciples of Jesus must question the beliefs and assumptions of their society. In the future, God will intervene in the person of the Lord Jesus and do what human beings cannot do, by rooting out the causes of oppression — which Luke leaves no doubt are the powerful people (1.52) – and by removing patriarchy in its entirety, replacing it with the messianic kingdom of his Son.

JEWS AND GENTILES IN LUKE

Luke unquestionably reflects Jewish eschatological beliefs. We have seen this in 13.34–5. Chapter 22 develops this approach when, in 22.20, Jesus says that his death inaugurates the new covenant, which for Luke has clear eschatological overtones (not least in terms of the forgiveness of sins); and in 22.30, where Jesus designates the tribal heads of the restored Israel in advance of his forthcoming death. Luke cannot be understood at all without a recognition of what these Jewish hopes contribute to the plot.

It is certain also that Luke takes an interest in the Gentiles. Whether or not he is *more* interested in the Gentiles than are the other Synoptists (which has sometimes been claimed) is less important than the demonstration that, for Luke, the Gentiles are assessed as regards salvation in precisely the same terms as the Jews. Time and again in the Gospel it is the faith which people show in Jesus which results in their healing. This is perhaps most obvious in the statement of the Roman centurion in chapter 7, 'say the word and my servant will be cured' (7.7), to which Jesus responds: 'not even in Israel have I found such faith' (7.9). That the demand for faith is such a frequent element in the miracles reminds the reader that *this* is the way in which one gains initial entry to the Christian community. The same is true in Acts. In Acts 14.9 the Lystran cripple is said to be healed because he has the faith (*sc.* in Jesus) that he will be cured. It is implied that, without such faith, there would be no cure. There is even perhaps the sense in which is true to say that, for Luke, the miracles are parables of what it means to receive salvation in Jesus. Those whom Jesus heals are types, by which I mean undeveloped characters, whose healing shows that the eschatological vision of Isaiah 61 (4.18–19) is being realized. It is implied that, in responding well to Jesus, these people respond to the kingdom of God. They are included in the Christian community because that community is made up of people who have faith in Jesus.

The question that has often been asked is whether Luke sees the Gentiles as the *replacement* for the Jews as God's people and where in consequence the Jews fit into Luke's economy of salvation. Some scholars think that Luke makes the *Gentiles* the chosen people of God and regards the Jews as excluded from the original divine promise to Israel.[14] This seems to me an incautious assessment of the evidence. It is based especially on two passages in Acts. Acts 13.46 reports the words of Paul and Barnabas: 'It was necessary . . . that the word of God should be declared to you first. But since you reject it and judge yourselves unworthy of eternal life, we now turn to the Gentiles.' 18.6 is similar in tone. Paul says: 'From now on I shall go to the Gentiles!' But this is not the complete picture of the Jews and the Gentiles which emerges from Luke's corpus. A different attitude is suggested by two other passages. In the *Nunc Dimittis* Simeon states that the coming of Jesus is an act of deliverance which represents 'a light that will bring revelation to the Gentiles, and glory to your people Israel' (Luke 2.32). Here, the Gentiles and Israel are mentioned as parallel constructs, quite without the belief that the one has supplanted the other. At the end of Acts, Paul 'proclaimed the kingdom of God and taught the facts about the Lord Jesus Christ quite openly and without hindrance' (Acts 28.31). This is after Luke says that he has preached to the local Jewish leaders (Acts 28.17). Of the results of this preaching it is said: 'Some were won over by his arguments; others remained unconvinced' (Acts 28.24). Acts closes with Paul preaching as much to the Jews as to the Gentiles and with an acknowledged Jewish response in Rome. One can hardly conclude from this that Luke thinks the Jews are left behind in God's offer of salvation. They continue to feature there, otherwise Paul's preaching to them is inexplicable. Acts 13.46 is probably better understood as a declaration of Paul's mission policy and not as a theological statement that the Jews have been excluded from the kingdom.[15]

Luke is nevertheless emphatic that the eschatological climax will take place according to a fundamentally Jewish scheme. This scheme is determined by the fulfilment of Hebrew prophecy where hopes about the temple and the restoration of the tribes predominate. The impression gained from this, as from Paul in Romans 9–11, is that the Gentiles are not so much the replacement for Israel as their concomitants whose inclusion is itself the fulfilment of prophecy. The Gentiles are incorporated in salvation because this is what Jewish eschatological tradition believed would happen at the end-time. This does not mean, either that the Jews are excluded from salvation, or that the eschatological hope has been transferred from its fundamentally Jewish context. Luke, like Paul, places Jews and Gentiles on an equal footing before God and makes the response of faith in Jesus determinative. This is a direct fulfilment of the context in which the words in 19.46a ('my house shall be a house of prayer') were originally spoken: 'So too with the foreigners who give their allegiance to me, to minister to me and love my name and become my servants, all who keep the sabbath unprofaned and hold fast to my covenant: these shall I bring to my holy hill and give them joy in my house of prayer. Their offerings and sacrifices will be acceptable on my altar; for my house will be called a house of prayer for all nations' (Isaiah 56.6–7). The Gentiles, included in salvation with the Jews, form part of the prophetic hope that is cited by Jesus himself.

It would be rash, therefore, to suggest that Luke sees Israel as excluded from its original status as the people of God. Having said this, the status of the people of God is undoubtedly redefined in the Gospel. The Gentiles now form as much part of God's people as the Jews. The only relevant criterion is that of faith. The tribal presidents are nevertheless all Jewish (22.30). This is an indication of the way that Jewish structures continue to dominate Luke's eschatology.

AN ESSAY IN THE HISTORY OF SALVATION?

One of the most influential approaches to Luke has been Hans Conzelmann's suggestion that the Gospel embodies an understanding of 'salvation history' where God's salvific action is broken up into three discernible stages: 'We see also how, by removing the End to a greater distance, a more reflective attitude emerges, as a result of which the individual events are separated. This development is parallel to the other developments, by which the past is broken up into its separate component parts. Thus we see how the whole story of salvation, as well as the life of Jesus in particular, is now objectively set out and described according to its successive stages.'[16] The three stages which Conzelmann has in mind are the periods of Israel, Jesus and the church. This scheme determines the original German title of Conzelmann's book which, if translated literally into English, is called 'The Middle of Time'.

Part of the force of Conzelmann's argument rests with the fact of Acts. Acts was rather obviously conceived as a companion to the Gospel. This implies that Luke thought the writing of the Gospel by itself was not enough. Acts notionally describes the history of the primitive church but the portrait is a selective one and we have seen that Luke's writing of history as such is by no means necessarily an indication of his belief in the substantially delayed return from heaven of Jesus. I have argued that the conclusion of Acts with Paul's preaching in Rome is itself an eschatological sign. The whole history that Acts tells is an eschatological one. The accent in the two-volumed series falls much more on 'the events that have taken place among us' (Luke 1.1) than on the unspecified period which must elapse before the end. This retrospective interest is confirmed by my reading of Luke 21 where Luke presents many of the eschatological signs as accomplished already.

It is certainly true to say that Luke discerns different stages in the redemptive process. This is illustrated most obviously by 16.16: 'The law and the prophets were until John: since then, the good news of the kingdom of God is proclaimed, and everybody forces a way in.' This verse distinguishes the period of the kingdom of God from the history of Judaism which preceded it. John is ranked with the law and the prophets on the grounds that he heralds the kingdom (although he is not thereby *excluded* from the kingdom). The kingdom of God is distinguished from earlier Judaism (with the qualification introduced by 16.17) because it represents the eschatological age, not least in terms of the social convictions that Jesus articulates. This verse seems to acknowledge *two* crucial periods in Jewish history, not three. The decisive change comes with Jesus for with him the kingdom of God is held to be present. The preaching of the church is a continuation of the mission of Jesus and not a *tertium genus* for it stands on the same side of the divide established by 16.16. The end of Acts will show that history is moving towards its conclusion and offers little support for the view that the end will be substantially delayed.

The distinction between 'then' and 'now' in 16.16 is thus the key to Luke's understanding of history. Although Luke recognizes that the (earthly) life of Jesus lay in the past, and that his return is taking longer to happen than had been expected, it is probably wrong to distinguish too precisely between the time of Jesus and the period of the church in his work. Both of them belong to the eschatological age. The conclusions of Luke's two books show that different stages in the eschatological process have been completed. At the end of Luke, the kingdom has been announced and the new covenant inaugurated. By the end of Acts, the offer of salvation has been made in the Roman capital and the Gentiles are included in the offer of salvation. This means that the age is drawing towards its eschatological climax. The real distinction in Luke is between the periods of Judaism and of Christianity, its eschatological fulfilment.

One should therefore perhaps beware of Conzelmann's *three*-age scheme given the contention of this book that Luke has not abandoned an imminent eschatology.

LUCAN ETHICS

We have seen that Luke includes a fair amount of ethical teaching. This is distributed across the Gospel, sometimes in concentrated passages. Ethics in Luke are mostly attributed to Jesus as speaker. Luke is not first and foremost a compendium of Christian ethics but a Gospel which tells a story. The ethical sections form one part of that narrative. They reveal the authority of Jesus as a teacher from the recent past whose words are decisive for the readers of the Gospel. The ethics cohere with and support the Gospel's central theme that the kingdom of God has arrived. They have no meaning apart from this consideration.

The ethics of Luke's Jesus are grounded in eschatology. An example of this is Jesus' attitude to the question of divorce. Moses permitted divorce for unchastity in Deuteronomy 24.4. The historical Jesus never, so far as we know, annulled the Mosaic regulation. Luke records him as intensifying it. In 16.18, Jesus says that: 'a man who divorces his wife and marries another commits adultery; and anyone who marries a woman divorced from her husband commits adultery'. The implication of this saying is that, in the Christian dispensation, those who become divorced are not free to remarry. This apparently 'hard-line' attitude is probably to be understood against the backcloth of the belief that the kingdom was impending. The nearness of the kingdom challenges human relationships and leads to the belief that marital relationships represent a complication in view of its imminence.

Luke retains belief in the return of Jesus despite his acknowledgement of delay (19.11). This consciousness of delay does in fact affect his presentation of ethics, as we can see for instance in 17.3b–4 which I have suggested represents the beginning of a Christian penitential system. Nevertheless, concepts such as patience (8.15) and readiness (21.36) are crucial ones in the Gospel. Readers are constantly reminded that, since they do not know when the Son of Man will appear, they must hold themselves in readiness lest they be excluded from the kingdom. It is doubtless also true to say that these Lucan virtues lend themselves to a somewhat different interpretation once the hope for the imminent consummation of eschatology recedes into the background. They pass over into the cardinal virtues which the Christian tradition has long enjoined. In this sense, Luke does much to resource the subsequent tradition. We should not, however, let this observation obscure the original eschatological focus of his ethics.

In Acts one finds that, as in Paul, the concept of the indwelling Spirit is the major ethical impetus. The Spirit is God's gift to replace the ascended Jesus in the Christian communities (Luke 24.49). Time and again in Acts we read of the Spirit motivating the followers of Jesus in their mission and evangelism. His working is accompanied by powerful miracles. Perhaps it is true to say that this dimension is not so prominent in Luke. One might be tempted to explain this difference with reference to a passage from the Fourth Gospel: 'The Spirit had not yet been given, because Jesus had not yet been glorified' (John 7.39). Luke preserves the historical sense that the Spirit is given only *after* the ascension of Jesus. The Spirit in Luke resides especially with Jesus and inspires his proclamation of the kingdom. It is important to observe, however, that references to the Spirit helping Christian believers are not entirely absent there. 12.12 says of believers on trial for their faith in Jesus: 'When the time comes the Holy Spirit will instruct you what to say'. Here, we find the perspective of the Acts of the Apostles read back into the Gospel of Luke.

An area for special consideration is the question of what extent Luke regards the Jewish Law (with its moral, as well as other, precepts) as binding on his readers. 16.17 states that the Law is by no means abrogated but in practice it plays little part in what Jesus tells his disciples. There is an obvious difference here from what Matthew's Jesus says in Matthew chapter 5. The emphasis in Luke falls much more strongly on *Jesus* as the teacher of ethical principles. Perhaps this is more a reflection of Luke's orientation to the Hellenistic world than a fundamental antipathy to the Law of Moses. The different orientation is evident again in the Lucan regulation about divorce (16.18). Jesus says (16.17) that 'it is easier for heaven and earth to come to an end than for one letter of the law to lose its force'; but he goes on to offer his own regulation about divorce which represents an intensification of the Mosaic rule, and not a simple continuation of it (16.18). Luke here shows no interest in the contemporary rabbinic understanding of Moses which is the major feature of the Matthaean treatment of the question of divorce (Matthew 5.31–2). If Luke writes with a knowledge of Matthew, we should probably regard this as a qualification of Matthew's perspective in this respect. The qualification shows a willingness to set rabbinic debate to one side and to present Jesus as an ethical teacher whose sayings relate to the kingdom of God.

Ethical teaching is imparted also by the narrative in Luke. The parable of the good Samaritan demonstrates the need for love (as a criterion that over-rides other distinctions). The parable of Dives and Lazarus warns against the selfish love of riches which promotes the disenfranchisement of others. Ethical admonition seems to be the point of parables such as these. They demonstrate the kind of behaviour that is appropriate to the kingdom.

Although it is wrong to call Luke a political 'tract', still less a 'manifesto', the Gospel does include material which explains that the Romans (and all educated pagans) have nothing to fear from the Christians. The background to this strand is the general suspicion in which the Christians were held in the first century. Luke records Jesus as teaching that Caesar should receive his due (20.25) and he insists that Pilate, Herod and more than one Roman centurion find Jesus an innocent and even an admirable character. We should probably not suppose that Luke was written for those beyond the Christian community but the fact that such information is included shows that the Gospel addresses important questions of civic loyalty and service, given that Christians saw themselves as members of the kingdom *of God* who awaited a heavenly Messiah. Luke advocates a civic conservatism in which Christians, in their attitude to the state, are told to accept things as they are — but with the scarcely veiled indication that a change is impending which supplies the logic for the Christian questioning of the values of the social order.

Finally, we must consider the extent to which Luke's ethical stance represents a change from the ethical position likely to have been advanced by the historical Jesus. I argued earlier that Jesus' ethics were dominated by the belief that the kingdom of God represented an alternative model of society: one in which the traditional concept of patriarchy, with its basis in the village unit of rural Palestine, was being replaced by the new belief in mutuality and the fatherhood of God. The basis of Pauline Christianity, to which Luke's Gospel is clearly related, is the city and not the Palestinian village. The kind of society one finds in the Asian cities was rather different from Palestine. Christianity in the Roman cities was principally fostered in 'the household'. A Roman 'household' was a much broader entity than the modern European 'nuclear family'. It included slaves, former slaves, business associates and tenants. Wayne Meeks describes the archaeological evidence for such households which has been discovered in Pompeii and on Delos: 'The floor plans of some of the houses that have been excavated . . . can be read as a physical diagram of some of these relationships: private rooms and offices for the head of the house; a section of the house probably for the women or children; apartments for slaves; rented rooms; on the street side a shop or two, perhaps a tavern or even a hotel, sometimes connecting with the atrium; and, centrally located, a dining room in which the *paterfamilias* might enjoy the company of his equals and friends from other households, or entertain his *clientela*, or do both at once (with each assigned his fitting place).'[17]

We can make sense of a passage such as 14.26 (the call to hate one's family) on the lips of Jesus under the assumption that he is speaking in hyperbolic terms about the renewal of society and not about relations between individuals as such. One wonders, however, what Luke's urban readers would have made of the command to hate one's family for the sake of the kingdom. The verse has been compared with a Greek philosophical tradition, reaching back to Socrates, which devalues family loyalties in the name of a single-minded devotion to truth. That does not, however, make it any easier to translate 14.26 into the language of city social relations in the first century. The palpable fact is that Pauline Christians derived much support from their 'households', or families, and that these were the nucleus of the religion as it developed in the Hellenistic cities. It is probably true to say that certain aspects of Jesus' ethics proved as confusing in the first century as they do today. This confusion was due to the shift from the village to the urban setting which happened as Christianity expanded beyond the confines of Palestine.

Luke himself is not unmindful of this shift. One of his favourite images is the dinner-party where Jesus sits and talks, and sometimes works miracles. This presents Jesus in the familiar Hellenistic guise of the teacher. It is here that much ethical teaching is imparted. The first half of chapter 14 is an example of this approach. Jesus is dining with a Pharisee when he notices guests trying to secure the places of honour (14.7). He tells the parable of the wedding feast in which the host demotes a guest. This leads to the conclusion (14.11) that 'everyone who exalts himself will be humbled; and whoever humbles himself will be exalted'. The conclusion is reinforced in the saying about inviting the poor, the crippled, the lame and the blind (14.13) which directly echoes the citation of Isaiah 61 in 4.18–19. It is in turn followed by another parable of a wedding feast which the original guests refuse to attend (14.15–25).

The fact that Luke is so conspicuously interested in parties shows how far the ethics of the city undergird his Gospel. Jesus appears here as a dinner-party speaker who uses dinner-party illustrations to undergird the call for humility. This suggests rather strongly that the call for the abandonment of household structures has not been heeded. We do not know the precise circumstances to which Luke's Gospel was addressed but I have suggested (following Dawsey) that they were such that the author deemed the readers in need of a reminder about humility and service. 14.11 to this extent appears to stand at the ethical heart of the Gospel. Characteristically, Luke repeats it in 18.14 to reinforce the call for humility in the minds of his readers.

It is fascinating to speculate on how 14.11 might be translated into concrete social terms as regards the Lucan communities. It presupposes a situation where some had tried to claim a greater position than they were entitled to. We must ask who is criticized here. It is tempting initially to conclude that the saying is set against the relatively poor who are trying to use Christian commonality as an excuse for acting above their station. But this conclusion must almost certainly be resisted. It is not normal for slaves to be invited to a wedding feast. They generally wait on tables. Those who are criticized by the parable are more likely the middle-placed people who think they have much to gain by contact with the *paterfamilias*. The parable potentially applies to the *paterfamilias* too for one can conceive of situations where he would be a relatively junior member of a social gathering. The parable and the appended saying are more likely addressed to those nearer the top of the Christian household than at the bottom. They warn such people not to presume on their social superiority in dealing with other people, including members of their own household. This brings Luke close to what Paul says in Galatians 3.28 that 'there is no such thing as Jew and Greek, slave and free, male and female; for you are all one person in Christ Jesus'. The lesson which Christian households had to learn, apparently, was that social position was a subordinate factor to the common status that one enjoyed in Christ. (We should observe, however, that it evidently never occurred to the early Christians that slavery should be abolished.)

THE TEMPLE

I return, finally, to the temple which I have held to be a major theme in Luke. The question arises of why Jesus should express such vehemence towards the holy building. Part, but only part, of the answer lies in the observation that he is following the precedent of Jeremiah. In order to understand the full reason for his antipathy, we must consider the comparatively short history of the building in question.

The first temple was built by Solomon in the tenth century BCE. It was subject to continual alteration during the four centuries of its existence and destroyed by the Babylonians in 587 BCE. When the Israelites returned from exile in 537 BCE the temple remained desolate while other parts of the city were rebuilt. This is the situation criticized by Haggai whose chiding was instrumental in the reconstruction of the temple in 520 BCE. This temple in turn was desecrated by Antiochus Epiphanes in the second century BCE (the event described in the book of Daniel). It was rededicated and progressively fortified under the Hasmonaean dynasty. This, however, did not prevent its invasion by Pompey in 63 BCE nor its capture by Herod the Great in 37 BCE.

Herod set about rebuilding the temple according to a grandiose scheme. Although he decided, on the basis of the Hebrew Bible, that the temple building must have the same dimensions as its predecessor, he decided to raise the platform to create an immense edifice that dwarfed what had stood there before. The temple itself took only eighteen months to construct. The whole project, by contrast, took forty-six years as we know from John 2.20.

This means that Herod's grand design was finished barely years before the ministry of Jesus. Herod did not live to see it finished. This is the temple that Luke mentions. Its construction would have been a familiar sight to everyone who journeyed to Jerusalem, as Jesus did. The temple to this extent was the living and permanent embodiment of the Herodian dynasty. It symbolized the burden of taxation which had been imposed to fund its erection (cf. Josephus *Ant.* 17.205, 317–21). Herod even plundered David's tomb and stole 3,000 talents to do this (Josephus *Ant.* 16.179–82). One can imagine that Jesus might have developed a natural antipathy to the Herodian temple because it was a living demonstration of an order which he considered exploitative and unsavoury. This might in turn explain why he condemned the present temple in 13.35, and hoped for a perfect replacement which God would introduce. The exploitative nature of the social structures in first-century Palestine must not be ignored in the attempt to reconstruct the background to the Gospels. They do much to explain why Luke says that the temple must be replaced (but not, significantly, removed).

Chapter 6

A reading of readings

The final chapter of this book sets out to examine some of the, by now, quite substantial secondary literature on Luke. Only a zealous research student can honestly claim to have read everything that there is. I am happy to plead my own deficiency in this area. The tide of scholarship has not begun to recede. If anything, the breakers are coming in even faster than before.[1] What follows is therefore a selective reading which examines only some of the books and commentaries that have been produced in the wake of Conzelmann. I hope, however, that I have managed to include many of the important works. I shall try to explain briefly what they say and in places add my own commentary to the argument. I begin with books about Luke and proceed at the end of the chapter to commentaries on Luke.

CONZELMANN (1953, 1960)

No-one who makes a serious study of Luke can ignore the work of Hans Conzelmann. Conzelmann's *Die Mitte der Zeit* (1953), which was translated into English under the title *The Theology of St Luke* (1960), advocates a view of the Gospel as having abandoned imminent eschatology in favour of a view of 'salvation history' in which the period of the church is regarded as a substantial one and the return of Jesus far from an imminent possibility. In this context Conzelmann draws attention to Lucan ethics, particularly the virtue of endurance, as an important factor which sustained the church during a period of persecution.

It is not perhaps said often enough that Conzelmann's book does not make for easy reading. It is neither a guide to Luke's thought nor a full-scale commentary on Luke (or reading of Luke) but a redaction-critical study which examines the way that Luke handles his received material to produce a new story about Jesus. The following sentence is typical of Conzelmann's approach. In his discussion of Luke 21 Conzelmann observes: 'Whereas Mark goes on to give a fuller description of the eschatological events, Luke now gives a polemical excursus about matters which are mistakenly included among the eschatological events, namely the destruction of Jerusalem and the Temple. In this way eschatology is lifted out of any historical context, and is removed from all events which take place within history. Thus the apocalyptic allusion in Mark xiii, 14 disappears, because one cannot "read" of such a thing (N.B. Luke's concept of Scripture) and because it has nothing to do with the Eschaton' (p.128).

Here Conzelmann explains how Luke modifies Mark to provide a new explanation of eschatology. Leaving aside the question of whether Conzelmann is right in his exegesis of Luke 21, the citation shows his redactional interest lies in Luke's handling of his sources. For a generation that is accustomed to a broader style of interpretation this approach can seem a little specialized or even restricted.

Conzelmann's book falls into five parts. The first part is a study of 'geographical elements in the composition of Luke's Gospel' (pp. 18–94). Here, the author offers an exegetical study which notes the main features of the text. No conclusion as such is offered; the material has the air of a preliminary exegesis which paves the way for further discussion.

The second part (pp. 95–136) deals with the question of Luke's eschatology. Here Conzelmann advances his well-known thesis that a change has taken place in Luke's understanding of the 'last days'. 'If we wish to see the peculiar features of his conception,we have to reckon with discrepancies between the ideas in the sources and his own ideas. . . . For example, in the quotation from Joel in the story of Pentecost (Acts ii, 17ff.), the Spirit is thought of as a sign of the End, in the source and also in Luke, but the interpretation is different in each case. In their original sense the "last days" have not yet been expanded into a longer epoch, which is what happens in Luke's conception of the Spirit and of the Church. . . . The Spirit Himself is no longer the eschatological gift, but the substitute in the meantime for the possession of ultimate salvation' (p. 95). By this Conzelmann means that Luke has altered his received understanding of eschatology to accord with his own belief that the return of Jesus will be delayed. 'As the End is still far away, the adjustment to a short time of waiting is replaced by a "Christian life" of long duration, which requires ethical regulation and is no longer dependent upon a definite termination' (p. 132).

This view is developed in part 3 of the book which Conzelmann calls 'God and Redemptive History' (pp. 137–69). 'As the life of the world continues, there arise certain problems concerning the relation of the Church to its environment, which had remained hidden at the beginning because of the belief that the End was imminent. It is a question mainly of the relationship of the Church with Judaism and with the Empire. . . . Luke . . . lays as the foundation of his defence of the Church a comprehensive consideration of its general position in the world; he fixes its position in respect of redemptive history and deduces from this the rules for its attitude to the world. This is an original achievement' (p. 137). Conzelmann argues further (p. 150) that Luke thinks history has three phases: the period of Israel, represented by the Law and the Prophets; the period of Jesus, which gives a foretaste of future salvation; and the period between the coming of Jesus and his Parousia or return, the age of the church and the Spirit, which Luke never says will be short. This places Jesus in the centre of history, hence the original German title of the book. Conzelmann thinks that only the *idea* of the people of God, and not the details of Israel's history, are found in Luke's interpretation so that the church is now the people of God (p.167).

Part 4 ('The Centre of History', pp. 170–206) deals with the place of Jesus in the divine purpose. For Luke Jesus is already on earth Christ, Son and Lord (p. 176) but his subordinate position to God is maintained as a matter of principle (p. 177). The ascension is a critical moment because it marks the limit of Jesus' stay on earth and the beginning of his heavenly reign. From now on, Jesus needs a substitute for his 'real presence', which is supplied by the Spirit who is given to the church (p. 204). Conzelmann notes, I think correctly, that '[Luke] is no longer aware of the original peculiarities of titles such as "Son of Man", etc. He has taken them over from the tradition and interprets them according to his own conceptions' (pp. 170–1). 'The complex of events, Resurrection–Ascension–Pentecost, forms a clear division between the two epochs. Before his exaltation Christ is the only bearer of the Spirit, but in a special sense, for he is not under the Spirit. . . . His endowment with the Spirit is differentiated from the later outpouring upon the community by the very manner in which the Spirit appears. He comes to him in "bodily form". Jesus is not baptized "with fire", as is the community' (p.179). 'The place of Jesus in the course of redemptive history does not depend on any idea of pre-existence . . . In the foreground stands the definition of the relation to Israel and, of course, to the subsequent period of the Church' (p.185).

The fifth and final part of the book assesses the theme of 'Man and Salvation: The Church' (pp. 207–34). 'Luke does not directly define the position of the individual in the course of redemptive history. Instead his position is defined as a mediated one, for he stands within the Church, and thereby in a definite phase of the story. The Church transmits the message of salvation. . . . This transmission by the Church makes it possible for the individual's remoteness in time from the saving events of past and future, from the time of Jesus and from the Parousia, to be no hindrance to him. Instead of the nearness of these events there is the Church with its permanent function. In the Church we stand in a mediated relationship to the saving events . . . and at the same time in an immediate relationship to them, created by the Spirit, in whom we can invoke God and the name of Christ; in other words, the Spirit dwells in the Church, and is imparted through its means of grace and its office-bearers' (p. 208). The church constitutes the third historical period and its life is determined by persecution (pp. 209–10). 'Both the content of the proclamation and also the act of proclaiming are described in stereotype concepts which are current in the Church and therefore do not require any closer definition by the one who employs them' (p. 218). Conzelmann proceeds to examine these stereotyped phrases (pp. 218–25). 'With the decline of the expectation of an imminent Parousia, the theme of the message is no longer the coming of the Kingdom, from which the call to repentance arises of its own accord, but now, in the time of waiting, the important thing is the "way" of salvation, the "way" into the Kingdom. . . . Here Luke gives greater attention to the individual element in the hope, the personal assurance of one's resurrection, than to the cosmological element. The message to man reveals to him his situation, by informing him of the Judgement to come and by revealing the fact that he is a sinner' (p. 227). 'The fact of the future life is no longer dependent on the imminence of God's reign; and as a promise it can surmount the passage of time' (p. 230).

Conzelmann's book draws attention to the issue of eschatology as the most significant theme that Luke reworks from his sources. Conzelmann argues that Luke does this because he is writing for a time when the delayed return of Jesus was coming to be accepted, albeit with resignation. The emergence of a new situation means that a different response is needed than that provided by the earlier Gospel(s). Luke's shift in understanding has the effect of placing the historical Jesus in the *middle* of history, not in its immediate climax, and of drawing attention to the church as the body that proclaims the message of salvation and is guided by the Holy Spirit who replaces the ascended Jesus on earth.

My reading of Luke takes a different view of his eschatology. I agree with Conzelmann that Luke, like all primitive Christian writers, maintains a prudent ambiguity about when Jesus will return but I think that the references to delay are retrospective and do not necessarily anticipate a further hiatus. I base my argument on chapters 19 and 21 in particular. 19.11–27 is a story told by Jesus about the noblemen who goes on a long journey. This story counters the view that the kingdom of God will appear when Jesus reaches Jerusalem (19.11). I think this refers the 'long journey' of 19.12 to the period between the ministry of Jesus and the readers' own present. This is why the emphasis falls on the certainty of the nobleman's return as king (19.15) and the judgment that will ensue from this. The parable implicitly warns the readers to expect the king's return given that his absence has been a long one. I cannot but find an implied note of imminence here. The warning of judgment also seems set against the view that there will be a further delay. I thus agree with Conzelmann that 19.11 is a significant verse for Lucan eschatology but disagree with him about the time to which it refers.

Nor can I agree with Conzelmann's interpretation of Luke 21. Conzelmann thinks that 'eschatology is lifted out of any historical context, and is removed from all events which take place within history' (p.128). My exegesis, by contrast, shows that chapter 21 is conceived with history fully in mind. The focal point of the chapter, which determines its interpretation, is 21.6–7. Here Jesus predicts that the stones of the temple will be cast down. The disciples ask when this will happen. Jesus replies with the Lucan version of the Synoptic eschatological discourse. 21.6 must not be confused with the Roman destruction of Jerusalem which is mentioned by 21.20. 21.20 has the form of an historical review and describes an event which has taken place already. The destruction of Jerusalem is thereby made a *sign* of the end. It is followed in Luke's scheme by portents in the heavens (21.25) which are said to herald the Son of Man's return from heaven (21.27). The discourse concludes with the comment: 'when all of this begins to happen, stand upright and hold your heads high, because your liberation is near' (21.28).

This progress of thought means that, far from excluding the historical past from eschatology, Luke makes it part of the signs of the end. Luke alone of the Synoptists includes a reference to the Roman destruction of Jerusalem. This addition is a striking one. It makes the recent past a sign that Jesus will return. The key to understanding the chapter lies in the recognition that 21.6 must be interpreted with reference to 13.35 and 20.17 and not to 21.20. Eschatology dominates the picture, and the picture is constructed on the basis of an historical review.

I have also criticized Conzelmann's view that the Lucan churches are characterized by 'persecution'. This needs more cautious statement. It is inaccurate to speak of Roman persecution of the Christians in the first century (except for 64 CE). This includes the reign of Domitian where the evidence for a formal persecution is scanty. There was, no doubt, local Jewish agitation throughout the first century and perhaps other sporadic opposition. But whether this can be called 'persecution' is an open question and I should prefer to use the phrase 'local opposition'. An accurate picture of Luke's churches must also examine recent research, especially that undertaken by Wayne Meeks, about the social position of the Christians in the cities of the Roman empire. There was something in their self-understanding which encouraged the maintenance of high social boundaries in respect of outsiders. These were reinforced by the rituals of the Christian religion, not least by the ritual of baptism. We should not confuse the Christian sense of being a small, rather inward-looking community with the experience of persecution – especially not on the basis of the minority consciousness that emerges from much Christian literature.

I have also raised questions about Conzelmann's view of Lucan ethics and ecclesiology. I am by no means convinced that Luke has removed the eschatological basis of the ethical imperative although I accept that in places eschatology is not heavily foregrounded in the demand for ethical action. I think that the Beatitudes and Woes in chapter 6 represent the heart of Luke's ethical teaching. The reason given there for adopting humble behaviour is that only this will secure final membership of the kingdom of God. That ethics are related to the kingdom, as they are in the Lord's Prayer, is left in no doubt by this passage. The correlative of ethical laxity is eschatological judgment by the Son of Man (9.26). Luke warns his readers about this point (13.25b).

BARRETT (1961)

The next year C. K. Barrett published his short book, *Luke the Historian in Recent Study* (London: Epworth Press, 1961). This book, as its title suggests, is an examination of Luke's claim to write history. Barrett spawned a succession of later studies, not the least of which is Loveday Alexander's work on the Lucan Preface which I mentioned in Chapter 1. Barrett's book is now perhaps rather dated; but it deserves study because of its articulation of a well-known case, and also for its discussion of literature which had previously been available only in German.

MARSHALL (1970)

We jump almost a decade to consider the work of Howard Marshall. Marshall's book has in some sense been superseded by later literature but I mention it here because it continues to be used by students; especially by those of an Evangelical persuasion.

Marshall includes a discussion of the nature of history and a review of Luke's qualities as an historian. The answer that Marshall reaches is (predictably) a conservative one. Against those, like J. C. Hurd, who question the historical value of Acts as a source for early Christianity, Marshall comments: 'we do not want to make exaggerated claims for his reliability, nor to suggest that his views of the historian's task were identical with those of the modern historian. But it is unfair to suggest that he is a thoroughly tendentious and unreliable writer, freely rewriting the history of the early church in the interests of his own theology . . . there is in our judgment sufficient evidence in his favour to demand a more positive evaluation of his historical ability' (p. 75).

It is worth mentioning in this connection, although it technically lies beyond the scope of this book, that the question of the reliability of the Lucan writings has been examined much more recently in a collection of studies published under the auspices of Tyndale House in Cambridge with which Marshall has connections. The question of 'Acts and the Ancient Historical Monograph' is examined by Darryl W. Palmer in the volume edited by B. W. Winter and A. D. Clarke, *The Book of Acts in its Ancient Literary*

Setting (Grand Rapids: Eerdmans, 1993). The final volume in this series had yet to be published when this book was written.

JERVELL (1972)

I mention briefly the work of Jacob Jervell. His *Luke and the People of God* (Minneapolis: Augsburg, 1972) has in many ways also been superseded by later literature, but Jervell is a perceptive commentator whose insights deserve consideration. Jervell discusses the problem of 'the restoration of Israel and salvation for the Gentiles' (pp. 41–68), where he argues that Luke knows only one Israel, i.e. the Jewish people, so that the Gentile mission forms a difficult problem for him (p. 68). He thinks Luke argues that the apostles have already completed the mission to Jews: 'the conversion of Gentiles is itself a fulfilment of the promises to Israel so that the apostolic mission to Jews turns out indirectly to be Gentile mission' (p. 68).

The most interesting part of Jervell's book to me is the chapter entitled: 'The Twelve on Israel's thrones: Luke's understanding of the apostolate' (pp. 75–112). Here he argues for a link between the Twelve and Israel which I think is correct. In this context Jervell presents the church as the restored Israel.

WILSON (1973)

The other side of this picture is provided by Stephen G. Wilson. His book examines the question of *The Gentiles and the Gentile Mission in Luke-Acts* (SNTSMS 23; Cambridge: Cambridge University Press, 1973). Wilson shows how Luke justifies the Gentile mission by showing that it is 'rooted in the words of Jesus, as a promise in his earthly ministry and as a command after the Resurrection' (p. 243).

MADDOX (1982)

A book which I have long found useful is Robert Maddox's *The Purpose of Luke-Acts* (Edinburgh: T. & T. Clark, 1982). This book deals with many issues of Lucan interpretation, including questions of Luke's eschatology and setting, in a helpful and illuminating way. Not the least important part of the book is the way in which it summarizes scholarly literature in its different chapters on the period before the early 1980s. Maddox's view of Lucan eschatology is that Luke's emphasis lies in the reality of the present fulfilment of eschatological hopes (p. 145). He thinks that Luke was written to reassure the Christian community about the significance of the tradition of faith in which it stood: 'Luke encourages his readers not only to look forward with hope to the consummation of all things at the End, but also to appreciate that "salvation", the grace and power of God in action, is a *present reality* in which they already stand' (p. 187).

TALBERT (1982)

C. H. Talbert has written or edited several books on Luke but for our purposes the most significant is his *Reading Luke: A Literary and Theological Commentary on the Third Gospel* (1982). It is interesting that Talbert spends very little time on introductory preamble. There is, for instance, no initial attempt to explain the mechanics of the plot. Talbert is already reading Luke 1 on p. 7! This is not quite a sequential reading. Talbert arranges the Lucan material according to themes. Thus he places together all the material that deals with 'John, prototype of the Christian Evangelist'. Nor does it read the whole Gospel; I can see no discussion of 13.35 listed in the table of contents. Talbert's reading of Luke works from the belief that it belongs to the genre of ancient biography.

DAWSEY (1986)

Dawsey we have considered already. His book must be read by everybody who wants to gain a deeper understanding of Luke. Dawsey exposes the tensions in the narrative, especially the way in which the narrator adopts a different stance from the implied author.

SANDERS (1987)

I have already mentioned Jack Sanders' book on *The Jews in Luke-Acts*. This differs from earlier work on the subject (e.g. Jervell) in that it sees Luke as roundly condemning the Jews for their rejection of Jesus. Sanders sees Luke as supplying further evidence for the development of an anti-Jewish perspective in the literature of primitive Christianity.

ESLER (1987)

Esler (*Community and Gospel in Luke-Acts*) brings socio-scientific methodology to bear on the Lucan corpus. Esler sees Luke-Acts as written for a Christian community in a Hellenistic city of the Roman East, which was experiencing difficulties from within and opposition from without, which threatened its continued existence and unity. Esler thinks that this predicament originated largely in the very mixed nature of the individuals who comprised its membership. This mixture can be seen both on the axis of their prior religious affiliation, which ranged from pagan idolatry to conservative Judaism, and on the socio-economic axis, which extended from the wealth and power of senior Roman figures to the poverty of the city's beggar population.

Esler argues that Luke responded to the first of these problems by re-writing early Christian history to present the phenomenon of table-fellowship between Jews and Christians as inaugurated by Peter with divine permission. Luke responds to the second by intensifying the preference for the poor which he found in Mark and reassuring them of their privileged position in the scheme of salvation inaugurated by Jesus. On the political level, Luke's message for the Romans in his community is that there is no clash between Christianity and Rome. To this extent Luke's theology is moulded by the social and political forces that operated upon his community.

FITZMYER (1989)

An important introduction to the various Lucan themes is Fitzmyer's *Luke the Theologian: Aspects of his Teaching* (London: Geoffrey Chapman, 1989). This, as its title implies, considers some of the theological motifs that we encounter in the Gospel. Much of the material is covered in other books, although arguably rather less well. There is an interesting chapter on 'Mary in Lucan Salvation History' and another on 'the Lucan picture of John the Baptist as Precursor of the Lord'. It is unfortunate, perhaps, that Fitzmyer shows no knowledge of Dawsey's work. But his book is easy to read and serves as an admirable introduction to Lucan theology. It is not, however, in any sense a 'literary' reading of Luke.

GOULDER (1989)

Michael Goulder is an able and significant figure in British New Testament scholarship. His *Luke – A New Paradigm* falls within the province of redaction criticism. It follows that those who want a holistic commentary on Luke will be disappointed by this book. That is not what Goulder sets out to provide. On the other hand, those who are prepared to work through two detailed volumes will find a journey that is magisterially conducted with a conclusion powerfully argued. One does not have to agree with every aspect of Goulder's conclusion to recognize that this is a significant book. Its section-by-section analysis makes it much easier to read than, say, Conzelmann, who also writes from the perspective of redaction-criticism.

NEYREY (1991)

Jerome H. Neyrey has edited a valuable collection of essays in *The Social World of Luke-Acts: Models for Interpretation* (Peabody: Hendrickson, 1991). Study of the social world in which the different documents came to birth is an increasingly important aspect of New Testament research. Readers of Luke-Acts will find much to stimulate them here. Of particular interest are the essays by Malina and Neyrey on 'Honor and Shame in Luke-Acts: Pivotal Values of the Mediterranean World' (pp. 25–65); by Rohrbaugh on 'The Pre-industrial City in Luke-Acts: Urban Social Relations' (pp. 125–49); and by Robbins on 'The Social Location of the Implied Author of Luke-Acts' (pp. 305–32). The nature of this volume means that it ought to be required reading for those who want to gain a contemporary understanding of the Gospel.

FRANKLIN (1994)

The penultimate book to be considered is Eric Franklin's *Luke: Interpreter of Paul, Critic of Matthew* (1994). Franklin, like Goulder, is a senior British New Testament scholar who has spent much of his life teaching in a theological college. Franklin argues that Luke interprets Matthew (which, obviously, he therefore knew) but criticizes Paul. The nature and significance of Franklin's argument merits a little investigation.

Franklin begins his Pauline section with a study of Acts 15, the report of the so-called Jerusalem Conference. He cites F. F. Bruce's (rather grudging) admission that Paul may not actually have been at the Conference and poses the problem in the following way: 'Acts 15 is in every sense pivotal for Luke's picture of Paul in Acts. If he has got Paul to a meeting at which he was not present and doing something which he is wholly unlikely to have done – let alone going around and imposing that something on others – there seems little ground for defending the historicity of Luke's picture of Paul. In some way, the Paul of Acts is not the real Paul' (pp. 43–4).

This leads Franklin to conclude (chapter 3) that Luke has a clear understanding of Paul's position on the Law. This is that the Law no longer has a part in defining the boundaries of the people of God. The historical Paul did not accept the apostolic decree; the Paul of Acts by contrast does.

Luke makes Paul preach to Israel (chapter 4) for he (Luke) has a continuing concern with the Jewish people. The final section of Acts shows that Luke has not written the Jews off. 'There is nothing to suggest that Rome marks the end, either of God's concern, or of his mercy towards the Jews' (p. 103).

Franklin explains the prominence of Paul in Acts in the following way: 'Paul, then, is not climactic for Acts, let alone for Luke-Acts as a whole. He is rather supremely illustrative of the purpose of Luke-Acts. He is drawn into Luke's overall purpose which is to express his understanding of the significance of Jesus and of the events which have come about as a result of him . . . Luke's primary purpose was nothing less than a presentation of the truths of the gospel as he understood it' (p. 135).

Our interest here lies rather more with Franklin's evaluation of Matthew which he presents in the second half of the book. Franklin begins from the premise that both Gospels were addressed to mixed communities where what was a strong Jewish outlook was developing into a situation where the church was becoming predominantly Gentile in its concerns (p. 165). Luke is not hostile to his predecessors but he is critical of them in certain respects (pp. 171–2). The first area is in his treatment of the Pharisees. Luke is much less negative to them than Matthew or Mark (chapter 8). 'Luke sees the Pharisees, not as representatives of any contemporary group – though there was no doubt Pharisaic activity in his time – but as figures primarily from the past, as representatives of that group who by their piety, their zeal, their covenantal seriousness, and their response to Israel's election should have been those who would have been expected to respond to Jesus to see the Law and prophecy taken up and fulfilled in him. The tragedy is that they had not, that though they had a natural affinity with Jesus and with the proclamation about him, they had been unable to take on board the newness within the continuity that the coming of Jesus meant' (pp. 196–7). Luke chapter 11 differs from the Matthaean parallel (Matthew 23.1) because it is addressed directly to the Pharisees and not to the crowds and disciples *about* the Pharisees.

Allied to this is Luke's treatment of the Law (chapter 9). Luke sees Christianity as the fulfilment of Judaism in such a way as to make him detect an over-riding continuity between the two religions. Nevertheless, Luke is aware that the Mosaic regulations have been waived for Gentile converts to Christianity. This leads him to reshape much of the old as it is caught up in the new. That is evident especially in 16.16–17. 16.16 expresses the discontinuity between Judaism and Christianity. 16.17, however, puts constraints on the freedom offered by the new religion: 'The old must not be dismissed as outmoded. It must be caught up in the new and that means that the Law is not to be set aside, to be dismissed as of no consequence, as bringing nothing into the new age. Freedom from its rules must not be interpreted as licence to reject its outlook, it points to the means of love of God and neighbour' (p. 205). 'There is in Luke . . . something of a lightness of touch towards the Law as this is compared with Matthew on the one hand and with Paul and Mark on the other' (p. 211).

Luke has 'a less clearly defined division between Jesus and the people of Israel as a whole than does Matthew' (p. 212). The genealogy shows that 'his sonship has implications not only for all Israel but for all mankind. . . . Jesus is seen to be restoring the potentiality that is in Israel and in mankind as a whole' (p. 215). 'Luke's understanding of the attitude of God to Israel in the light of the coming of Jesus is set out in his account of the rejection at Nazareth which for him is, as is usually acknowledged, given programmatic significance (4.16–30)' (p. 225). Franklin criticizes (Jack) Sanders' interpretation of Luke 4 that it was written 'to show how God's will was carried out in the Jewish rejection of salvation and the consequent Gentile mission' (p. 226; citing Sanders, p. 168). Franklin himself offers a more moderate conclusion: 'Jesus is rejected by his people; they set out to destroy him; he however turns upon them to stop their intention from being realized and so to pass through them to go on his way' (p. 228). This means that

'Luke's telling of the story does not find its significance in Jesus' rejection of the Jews but in their rejection of him' (p. 229). The Nazareth episode indicates that 'Jewish rejection does not mean that all is brought to nothing' (p. 229). It is rather 'an attempt to understand and to counter the problems raised by the Jewish rejection of him' (p. 231).

Franklin next turns his attention to the problem of Lucan eschatology: 'the fact of Acts . . . does not mean that Luke has necessarily abandoned belief in an early parousia. . . . His story of the past means that the hope grounded on that past could as well have been a hope in an early parousia as in the continuation of the world and of history' (p. 259). 'The parousia . . . retains its place in Luke's expectations, and belief in its nearness continues to exercise a controlling influence over his understanding of the nature of the work of God in Christ and of the nature of Christian hope' (p. 263).

The final part of Franklin's book presents a survey of Luke's use of Matthew. He concludes that Luke *did* know Matthew and that his divergences from Matthew are in consequence significant. He adds, however, that 'Luke basically approved of neither the way Matthew resolved the historical difficulties encountered by his church nor the basic theological outlook which resulted from such a resolution' (p. 310). Franklin continues: 'While he regarded Mark's Gospel as a witness which merited great respect but which the passing of time made inadequate as a basis for commending continuing belief in Jesus in the light of new circumstances and changed problems, he found Matthew's attempt to meet the need posed by those very circumstances and problems inadequate, if not downright wrongheaded, in its resulting attitude to the Law, to the Jews, and in its eschatological interpretation of the present times. If Mark was inadequate and needed updating, Luke recognized Matthew as such an updating of Mark but one which in fact was misguided' (p. 311).

Franklin finds the basis of this unease in Luke's presentation of eschatology: 'Luke sees eschatology as being less realized in the present than does Matthew and he therefore accepts the parousia as having a positive role. It retains the aspect of hope in a way that Matthew's emphasis upon its judgmental role does not' (p. 312). Luke also disliked Matthew because it 'represented a tradition which had diverged forcefully from that expressed by his hero Paul' (p. 314).

Franklin explores these differences in the rest of his book. Chapter 14 examines the question of the discourses of Jesus in the two

Gospels, including of course the Lucan Sermon on the Plain (chapter 6). 'Luke's form of the sermon is best understood as a conscious reaction against that found in Matthew. It omits what its own understanding deems unacceptable' (p. 322). Chapter 15 studies the central section of Luke. Franklin cites the research of Evans and Moessner concerning the projected Deuteronomistic influence on Luke but concludes: 'In spite of the close Deuteronomistic connection, this is not enough to suggest that Deuteronomy of itself exerted the final control over the order of Luke's central section. Material in that section is linked to a Deuteronomic parallel but it is not wholly controlled by it. The closeness of parallelism does not extend throughout the narrative' (p. 336). He proceeds through the narrative and shows how and where the Matthaean viewpoint is corrected. Chapter 16 does the same for the Infancy and Resurrection narratives. Franklin concludes that 'Luke . . . is much clearer about the virginal conception than is Matthew' (p. 359).

Chapters 17 and 18 summarize the results of the study. 'Both the shape and the contents of Luke's Gospel are best explained on the supposition that Luke knew Matthew's Gospel as well as Mark's and that, while the latter was his primary source, he used Matthew as a second source with which to expand and update Mark' (p. 367). He assumes in this that a large question must be raised against the existence of Q (p. 369). Luke is consistently less hostile to the Jewish people than is Matthew; he is also somewhat less confident about the present (p. 371). His understanding of the significance of Jesus' life is very different, but his church situation is actually quite similar (pp. 371–2). So, too, Luke emphasizes the ascension in a way which Matthew does not (p. 375).

I warmly commend Franklin's book. Its style may be a little ponderous, but Franklin has devoted his entire career to study of the Lucan literature. Franklin is one of the major scholars with whom Lucan interpreters must reckon.

MOORE (1989, 1992, 1994)

Finally, Stephen Moore. I have mentioned Moore's work throughout this book and acknowledged what I have learned from it. I shall briefly explain what Moore's books contain and present my response to them.

Literary Criticism (1989) ought to be standard reading for everybody who is interested in this aspect of Gospel research. Moore has read widely in the field and presents his insights with wit and imagination. I particularly appreciated his introduction to narrative criticism (part I) which will help all readers of the Gospels to see the underlying philosophy of this approach and the presuppositions which it deconstructs. Part II is a series of readings of biblical literature which includes such topics as 'Do critics make or do they find?', and (most intriguingly) 'The failure of Johannine irony'. Here again is invaluable material for readers to ponder.

Moore's third book, *Poststructuralism* (1994), is again an important text. It offers an introduction to Derrida and Foucault and includes perceptive material on deconstruction and its value for Gospel scholarship. Moore takes on an earlier generation of literary critics, such as Culpepper, in his denial (p. 74) that the Fourth Gospel is an homogeneous and ordered text. Moore also introduces Foucault and his concern to show how discourses of knowledge produce the effects which they describe (pp. 83–117).

Moore's second book, *Mark and Luke* (1992), caused me the greatest problems of the three. Perhaps this is because I am myself a newcomer to poststructuralism. I wonder, however, whether Moore's undoubted wit and flair with words militates to some extent against the impact of his book. Consider the following sentence from the chapter entitled 'Look-Ax: Luke's Cutting Glance': 'But even if Look *is* God in his wor(l)d, Third Person of the Blessed Trinity – Author, Jesus, narrator – he nevertheless works a nine-to-five job. Thanks to the device of omnipresence, the Lucan Author can assume a secret identity in his written wor(l)d, can be transformed from a mere earwitness ("I have heard from some who were told by others who were there" – see Luke 1:2) into an eyewitness, can present the Good News as the Six O'Clock News. And the reader is made an eye-and-ear witness by extension, thanks to the roving camcorder and floating mike Luke has become' (p. 136). My problem with this is that, whatever one makes of the content, one is forever tripping over the words and images in a way that initially obscures, rather than advances, the flow of thought. Having said this, the book has many of the merits of Moore's two other volumes and many may find the style attractive. One wants to guard against the impression, however, of merely playing with words. This may prejudice some readers against a particular work of scholarship.

WHICH COMMENTARY SHOULD I USE?

And so to the question of commentaries. One of my personal favourites is that by Caird (1968) which is now unfortunately out of print. It is clear and concise but not a verse-by-verse exposition of the text. It has now been replaced by Evans (1990) which is longer than Caird's but follows the same format.

Among other commentaries students must choose between those by Roman Catholic and Evangelical writers. In the former category is the two-volume commentary by Joseph Fitzmyer (1981, 1985). This should be regarded as standard reading by anyone who is seriously interested in Luke. Marshall's commentary (1978) was for a long time also regarded as standard reading but it has now perhaps been replaced by the three volumes written by Nolland in the Word series (1989–93). Both contain invaluable bibliographical information. Nolland's exegesis (like Marshall's) is never less than worthy.

Students should, as a matter of course, ensure that they use more than one commentary and more than one book about Luke. Fitzmyer and Nolland would make a good balance but all the literature mentioned in this chapter can appropriately be consulted too.

Notes

1 AN INTRODUCTION TO THE TEXT

1 I want to acknowledge at the outset how much I have learned from Stephen D. Moore, particularly from his two books, *Literary Criticism and the Gospels: The Theoretical Challenge* (New Haven and London: Yale University Press, 1989) and *Poststructuralism and the New Testament: Derrida and Foucault at the Foot of the Cross* (Minneapolis: Fortress Press, 1994).

2 For an introduction see Mark A. Powell, *What is Narrative Criticism?* (Minneapolis: Fortress Press, 1990). I review this book below.

3 For earlier treatments see O. C. Edwards, *Luke's Story of Jesus* (Philadelphia: Fortress Press, reprinted 1989); W. S. Kurz, *Reading Luke-Acts: Dynamics of Biblical Narrative* (Louisville: Westminster/John Knox Press, 1993); and C. H. Talbert, *Reading Luke: A Literary and Theological Commentary on the Third Gospel* (New York: Crossroad, 1982).

4 This point is recognized by James M. Dawsey in his book, *The Lukan Voice: Confusion and Irony in the Gospel of Luke* (Macon: Mercer University Press, 1986). I provide the details of Dawsey's argument in Chapter 2.

5 On the relations between the two see H. Koester 'Apocryphal and Canonical Gospels', *HTR* 73 (1980), pp. 105–30. Valuable too is Koester's book *Ancient Christian Gospels: Their History and Development* (London: SCM Press and Philadelphia: Trinity Press International, 1990).

6 We know this from the second-century apocalypse called *The Ascension of Isaiah* which uses the oral tradition and at least some of the Gospels. On this text see J. M. Knight, *The Ascension of Isaiah* (GAP 2; Sheffield: Sheffield Academic Press, 1995).

7 Mark 16.8b–20 almost certainly represents a later addition to the Gospel.

8 Richard Burridge, *What are the Gospels? A Comparison with Graeco-Roman Biography* (SNTSMS 70; Cambridge: Cambridge University Press, 1992), pp. 128–53.

9 G. N. Stanton, *The Gospels and Jesus* (Oxford: Oxford University Press,

1989), p. 19. See also D. L. Barr and J. L. Wentling, 'The
Conventions of Classical Biography and the Genre of Luke-Acts', in
C. H. Talbert (ed.), *Luke-Acts: New Perspectives from the Society of
Biblical Literature Seminar* (New York: Crossroad, 1984), pp. 63–88.

10 On this point see E. P. Sanders and M. Davies, *Studying the Synoptic
Gospels* (London: SCM Press, 1989) p. 287.

11 C. H. Talbert, *What is a Gospel? The Genre of the Canonical Gospels?*
(Philadelphia: Fortress Press, 1977), p. 134.

12 This temptation is ably circumvented by Sanders and Davies,
Studying the Synoptic Gospels, pp. 252–98.

13 Ibid., pp. 276–8.

14 Ibid., p. 278.

15 See L. C. A. Alexander, *The Preface to Luke's Gospel: Literary Convention
and Social Context in Luke 1.1–4 and Acts 1.1* (SNTSMS 78;
Cambridge: Cambridge University Press, 1993).

16 Talbert, *What is a Gospel?*, Chapter 4.

17 E.g. by H. J. Cadbury, *The Style and Literary Method of Luke* (HTS 6;
Cambridge Mass.: Harvard University Press, 1920), pp. 39–72.

18 This explanation of the omission was proposed by J. Jeremias in his
The Eucharistic Words of Jesus (ET London: SCM Press, 1966),
pp. 138–59.

19 G. M. Styler, 'The Priority of Mark', in C. F. D. Moule, *The Birth of
the New Testament* (London: A & C Black, third edition, 1981),
Excursus IV, pp. 285–316.

20 Ibid., p. 305.

21 See C. M. Tuckett, *Q and the History of Early Christianity: Studies on Q*
(Edinburgh: T. & T. Clark, 1996).

22 Sanders and Davies, *Studying the Synoptic Gospels*, pp. 67–83.

23 'St. Mark's Knowledge and Use of Q' in W. Sanday (ed.), *Oxford
Studies in the Synoptic Problem* (Oxford: Clarendon Press, 1911),
pp. 165–83.

24 Sanders and Davies, *Studying the Synoptic Gospels*, pp. 84–92.

25 Ibid., pp. 93–7.

26 Ibid., p. 92.

27 Eric Franklin, *Luke: Interpreter of Paul, Critic of Matthew* (JSNTSS 92;
Sheffield: Sheffield Academic Press, 1994).

28 Ibid., p. 164.

29 Ibid., chapter 17.

30 Ibid., p. 373. He criticizes M.D. Goulder's *Luke: A New Paradigm*,
two vols. (JSNTSS 20; Sheffield: Sheffield Academic Press, 1989). For
a more detailed review of Goulder see M. S. Goodacre, *Goulder and the
Gospels: An Examination of a New Paradigm* (JSNTSS 133; Sheffield:
Sheffield Academic Press, 1996).

2 LUKE AS A NARRATIVE

1 See W. A. Maier, *Form Criticism Reexamined* (St Louis: Concordia,
1973); K. Berger, *Einführung in die Formgeschichte* (Tübingen: Francke,

1987) and *Formgeschichte des Neuen Testaments* (Heidelberg: Quelle and Maier, 1984).

2 Rudolph Bultmann, *The History of the Synoptic Tradition* (1921; ET Oxford: Basil Blackwell, 1972).

3 Martin Dibelius, *From Tradition to Gospel* (1919; ET London: Nicholson & Watson, 1934).

4 See N. Perrin, *What is Redaction Criticism?* (London: SPCK, 1970).

5 H. Conzelmann, *The Theology of Luke* (ET London: Faber and Faber, 1960) and Willi Marxsen, *Mark the Evangelist: Studies on the Redaction History of the Gospel* (ET Nashville and New York: Abingdon, 1969).

6 See the review of this method by Stephen D. Moore in his *Literary Criticism and the Gospels: The Theoretical Challenge* (New Haven and London: Yale University Press, 1989), pp. 3–7.

7 Ibid., p. 9.

8 R. A. Culpepper, *Anatomy of the Fourth Gospel: A Study in Literary Design* (Philadelphia: Fortress Press, 1983).

9 Ibid., p. 4.

10 Mark A. Powell, *What is Narrative Criticism?* (Minneapolis: Fortress Press, 1990).

11 Ibid., p. 19.

12 Ibid., p. 35.

13 Moore, *Literary Criticism*, p. 172.

14 The phrase is noted by Moore, *Literary Criticism*, p. 175.

15 With due acknowledgement to Stephen Moore.

16 F. K. Stanzel, *A Theory of Narrative* (ET Cambridge: Cambridge University Press, 1984) p. 4.

17 M. Bal, *Narratology: Introduction to the Theory of Narrative* (ET Toronto: Toronto University Press, 1985) p. 5.

18 Wayne Booth, *The Rhetoric of Fiction* (Harmondsworth: Penguin Books, second edition, 1991), p. 72.

19 William Kurz, *Reading Luke-Acts: Dynamics of Biblical Narrative* (Louisville: Westminster/John Knox Press, 1993), pp. 10–12.

20 Ibid., p. 11.

21 J. M. Dawsey, *The Lukan Voice: Confusion and Irony in the Gospel of Luke* (Macon: Mercer University Press, 1986), pp. 110–24.

22 Ibid., pp. 1–14.

23 Ibid., p. 12.

24 Eduard Norden, *Die Antike Kunstprosa vom 6en Jahrhundert vor Christus bis in die Zeit der Renaissance* (Stuttgart: B. G. Teubner, 1958), vol. ii, p. 483; reported by Dawsey, *Lukan Voice*, p. 19.

25 Dawsey, *Lukan Voice*, p. 21.

26 Ibid, pp. 25–6

27 Moore, *Literary Criticism*, p. 33.

28 Dawsey, *Lukan Voice*, pp. 43–71.

29 Ibid., pp. 115–17.

30 Ibid., p. 41.

31 Ibid., p. 49.

32 Ibid., p. 88.

33 See e.g. W. Iser, *The Act of Reading: A Theory of Aesthetic Response* (ET London: Routledge & Kegan Paul, 1978); and cf. J. L. Staley, *The Print's First Kiss: A Rhetorical Investigation of the Implied Reader in the Fourth Gospel* (SBLDS 82; Atlanta: Scholar's Press, 1988).

34 Kurz, *Reading Luke-Acts*, pp. 12–16; citing Fitzmyer's commentary.

35 Dawsey, *Lukan Voice*, pp. 139–42.

36 Ibid., p. 149.

37 Ibid., p. 155.

38 The evidence is examined in a stimulating way by E. P. Sanders, *Jesus and Judaism* (London: SCM Press, 1985), pp. 61–90.

39 Ibid., pp. 98–106.

40 J. Klausner, *The Messianic Idea in Israel* (London: George Allen & Unwin, 1956), p. 9.

41 See the summary of scholarship in Sanders, *Jesus*, pp. 61–76, but also the reply by Craig A. Evans, 'Jesus' Action in the Temple: Cleansing or Portent of Destruction?', CBQ 51 (1989), pp. 237–70.

42 E. Lohmeyer, *Lord of the Temple: A Study of the Relation Between Cult and Gospel* (ET Edinburgh: Oliver & Boyd, 1961), pp. 44–5.

43 On this point see M. Hengel, *The Johannine Question* (London: SCM Press, 1989), pp. 68–72.

44 C. F. Evans, 'The Central Section of St. Luke's Gospel' in D. E. Nineham (ed.), *Studies in the Gospels: Essays in Memory of R. H. Lightfoot* (Oxford: Basil Blackwell, 1955), pp. 37–53. For a refinement of this theory, see D. P. Moessner, *Lord of the Banquet: The Literary and Theological Significance of the Lukan Travel Narrative* (Minneapolis: Fortress Press, 1989).

3 A READING OF LUKE

1 See J. M. Dawsey, *The Lukan Voice: Confusion and Irony in the Gospel of Luke* (Macon: Mercer University Press, 1986), p. 137.

2 Ibid., p. 132.

3 Ibid., pp. 62–70.

4 See Dawsey's discussion of it in his *Lukan Voice*, pp. 85–6. He cites the work of J. A. T. Robinson, 'Elijah, John and Jesus: An Essay in Detection', NTS 4 (1957–8), pp. 263–81.

5 J. A. Fitzmyer, *The Gospel According to Luke*, vol. 1 (AB 28; Garden City: Doubleday, 1981), p. 681.

6 See J. Jeremias, *The Parables of Jesus* (ET London: SCM Press, 1963), p. 131: 'the parable was addressed to men who were like the older brother, men who were offended at the gospel'.

7 E. P. Sanders, *Jesus and Judaism* (London: SCM Press, 1985), p. 309, cites Albert Schweitzer's belief that Judas betrayed the secret that the followers of Jesus thought of him as a king.

8 See J. Blinzler, *The Trial of Jesus* (ET Cork: Mercier Press, 1959), pp. 194–204.

4 ALTERNATIVE READINGS OF LUKE

1 D. J. A. Clines, 'Ethics as Deconstruction, and, the Ethics of Deconstruction', in J. W. Rogerson, M. Davies and M. D. Carroll (eds), *The Bible in Ethics: The Second Sheffield Colloquium* (JSOTSS 207; Sheffield: Sheffield Academic Press, 1995), p.104.

2 Ibid., p.104.

3 For earlier treatments of this issue see W. Schrage, *The Ethics of the New Testament* (ET Edinburgh: T. & T. Clark, 1988), pp. 158–9; L. Schottroff, *Let the Oppressed go Free: Feminist Perspectives on the New Testament* (ET Louisville: Westminster/John Knox Press 1993), esp. pp. 138–67 and T. K. Seim, *The Double Message: Patterns of Gender in Luke-Acts* (Edinburgh: T. & T. Clark, 1994).

4 For a reading of this material see J. C. Exum, 'The (M)other's Place', in her *Fragmented Women: Feminist (Sub)versions of Biblical Narratives* (Sheffield: Sheffield Academic Press, 1993), pp. 94–147.

5 THE THEMES OF LUKE'S GOSPEL

1 For this approach to Luke see J.B. Green, *The Theology of the Gospel of Luke* (NTT; Cambridge: Cambridge University Press, 1995).

2 Stephen Moore, *Mark and Luke in Poststructuralist Perspectives: Jesus begins to Write* (New Haven and London: Yale University Press, 1992), p. 111.

3 In his book, Hans Conzelmann, *The Theology of St Luke* (ET London: Faber and Faber, 1960) pp. 95–136.

4 Robert Jewett, *The Thessalonian Correspondence: Pauline Rhetoric and Millenarian Piety* (Philadelphia: Fortress Press, 1986), pp. 161–78.

5 I say 'probably' because the scroll in question is unfortunately damaged.

6 Richard A. Horsley, *Sociology and the Jesus Movement* (New York: Continuum, second edition, 1994). By the same author see also *Jesus and the Spiral of Violence: Popular Jewish Resistance in Roman Palestine* (San Francisco: Harper & Row, 1987); and (with John S. Hanson), *Bandits, Prophets, and Messiahs: Popular Movements in the Time of Jesus* (Minneapolis, Chicago, New York: Winston Press: 1985).

7 Horsley, *Sociology*, p. 85.

8 Ibid., p. 86.

9 Ibid., p. 88.

10 Ibid., p. 94.

11 R. A. Horsley, *Galilee: History, Politics, People* (Valley Forge: Trinity Press International, 1995), pp. 189–221.

12 See B. J. Capper, 'Community of Goods in the Early Jerusalem Church', in W. Haase (ed.) *Aufstieg und Niedergang der römischen Welt*, II.26.2 (Berlin and New York: de Gruyter, 1995), pp. 1,730–74. For the description of this evidence in the Lucan literature see P. F. Esler, *Community and Gospel in Luke-Acts: The Social and Political Motivation of Lucan Theology* (SNTSMS 57; Cambridge: Cambridge University Press, 1987).

13 Horsley, *Sociology*, p. 122.
14 See e.g. J. T. Sanders, *The Jews in Luke-Acts* (London: SCM Press, 1987), p. 303.
15 For a different understanding see Robert L. Brawley, *Luke-Acts and the Jews* (Atlanta: Scholars Press, 1987).
16 Conzelmann, *Theology*, p. 132.
17 Wayne Meeks, *The First Urban Christians: The Social World of the Apostle Paul* (New Haven and London: Yale University Press, 1983), p. 30. Meeks is a penetrating commentator on primitive Christian social ethics. See also his *The Moral World of the First Christians* (Philadelphia: Westminster Press, 1996) and *The Origins of Christian Morality: the First Two Centuries* (New Haven and London: Yale University Press, 1993).

6 A READING OF READINGS

1 See for instance C. M. Tuckett (ed.), *Luke's Literary Achievement: Collected Essays* (Sheffield: Sheffield Academic Press, 1995).

Bibliography

Alexander, L. C. A., *The Preface to Luke's Gospel: Literary Convention and Social Context in Luke 1.1–4 and Acts 1.1* (SNTSMS 78; Cambridge: Cambridge University Press, 1993).

Attridge, H., *The Epistle to the Hebrews* (Hermeneia, Philadelphia: Fortress Press, 1989).

Bal, M., *Narratology: Introduction to the Theory of Narrative* (ET Toronto: Toronto University Press, 1985).

Bammel, E., Πτωχός, in G. Friedrich (ed.), *Theological Dictionary of the New Testament* (ET Grand Rapids: Eerdmans 1968), vol. vi, pp. 888–915.

Barr, D. L. and Wentling, J. L., 'The Conventions of Classical Biography and the Genre of Luke-Acts', in C. H. Talbert (ed.), *Luke-Acts: New Perspectives from the Society of Biblical Literature Seminar* (New York: Crossroad, 1984), pp. 63–88.

Barrett, C. K., *Luke the Historian in Recent Study* (London: Epworth Press, 1961).

Berger, K., *Formgeschichte des Neuen Testaments* (Heidelberg: Quelle and Maier, 1984).

—— *Einführung in die Formgeschichte* (Tübingen: Francke, 1987).

Blinzler, J., *The Trial of Jesus* (ET Cork: Mercier Press, 1959).

Booth W. A., *The Rhetoric of Fiction* (Harmondsworth: Penguin Books, second edition, 1991) .

Borgen, P., 'God's Agent in the Fourth Gospel', in J. Neusner (ed.), *Religions in Antiquity: Essays in Memory of Erwin Ramsdell Goodenough* (SHR 14; Leiden: E. J. Brill, 1968), pp. 137–48.

Brawley, R. L., *Luke-Acts and the Jews: Conflict, Apology and Conciliation* (SBLMS 33; Atlanta: Scholars Press, 1987).

Bultmann, R., *The History of the Synoptic Tradition* (1921; ET Oxford: Basil Blackwell, revised edition, 1972).

Burridge, R., *What are the Gospels? A Comparison with Graeco-Roman Biography* (SNTSMS 70; Cambridge: Cambridge University Press, 1992).

Cadbury, H. J., *The Style and Literary Method of Luke* (HTS 6; Cambridge Mass.: Harvard University Press, 1920).

Caird, G. B., *The Gospel of St. Luke* (Pelican Gospel Commentaries: London: SCM Press, reprinted 1968).

Capper, B. J., 'Community of Goods in the Early Jerusalem Church', in W. Haase (ed.) *Aufstieg und Niedergang der römischen Welt*, Volume II.26.2 (Berlin and New York: de Gruyter, 1995), pp. 1,730–74.

Clines, D. J. A., 'Ethics as Deconstruction, and, the Ethics of Deconstruction', in J. W. Rogerson, M. Davies and M. D. Carroll (eds), *The Bible in Ethics: The Second Sheffield Colloquium* (JSOTSS 207; Sheffield: Sheffield Academic Press, 1995), pp. 77–106.

Collins, A. Y., *Crisis and Catharsis: The Power of the Apocalypse* (Philadelphia: Westminster Press, 1984).

Conzelmann, H., *The Theology of St Luke* (ET London: Faber and Faber, 1960).

Culpepper, R. A., *Anatomy of the Fourth Gospel: A Study in Literary Design* (Philadelphia: Fortress Press, 1983).

Dawsey, J. M., *The Lukan Voice: Confusion and Irony in the Gospel of Luke* (Macon: Mercer University Press, 1986).

Dibelius, M., *From Tradition to Gospel* (1919; ET London: Nicholson & Watson, 1934).

Drury, J., *Tradition and Design in Luke's Gospel: A Study in Early Christian Historiography* (London: Darton, Longman and Todd, 1976).

Dunn, J. D. G., *Baptism in the Holy Spirit* (SBT second series 15; London: SCM Press, 1970).

Edwards, O. C., *Luke's Story of Jesus* (Philadelphia: Fortress Press, reprinted 1989).

Esler, P. F., *Community and Gospel in Luke-Acts: The Social and Political Motivations of Lucan Theology* (SNTSMS 57; Cambridge: Cambridge University Press, 1987).

Evans, C. A., ' "Jesus" Action in the Temple: Cleansing or Portent of Destruction?', CBQ 51 (1989), pp. 237–70.

Evans, C. F., 'The Central Section of St. Luke's Gospel' in D. E. Nineham (ed.), *Studies in the Gospels: Essays in Memory of R. H. Lightfoot* (Oxford: Basil Blackwell, 1955), pp. 37–53.

―――― *Saint Luke* (Trinity Press International New Testament Commentaries; London: SCM Press and Philadelphia: Trinity Press International, 1990).

Exum, J. C., 'The (M)other's Place', in her *Fragmented Women: Feminist (Sub)versions of Biblical Narratives* (JSOTSS 163; Sheffield: Sheffield Academic Press, 1993), pp. 94–147.

Fitzmyer, J. A., *The Gospel According to Luke* (Anchor Bible series vols 28, 28a; Garden City: Doubleday, 1981 and 1985).

―――― *Luke the Theologian: Aspects of His Teaching* (London: Geoffrey Chapman, 1989).

Franklin, E., *Luke: Interpreter of Paul, Critic of Matthew* (JSNTSS 92; Sheffield: Sheffield Academic Press, 1994).

García Martínez, F., *The Dead Sea Scrolls Translated: The Qumran Texts in English* (ET Leiden: E. J. Brill, 1994).

Goodacre, M. S., *Goulder and the Gospels: An Examination of a New Paradigm* (JSNTSS 133; Sheffield: Sheffield Academic Press, 1996).

Goulder, M. D., *Luke: A New Paradigm* (JSNTSS 20; two vols; Sheffield: Sheffield Academic Press, 1989).

Green, J. B., *The Theology of the Gospel of Luke* (NTT; Cambridge: Cambridge University Press, 1995).

Hengel, M., *Crucifixion* (ET London: SCM Press, 1977).

—— *The Johannine Question* (London: SCM Press, 1989).

Horsley, R. A., *Jesus and the Spiral of Violence: Popular Jewish Resistance in Roman Palestine* (San Francisco: Harper & Row, 1987).

—— *Sociology and the Jesus Movement* (New York: Continuum, second edition, 1994).

—— *Galilee: History, Politics, People* (Valley Forge: Trinity Press International, 1995).

Horsley, R. A. and Hanson, J. S., *Bandits, Prophets, and Messiahs Popular Movements in the Time of Jesus* (Minneapolis, Chicago, New York: Winston Press, 1985).

Hull, J. M., *Hellenistic Magic and the Synoptic Tradition* (SBT second series 28; London: SCM Press, 1974).

Hurtado, L. W., *One God, One Lord: early Christian devotion and ancient Jewish Monotheism* (London: SCM Press, 1988).

Iser, W., *The Act of Reading: A Theory of Aesthetic Response* (ET London: Routledge & Kegan Paul, 1978).

Jeremias, J., *The Parables of Jesus* (ET London: SCM Press, revised edition, 1963).

—— *The Eucharistic Words of Jesus* (ET London: SCM Press, 1966).

Jervell, J., *Luke and the People of God* (Minneapolis: Augsburg, 1972).

Jewett, R., *The Thessalonian Correspondence: Pauline Rhetoric and Millenarian Piety* (Philadelphia: Fortress Press, 1986).

Klausner, J., *The Messianic Idea in Israel* (London: George Allen & Unwin, 1956).

Knight, J. M., *The Ascension of Isaiah* (GAP 2; Sheffield: Sheffield Academic Press, 1995).

Koester, H., 'Apocryphal and Canonical Gospels', *HTR* 73 (1980), pp.105–30.

—— *Ancient Christian Gospels. Their History and Development* (London: SCM Press and Philadelphia: Trinity Press International, 1990).

Kurz, W. S., *Reading Luke-Acts: Dynamics of Biblical Narrative* (Louisville: Westminster/John Knox Press, 1993).

Lohmeyer, E., *Lord of the Temple: A Study of the Relation between Cult and Gospel* (1942; ET Edinburgh: Oliver & Boyd, 1961).

Maddox, R., *The Purpose of Luke-Acts* (Edinburgh: T & T Clark, 1982).

Maier, W. A., *Form Criticism Reexamined* (St Louis: Concordia, 1973) .

Mannheim, K., *Ideology and Utopia: an Introduction to the Sociology of Knowledge* (new edition, London: Routledge, 1991).

Marshall, I. H., *The Gospel of Luke: A Commentary on the Greek Text* (Exeter: Paternoster Press, 1977).

—— *Luke: Historian and Theologian* (Exeter: Paternoster Press, 1970).

Marxsen, W., *Mark the Evangelist: Studies on the Redaction History of the Gospel* (ET Nashville and New York: Abingdon, 1969).

Meeks, W. A., *The First Urban Christians: The Social World of the Apostle Paul* (New Haven and London: Yale University Press, 1983) .

—— *The Moral World of the First Christians* (Philadelphia: Westminster Press, 1986) .

—— *The Origins of Christian Morality: the First Two Centuries* (New Haven and London: Yale University Press, 1993).

Moessner, D. P., *Lord of the Banquet: The Literary and Theological Significance of the Lukan Travel Narrative* (Minneapolis: Fortress Press, 1989).

Moore, Stephen D., *Literary Criticism and the Gospels: The Theoretical Challenge* (New Haven and London: Yale University Press, 1989) .

—— *Mark and Luke in Poststructuralist Perspectives: Jesus Begins to Write* (New Haven and London: Yale University Press, 1992).

—— *Poststructuralism and the New Testament: Derrida and Foucault at the Foot of the Cross* (Minneapolis: Fortress Press, 1994).

Neyrey, J. H., (ed.), *The Social World of Luke-Acts: Models for Interpretation* (Peabody: Hendrickson, 1991).

Nickelsburg, G. W. E., *Jewish Literature between the Bible and the Mishnah* (Philadelphia: Fortress Press, 1981).

Nolland, J., *Luke 1.9.20/9.21–18.34/18.35–24.53* (Word Biblical Commentaries vols 35a, 35b, 35c; Dallas:Word Books, 1989–93).

Norden, E., *Die Antike Kunstprosa vom 6en Jahrhundert vor Christus bis in die Zeit der Renaissance* (two vols; Stuttgart: B. G. Teubner, 1958).

O'Toole, R. F. *The Unity of Luke's Theology: an Analysis of Luke-Acts* (Wilmington: Glazier, 1984).

Perrin, N.,*What is Redaction Criticism?* (London: SPCK, 1970).

Powell, M. A., *What is Narrative Criticism?* (Minneapolis: Fortress Press, 1990).

Robinson, J. A. T., 'Elijah, John and Jesus: An Essay in Detection', *NTS* 4 (1957–8), pp. 263–81.

Rowland, C. C., *The Open Heaven* (London: SPCK, 1982).

Sanders, E. P.,*Jesus and Judaism* (London: SCM Press, 1985).

Sanders, E. P. and Davies, M., *Studying the Synoptic Gospels* (London: SCM Press, 1989).

Sanders, J. T., *The Jews in Luke-Acts* (London: SCM Press, 1987).

Schottroff, L., *Let the Oppressed go Free: Feminist Perspectives on the New Testament* (ET Louisville: Westminster/John Knox Press 1993).

Schrage, W., *The Ethics of the New Testament* (ET Edinburgh: T.&T. Clark, 1988).

Seim, T. K., *The Double Message: Patterns of Gender in Luke-Acts* (Edinburgh: T. & T. Clark, 1994).

Staley, J. L., *The Print's First Kiss: A Rhetorical Investigation of the Implied Reader in the Fourth Gospel* (SBLDS 82; Atlanta: Scholar's Press, 1988).

Stanton, G. N., *The Gospels and Jesus* (Oxford: Oxford University Press, 1989).

Stanzel, F. K., *A Theory of Narrative* (ET Cambridge: Cambridge University Press, 1984).

Streeter, B. H., 'St. Mark's Knowledge and Use of Q' in W. Sanday (ed.), *Oxford Studies in the Synoptic Problem* (Oxford: Clarendon, 1911), pp. 165–83.

Styler, G. M., 'The Priority of Mark', in C. F. D. Moule, *The Birth of the New Testament* (London: A & C Black, third edition, 1981), Excursus IV, pp. 285–316.

Talbert, C. H., *What is a Gospel: The Genre of the Canonical Gospels?* (Philadelphia: Fortress Press, 1977) .

—— *Reading Luke: A Literary and Theological Commentary on the Third Gospel* (New York: Crossroad, 1982).

Thompson, L. L., *The Book of Revelation: Apocalypse and Empire* (New York and Oxford: OUP, 1990).

Tuckett, C. M., *Luke's Literary Achievement: Collected Essays* (Sheffield: Sheffield Academic Press, 1995).

—— (ed.), *Q and the History of Early Christianity: Studies on Q* (Edinburgh: T. & T. Clark, 1996).

Walaskay, P., *'And so we came to Rome'; The Political Perspective of St Luke* (SNTSMS 49; Cambridge: Cambridge University Press, 1983).

Wilson, S. G., *The Gentiles and the Gentile Mission in Luke-Acts* (SNTSMS 23; Cambridge: Cambridge University Press, 1973).

Winter, B. W., and Clarke, A. D., *The Book of Acts in its Ancient Literary Setting* (Grand Rapids: Eerdmanns, 1993).

Biblical index

1. Hebrew scriptures

Genesis
1.2   79
3   106
3.15   106
38.8   132

Exodus
8.19   108
16.4   80
17.1–7   80
23.20   15, 94

Numbers
14.34   80

Deuteronomy
8.3 (LXX)   80
9.10   108
10.18   93
18.15   63, 102
24.1–4   121
24.4   177
25.5   132
32.20   103

Judges
13   72

1 Samuel
1—2   72

15.10   77
16   75

2 Samuel
7.14   77

2 Kings
1.10   104
1.12   104

1 Chronicles
28.5   166

Psalms
2.7   79
47.2   167
107.29   98
110.1   132, 133
118.22   51, 131
118.26   117

Isaiah
1.3   75
2.3   62
8   131
8.14–15   51, 131
40   77
42.1   79
46.13   151
49.5   45
49.6   151
56.1–8   44
56.6–7   175

Ancient authors

General index